Translating Childhoods

THE RUTGERS SERIES IN CHILDHOOD STUDIES

The Rutgers Series in Childhood Studies is dedicated to increasing our understanding of children and childhoods, past and present, throughout the world. Children's voices and experiences are central. Authors come from a variety of fields, including anthropology, criminal justice, history, literature, psychology, religion, and sociology. The books in this series are intended for students, scholars, practitioners, and those who formulate policies that affect children's everyday lives and futures.

Edited by Myra Bluebond-Langner, Rutgers University, Camden, founding director of the Rutgers University Center for Children and Childhood Studies

Advisory Board
Joan Jacobs Brumberg, Cornell University
Perri Klass, Boston University School of Medicine
Jill Korbin, Case Western Reserve University
Bambi Schiefflin, New York University
Enid Schildkraut, American Museum of Natural History

Translating Childhoods

Immigrant Youth, Language, and Culture

MARJORIE FAULSTICH ORELLANA

RUTGERS UNIVERSITY PRESS
New Brunswick, New Jersey, and London

LIBRARY OF CONGRESS CATALOGING-IN-PUBLICATION DATA

Orellana, Marjorie Faulstich.
    Translating childhoods : immigrant youth, language, and culture / Marjorie
Faulstich Orellana.
        p. cm. — (The Rutgers series in childhood studies)
    Includes bibliographical references and index.
    ISBN 978–0–8135–4522–6 (hardcover : alk. paper)
    ISBN 978–0–8135–4523–3 (pbk. : alk. paper)
    1. Children of immigrants—Language.   2. Translating and interpreting.
3. Immigrants—Language.   4. Immigrant families.   I. Title.
    HQ792.U5O77 2009
    306.874086′912—dc22

                                                                    2008036401

A British Cataloging-in-Publication record for this book is available
from the British Library.

Copyright © 2009 by Marjorie Faulstich Orellana

Visit our Web site: http://rutgerspress.rutgers.edu

Manufactured in the United States of America

To my father, Charles Nicholas Faulstich

1918–2008

Contents

Acknowledgments   *ix*

Introduction

Chapter 1   Translating Frames

Chapter 2   Landscapes of Childhood

Chapter 3   Home Work

Chapter 4   Public *Para*-Phrasing

Chapter 5   Transculturations

Chapter 6   Transformations

Chapter 7   Translating Childhoods

Appendix A: Learning from Children   *127*
Appendix B: Transcription Conventions   *143*
Appendix C: Domains of Language Brokering   *144*
Notes   *147*
Bibliography   *163*
Index   *177*

Acknowledgments

This book was born out of research in three different communities over a twelve-year period, from 1995 to 2007. It is informed as well by my experiences as a teacher and community activist in Los Angeles throughout another decade (1983–1993). My understanding of children, childhoods, language and life have been influenced by countless people through the years, and I thank not only all the colleagues, students, teachers, family members and friends from many circles who have inspired me and catalyzed my thinking but also the many people who contributed directly to this project.

I began this project as a postdoctoral researcher on a study of "California Childhoods," sponsored by the MacArthur Foundation Research Network on Successful Pathways through Middle Childhood in a grant to Catherine Cooper and Barrie Thorne. The opportunity to do fieldwork in a community that was close to my heart under Barrie's inspiring mentorship was a gift, the spirit of which is at the core of this book. Anna Chee, Lucila Ek and Arcelia Hernández contributed to the early research in Los Angeles, and Wan Shun Eva Lam's work on language brokering in the Oakland site enriched my understandings of the practice. Through the MacArthur Foundation Network I learned from some of the best researchers of children's lives, including Shirley Brice Heath, Catherine Cooper, Greg Duncan, Cynthia García Coll, Jacqui Eccles, Hanne Haavind, John Modell, Barrie Thorne, and Tom Weisner. My work in Los Angeles also benefited from experiences I garnered as a teacher and activist in the "Madison" community from 1983 to 1993. Thanks to my colleagues in the Teachers Committee on Central America and the Human Rights Committee of UTLA, to Norma Chinchilla, who introduced me to the world of sociology through Central American solidarity work, and to all the "chapines" of the Guatemala Information Center.

For easing my crossing from teacher/activist to researcher and facilitating my own pathways of development, I am indebted to my graduate advisor at the

University of Southern California, Robert Rueda, as well as to Nelly Stromquist and Barrie Thorne. The introduction that Robert provided to sociocultural theory opened new worlds of understanding for me. Nelly's work reminded me to keep an eye on the global even as I focused on the local. Barrie showed me new ways of thinking about and studying children, childhoods, social categories, and social processes.

Taking a position at Northwestern University in 1998, I grew in ways I hadn't imagined through intellectual engagement with my colleagues in the School of Education and Social Policy. Special thanks to Carol Lee, for birthing "ChiLD" (The Center for Human Learning and Diversity") and to Kim Williams for conjoining our projects at "Regan." Many students assisted with gathering, processing, and analyzing data in Chicago: Jackie Azpeitia, Andrew Brantlinger, H. Julia Eksner, Lily González, Adelita Hernández, Lauren Hersh, Christine Li-Grining, Sean Morales-Doyle, Kate Pietsch, Nancy Randall, Erica Rosenfeld, and Nicole Wong. Lisa Dorner, María Meza, Lucila Pulido, and Jennifer Reynolds contributed over a long period, and enriched the project in important ways.

When I moved back to Los Angeles in 2003 to join the UCLA faculty, I carted mounds of data with me for analyzing, with help from UCLA students Paula Carbone, Stefanie Chiquillo, Jacqui Dwarte, Yvonne de la Peña, Inmaculada García Sánchez, Rosa Jimenez, Mouna Mana, Danny Martínez, Ramón Martínez, Mariana Pacheco, Teresa Palencio, María Rodriguez, and Angela Pineda. At UCLA, I benefit from participating in three groups that pushed my thinking about the inherently interdisciplinary issues I address in this book and offered forums to try out these ideas: The Migration Studies seminar series, the Culture, Brain and Development program, and the Relationship Studies Program. My homes in the Urban Schooling and Teacher Education programs of the Graduate School of Education and Information Studies helped me keep the faith that theory matters for creating a more just world and provided many supports for my work. Thanks especially to Kris Gutiérrez and Rashmita Mistry.

Funding agencies offered vital financial assistance for this research: The MacArthur Foundation; the National Institute for Child Health and Human Development (1 RO3 HD39510–10); the Spencer Foundation (National Academy of Education postdoctoral fellowship); the William T. Grant Foundation; Northwestern University; the Foundation for Psychocultural Research (Culture, Brain and Development program); the Academic Senate of UCLA; and the International Reading Association (Elva Knight Award).

A number of people read and commented on this book: Thanks to Ursula Aldana, Karla Alvarado-Goldberg, Mel Bertrand, Paula Carbone, Jaime del

Razo, Lisa Dorner, Julia Eksner, Kevin Escudero, Robert Faulstich, Inmaculada García Sánchez, Megan Hopkins, Christine Brigid Malsbary, Danny Martínez, Ramón Martínez, Jennifer Reynolds, Ana Soltero-López, Virginia Shiller, Barrie Thorne, Ericka Verba, Claudia Vizcarra, and the editors of this series, Myra Bluebond and Adi Hovav, as well as the two anonymous reviewers for Rutgers University Press. Many thanks to Megan Hopkins and Jacqui Dwarte for final preparations of the manuscript, especially contributions to the notes.

Family and friends have influenced, inspired, and nurtured me in ways that enriched this work. My children, Elisa Noemí and Andrés Gabriel, have undoubtedly been my greatest teachers about childhood. Self-dubbed "Guate-gringos," their unfolding, shifting processes of language learning, cultural formation, and identity construction offered me tremendous insights into the cultural and contextual complexities of development. Elisa models ways of writing with *corazón,* encouraging me to break out of the constricts of academic prose. Andrés knows this book will never compare with the Harry Potter series in terms of popularity, but he's still one of my biggest fans.

Nery Orellana has also taught me much about childhood and its variations. A *child* immigrant, having crossed the border at the age of sixteen, and the child *of* an immigrant who left him in Guatemala when she came to work in the Los Angeles garment industry, Nery's life experiences were very different from mine. His tales of swimming and canoeing alone in the ocean, hunting in the mountains, and managing his own machete at the age of six challenged my own narrow conceptions of childhoods. What I learned from him and his family—brothers and sisters, nieces and nephews, as well as the new second generation that is growing—factors into this book in profound ways. Thanks, too, for the cover art.

I owe thanks to my own family of origin for other lessons, first and foremost to my parents. I find it hard to imagine what daily life was like for my mother, Anna Faulstich, during my growing-up years; when I was born she had five children ranging in age from two to nine, and two more soon followed me. She and my father, Charles Faulstich, worked, scrimped, and saved to give me and my seven siblings opportunities they never had. They also gave me the moral foundation for a commitment to equity, compassion, and social justice that I have tried to bring into my academic work. The diversity in ways of growing up and/or being raised that my siblings and their families represent reminds me to neither homogenize any population's experience nor lose sight of individuals when describing groups. Special thanks to Ginny and Robert for their careful reading of the completed manuscript and other supports. Robert and his wife María Hon also provided me with a writer's retreat in their home in Costa Rica during a critical stage of my writing. Thanks to Mary Anne,

Ginny, Charles, Robert, John, Dot, Nancy, Marie, Ann, and Dick for love and all kinds of support through the years, and especially this last year.

My dear friend and fellow professor, Ericka Verba, deserves credit for many things: for encouraging me to move to California to teach in 1983; helping me to navigate the complex demands of Academia and Life, while always remembering what's really important; and reading several drafts of this manuscript with a keen editor's eye. Another dear friend, Claudia Vizcarra, lent her professional skills as a translator and shared her perspectives on the complexities of translation work. I wish I could name all the people who supported me while undergoing medical treatments this year, but I'll spotlight a few powerful women who filled my spirit and freed my energy in ways that made all the difference for finishing this book. Love and thanks to Chris Angelli, Lukaza and Suchi Branfman, Patti del Valle, Jacqui Dwarte, Lucila Ek, Inma García Sánchez, Cindy Harding, Libby Harding, Arcelia Hernández, Angela Hudson, Lisa Milinazzo, Angie Neff, Lisa O'Connell, Elisa Orellana, Carol Peterson, Olivia Regalado, Virginia Shiller, Heidi Tinsman, Ericka Verba, and Claudia Vizcarra.

I completed this book during the hardest period of my life. Thus it gives me satisfaction to see it come to fruition, as a counterbalance: a birth in a time of endings; a reminder of the inexorable forces of life that push through the darkest of times. The challenges I faced gave me a fresh perspective on the many different kinds of hardships that immigrant families manage as they strive to "salir adelante" ("to come out ahead"). I have learned so much from the children and families whose experiences I translate in this book, and there are no sufficient words to express my gratitude and love to them. As a small way of giving something back to children like the ones you meet in this book, I am donating my author royalties to a scholarship fund for immigrant youth.

Translating Childhoods

Introduction

F OR MORE than a decade, I have been documenting the work that the children of immigrants do as they use their skills in two languages to read, write, listen, speak, and do things for their families.[1] I refer to a practice that has variously been called Natural Translation, family interpreting, language brokering, and *para*-phrasing–terms I discuss further in chapter 1. Placing phone calls, taking and leaving messages, scheduling appointments, filling out credit card applications, negotiating sales purchases, soliciting social services, and communicating for their parents with teachers, medical personnel, and other authority figures are part of everyday life for the children whom you meet in this book. Twelve-year-old Jessica,[2] the daughter of immigrants from Mexico to Chicago, suggested such work in her description of a typical day in her life:

> Inside my house, I translate for my mom on the phone. But most of
> the time, I am either watching TV, on the computer, on the phone,
> eating and sleeping. That is basically what I do during the day. On the
> weekends, we just stay home and clean, after we are done with the
> chores, we go out to eat and get some movies to watch. Sometimes we
> go visit other people but I don't translate much with my dad around.
> If we are watching TV, and it's English, my mom asks us what they are
> saying so we have to tell her. Sometimes I also translate letters and
> bills. When I go to the pharmacy at Walgreen's, I have to translate for
> my mom. Usually the person that works there talks English, so my
> mom doesn't understand.

In this report, Jessica downplayed her work as a family interpreter. She emphasized that most often when she was home she just did "regular stuff" such as watch television, talk on the phone, eat, and sleep; like most of the children with whom I spoke, Jessica saw her translation work as "no big deal." Her mention of it was consistent with her overall presentation of herself as part of a collective, just as she used the word "we" when she spoke of her family's weekend activities of cleaning the house together. Jessica contributed her language skills to the collective needs of her household and family, as she spoke English for her mother on the phone, on errands to places like the local pharmacy, and when watching television shows in English with her family. She also leveraged her English literacy skills for the family, as she read and made sense of things that were delivered to the household in the mail, especially letters and bills.

In these ways, Jessica's work as a translator both shaped and was shaped by the routine practices of her household. It also both forged and was forged by her family's circumstances as immigrants to the United States. Children serve as language brokers because their families need their skills in order to accomplish the tasks of everyday life in their new linguistic and cultural context. Many teachers also need these children's skills. So too do doctors, dentists, salespeople, waiters, social service providers, and more. Because of this, I argue children's work should be considered as part of the labor cost equation in this current era of global economic restructuring in which many nations increasingly rely on an immigrant work force.

In turn, translation work shaped Jessica's childhood. Jessica was a typical American teenager in many ways: she enjoyed surfing the Internet, chatting with her friends on the phone or through Instant Messaging, watching movies, and going to the mall. But, like many in homes headed by immigrants (one in five households in the United States today)[3] she was frequently called on to speak and act in ways that are rarely demanded of children from nonimmigrant families. This mattered for her experiences of growing up, her understanding of what it meant to be a child, what she learned, and how she came to understand her place in her family and society.

In this book, I introduce you to children like Jessica with whom I spent a good deal of time over the last decade, talking with them about their engagement in this multifaceted social, cultural, and linguistic practice. I observed children in action and audiotaped their words in order to study what is involved in mediating between languages, cultures, and worldviews. I probed further into translation practices by means of a written questionnaire, interviews, and focus groups with dozens of children in several different kinds of immigrant communities in California and Chicago and by asking child translators to keep journals that recount their experiences. I also talked with teachers and parents, as well as young adults who offered their perspectives on the translation work they had done while growing up.

Most of the youth with whom I worked were from Spanish-speaking families—families who had immigrated from Mexico or Central America to the United States. A few came from other countries, including China, Hong Kong, and Korea. Though I focus on Latinos in this book, considering both variations and commonalities in the experiences of families from Mexico and Central America to Chicago and California, it is important to remember that the practice of family interpreting is not unique to people from any particular ethnic group or nation-state. It is ubiquitous in immigrant communities. Because children generally acquire the host country language more quickly than do their parents, in large part because they are compelled to attend school, their skills are called upon for family survival. Language brokering is a cultural practice that is shaped by the experience of being an immigrant. It is a practice in which children take the lead; it is not handed down from parents to children. Rather, it is invented by necessity in the immigrant context.

But perhaps because language brokers are children, whose actions often go unnoticed by adults, this work has received little attention to date. Indeed, children's language brokering is most notable for its absence of discussion, even in places where one might expect it to be addressed, such as in historical accounts of child migrants,[4] memoirs of immigrant childhoods,[5] and fiction about and by immigrant youth.[6] This parallels the invisibility of children's everyday work as translators today. At the same time, somewhat paradoxically, certain aspects of children's translation work have received considerable attention; for example, when children speak for their parents in medical settings.[7]

Overview of the Book

In chapter 1, I begin with this paradox. The central interpretive frame that informs my work, the critical social science of childhoods, can help us to explain not only why children's actions are often invisible but also why, when they deviate from accepted norms, those actions may become especially marked and cause adults great alarm. Examining the practice of language brokering through this lens, children emerge as actors and agents in a full range of institutional contexts, not just as schooled and domesticated objects of adults' socialization efforts. Their interactions with adults through this work make more evident the socially constructed nature of generational relations. Immigrant childhoods are good cases to think about constructions of normalcy and deviance in adult-child relations because the immigration experience may propel, or speed up, changes in family processes and intergenerational relationships and because the juxtaposition of the beliefs and practices of immigrants and others may help us to see the constructed nature of all such beliefs and practices.

But it's important to remember, too, that there is no singular experience of an immigrant childhood, even within a given nation state. Immigrants to the United States live in many different kinds of communities—including traditional urban centers that constitute "ethnic enclaves," mixed-ethnic urban communities, and historically white, English-speaking suburbs, small towns, and rural areas.[8] These local contexts shape the needs and opportunities for children to serve as translators, as well as their overall experiences of growing up. In chapter 2, I contemplate how immigrant childhoods play out in particular "landscapes" or social contexts, through a comparative analysis of three communities in which I worked over the last decade. These represent different kinds of receiving contexts for immigrants, ones that place different demands on child translators. How children's translation work is seen within each context also differs, based in part on local, sociopolitical histories of intergroup relations, or the fields of difference in each locale.

Chapters 3 and 4 offer overviews of the work that immigrant children perform as translators/interpreters for their families. I first illuminate in chapter 3 the largely invisible work of everyday translations that takes place in homes, as children answer the phone, read and decipher mail, and engage in other tasks for their families, a hidden kind of "homework" and "house work" that is performed by children. Drawing on interviews with many young people as well as observations in many homes, I describe variations and commonalities across households and communities.

In chapter 4 I follow children out into the public world, as they mediate between their families and public institutions, commercial establishments, and other strangers. Like their everyday translation work at home, children's mundane work in the public, such as making small purchases in stores is in many ways naturalized, normalized, taken for granted, and nearly invisible. In contrast, specialized encounters, such as translating in medical and legal situations, have received considerable attention in the popular press, probably because they challenge "mainstream" notions of children: what they should be allowed or expected to do, what they are capable of, and where, when, and how they should be seen or heard. I probe the meanings that children's work as translators takes on as children move from private to public spaces and across different domains, tasks, contexts, and relationships; I consider too how their work was seen within the local "fields of difference" across communities.

Parent-teacher conferences, which I study in chapter 5, offer a particularly interesting forum for examining how young people mediate between adults with different beliefs about children and childhoods. In these settings, children are multiply positioned—as mediators between their parents and teachers, coparticipants in the exchanges, and objects of these adults' evaluations. The

Ethnography really involves a process of translation.[10] As Benson Saler suggests, "The ethnographer is, metaphorically, a 'bridge-builder,' one that is charged with the task of facilitating a 'crossing' into the sensibilities and sensitivities of others. The major purpose of ethnographic bridges, of ethnographic monographs, is to allow the reading public to cross over to new understandings, new understandings of others and perhaps of themselves."[11] But many of the same challenges arise in reporting on observations and interviews as are found in translating information across languages for different audiences. How ideas are shared, stories are told, and information reported— in essence, how they are translated—is influenced by assumptions about audiences. Thus, before concluding this introduction, I want to make explicit my assumptions about my audience. Most readers will likely be English speakers in the United States or in other receiving areas for the new flows of immigration around the world, with advanced levels of formal schooling, from a range of disciplines and fields of study. Many will have little personal experience with translation or immigration, but I hope my audience will also include children of immigrants, themselves active translators.

By writing with multiple audiences in mind, I face similar challenges to those that translators encounter. How do I explain one set of ideas to people with different sets of values and assumptions, people who operate with divergent points of reference and disciplinary orientations, and people who are likely to experience the words in different ways? Fifteen-year-old Sammy described the complexity of translating for people from different social and cultural backgrounds: "It's hard choosing the right words, not to seem, or to swing, either way through the conversation." But Sammy was masterful in choosing his words, and he recognized the power of using words for particular effects. I take inspiration from him as I translate the experiences of child translators to my readers.

criteria that teachers and parents bring to those evaluations may differ and place child translators in particularly paradoxical positions. Much translat work happens at schools, and these conferences offer one window into the ch dren's work to connect homes and schools.

My aim in chapters 3, 4, and 5 is to make more visible the myriad of wa in which children use their knowledge of English to speak, read, write, listen and do things for their families; I thereby illuminate how children contribute not only to households and families but also to the functioning of institutions like schools and clinics as well as commercial establishments and society as a whole. In doing this, I view children as contributors to social processes just like other members of society. This counters the future-oriented focus of much research on children—one that presumes they are only "adults in the making" rather than authentic social actors in the here-and-now.[9]

At the same time, children's work as translators matters for their own processes of learning and development, and chapter 6 contemplates how translation experiences are implicated in maturation processes over the course of childhood and adolescence. Drawing on longitudinal data, I theorize different ways of understanding the changing nature of youths' engagement in translation practices and for considering what they learn from their work. I introduce sociocultural learning theory, a second theoretical framework that has been important for my research, and show how this framework has helped me to think about what children learn from their everyday experiences of translation, in both specific translation moments and through cumulative experiences over time. In this chapter, I also continue to probe the question of what counts as "normal" in child development and family processes by calling for expanded views of normalcy.

This theme continues as I wrap up the book in chapter 7. Here, I unpack the many ways that we can understand children's work as translators and interpreters. I suggest how to support children in their translation work rather than condemn it and call for the creation of more public spaces for children to engage in the same active, valued, and fully participatory ways that immigrant children operate in many households. In an era in which schools are struggling to provide children with service learning opportunities and otherwise encourage their civic engagement, we can learn from models of household and civic engagement that already exist.

Translating Childhoods

For those who are interested in details of the research process, I have included an appendix that documents my work as ethnographer in these communities.

Chapter 1   Translating Frames

Estela

At TEN YEARS old Estela was considered by her mother to be "the right hand" of the family. Estela used her knowledge of English to make and answer phone calls, schedule appointments, sort and decipher the daily mail, fill out forms, apply for credit, help her younger sister with homework, and read stories-in-translation to her youngest siblings. She also helped with general household tasks: washing dishes, vacuuming, and making purchases at the corner store. Like Jessica, the girl who drew a map to record her daily life translations, this seemed for the most part "just normal" to Estela, as it did for many of the other young translators with whom I talked.

As Estela grew older, her responsibilities grew as well. These changes were propelled by her family's changing circumstances: three younger siblings were born; her parents purchased a house; to pay the mortgage her father worked at three jobs, and her mother began working the night shift at Burger King. Estela's parents needed her help even more than they had when she was younger, and Estela was charged with caring for her sisters during after school hours; she monitored their homework, fed them the dinners that her mother prepared before leaving for work, cleaned up, and got the girls ready for bed. Estela continued to contribute her English skills to the household by running errands and translating interchanges at stores, restaurants, and other public places, as well as reading written information and making phone calls. Translation tasks were not separable from her other forms of household work. And as Estela's spheres of movement grew, she used her bilingual skills to negotiate meaning for a wider array of people, including her cousins, teachers, public service personnel, and strangers in public spaces. A challenge for Estela as she grew older, however, was that school *also* increased its demands on her time, and most of her teachers did not know about her responsibilities at home. Tension grew between Estela and her mother—fueled by the pressures that her family faced, in their struggles to "salir adelante" [to come out ahead] or even just to survive.

Meanwhile, most of Estela's peers in this mixed-income suburb—especially those in the middle school college preparation classes in which she was placed—were concentrating on activities intended to open pathways to college. Most of her classmates' parents, born in this country (Estela and her parents were born in Guanajuato, Mexico), had college degrees. These young people had homework support from their parents. Some had private tutors. They were not expected to *provide* such support to others. After school, they played on sports teams or in the orchestra, joined school clubs, or enrolled in the myriad of private program offerings available to young people in this community. Estela loved singing and acting and wanted to perform in the school musical, but she wasn't able to make the play rehearsals because of her home responsibilities. The drama teacher understood this and invited Estela to serve with her as an assistant director, which allowed her to participate whenever she was available.

Nova

Like Estela's status as the "right hand" of her family, Nova's position in his family was an honored one; at twelve his mother referred to him as "el hombrecito" or "the little man." Nova spoke for his parents at home, at school, and in stores, restaurants, and clinics; he negotiated the sale of a computer (at his insistence and largely for his own use); he assisted his father in applying for unemployment benefits and helped his parents to secure a mortgage when they bought their first home. Nova's mother delineated how her son spoke for her at a public Fourth of July celebration, when she felt too nervous to speak:

> Ahora tuvimos un percance aquí en el lago con unas personas que nos
> agredieron, y él habló con la policía. El tuvo que hablar con la policía
> por que nos estaban molestando. Nosotros estabamos allí bien, y yo le
> digo, porque yo como estaba, ya, este, yo tenía miedo de ver a esa
> gente yo ya ni podía ni hablar. Entonces le dije, "Mijo, ven y ustedes
> díganle, ustedes díganle lo que está pasando." Y ellos empezaron a
> decirle. Como Nova, empezó a decirle a la policía.[1]

[Now we had an incident here at the lake with some people who were attacking us, and he spoke with the police. He had to speak with the police because they were bothering us. We were fine there, and I, I tell you, because I was like, like, I was afraid because of seeing those people and I couldn't even speak. So I said to him, "My son, come and you (plural) tell them, you tell them what is happening." And they began to tell them. Like Nova, he began to tell the police.]

Cindy

Cindy,[2] who was fourteen at the time she was interviewed, was another girl whose translation work shaped her childhood. Cindy named many reasons why she liked her role as the family translator: she learned more about other people in her family and about herself (she got access to things she might not otherwise see, such as school and medical records and household bills); it made her feel smart; she learned more words in her two languages, English and Chinese; it cheered her up when she was in a bad mood or felt bad about herself; and it gave her time to communicate with her mother, who would sit and listen to her each evening after they went through the mail together. What she didn't like was being treated "like a kid," especially when she made phone calls. In many ways, she said she didn't feel like a kid; she felt that she was "on a higher level"; and she distinguished herself from other kids' experiences when she reflected:

> Sometimes I think I invaded people's privacy, like, they have to tell me over the phone, like deposit statements and stuff like that. I know exactly the house's wages and stuff like that, and I tell my parents, and they don't really care. I just know, and I translate it. While like other kids, they ask for things. I'm not trodding down people of my own age, but some people they just ask for things, like "Can I have a bike, can I go swimming, can I go to summer camp, can I have a new pair of Nikes?" . . . Their parents keep saying, "Do you know how hard I work for the money to pay the bills?" They don't know exactly how much is in their bank deposits, the bills and stuff. But *I* know personally because I write the bills. I write the checks.

Luz

Luz was eighteen years old when I talked with her about her household responsibilities. She was enrolled, on scholarship, in a prestigious private university twenty miles from her home, which she would never have known existed if one high school teacher had not urged her to apply.

As a child and continuing through college, Luz, like Estela, served as "la mano derecha" for her parents, who had immigrated from San Luís Potosí, Mexico, to Chicago shortly before she was born. Luz was a middle child, the one of three daughters that her family knew they could count on, and Luz had always played a central role as family translator, mentor for her younger sister, and supporter/counselor for her mother, who suffered from an advanced case of diabetes. During college Luz struggled to live within a meager budget—stretching her income from a work-study job to cover her own books and supplies as well as contribute to her parents' rent, food, and medical expenses—and to keep up with the demands of her coursework. She went home frequently to take her mother to the doctor, where she also served as her translator, and to deal with mail, bills, and the myriad of other English language and literacy tasks that are part of life in the modern age. During her senior year, Luz began commuting the long distance to and from school—first in her family's fifteen-year-old Chevrolet, and then, when it broke down, on a three-hour series of train rides. After four and a half challenging years, Luz graduated from college and began a career as a high school social studies teacher. She continued to care for her mother and began saving money to buy her family their first house.

Framing Translations

When I talk about the experiences of people like Estela, Cindy, Nova, and Luz, most adults who are outsiders to immigrant communities react with concern, pity, or dismay. They ask about the burdens translating places on children and the pressures children feel. Many people assume that translating gives young people more responsibility than they should ever have. This sense that children are somehow "out of place" when they take on family responsibilities like these is reflected in the terms "adultification" and "parentification" that psychologists use to label this as a form of "role reversal" that is detrimental to children's proper development and to normal, healthy family relationships.[3] This presumed deviance is based on the assumptions that when children speak, read, and write for their parents, parental authority is weakened and that children should be neither exposed to "adult" medical, legal, and financial information nor saddled with serious responsibilities at too young an age.

This perspective has roots in family systems theory in clinical psychology. However, the father of this school of thought, Salvador Minuchin, prefaced his discussion of the "parentified child":[4] "The allocation of parental power to a child is a natural arrangement in large families, in single-parent families, or in families where both parents work. The system can function well. The younger children are cared for and the parental child can develop responsibility, competence, and autonomy beyond his years." Following Minuchin's reasoning, taking on household responsibilities does not necessarily involve reversals of parent-child relations or a corresponding abdication of parental responsibility, and households that function according to norms that are different from current, dominant, or "mainstream" norms should not be assumed dysfunctional. This is important to keep in mind when evaluating crosscultural variations in child development and declaring what counts as deviant or normal, a point that I explore throughout this book, and return to especially in chapter 6.

The families that I worked with, in contrast with dominant understandings, generally treated children's translation work as unremarkable. Children were expected to help their families; people were expected to use their skills for the benefit of others; and family members were morally bound to work together for the collective good. It was not uncommon for children in Mexico and Central America to read and write things for their parents, when parents had had little opportunity to develop literacy skills through formal schooling. With life in their home countries as a point of comparison, translating became an extension of appropriate intergenerational relations into new circumstances.

The main complaint that I heard voiced by immigrant parents was about their children's resistance to translating; parents seemed to interpret such resistance as evidence that their children were not developing properly as obedient, helpful, and cooperative children who understood the importance of contributing to the family good. Sra. Gutiérrez, the mother of María, whom I introduce at the end of this chapter, pointed out on several occasions: "¿Ya ves, que ella no me quiere ayudar?" [Now do you see, that she doesn't want to help me?] Estela's mother made this complaint on more than one occasion. But these same parents also expressed pride in their children's skills and appreciation for their contributions. Nothing that parents said suggested that they thought it inappropriate to solicit their children's assistance. One day I rather overtly pressed Nova's mother to consider shifts in intergenerational power relations based on families' movement across cultural borders; still, Sra. Aguilera resisted my interpretation, in the following exchange:

MARJORIE: Y ¿Usted cree que cambia la forma de ser madre, estando aquí, con el inglés como idioma nacional, en comparación con como sería en México?

SRA. AGUILERA: No.

MARJORIE: Como aquí él habla por Ud. en público. Si fuera en Mexico no.

SRA. AGUILERA: No. Yo no cambiaría, yo todo es igual. Nada más que, pues—

MARJORIE: No es que él toma más responsabilidad.

SRA. AGUILERA: Sí, más responsabilidad, y más que le da gusto más, tú
    sabes que tienes un hijo que habla bien el inglés, que habla dos
    idiomas, o tal vez un día hable tres.

MARJORIE: Y no es que se siente uno más, menos poderoso.

SRA. AGUILERA: No.

MARJORIE: No.

SRA. AGUILERA: Yo me siento igual. Cuando a él lo veo que él está, me
    llena tanto como que me siento bien orgullosa de él. No tiene por
    que cambiar la manera de uno ser con ellos, ni ellos con uno. Sí,
    ellos cambian, pero él, yo no lo veo que ha cambiado así que se cree
    más importante.

[MARJORIE: Do you believe that your way of mothering changes, being
    here, with English as the national language, in comparison with
    what it would be like in Mexico?

SRA. AGUILERA: No.

MARJORIE: For example here he talks for you in public. If you were in
    Mexico no.

SRA. AGUILERA: No. I would not change, everything is the same. It's just
    that, well—

MARJORIE: It's not that he takes more responsibility.

SRA. AGUILERA: Yes, more responsibility, and what's more, one takes
    more pleasure, you know you have a son who speaks English well,
    who speaks two languages, or perhaps one day he'll speak three.

MARJORIE: And it's not that you feel more, less powerful.

SRA. AGUILERA: No.

MARJORIE: No.

SRA. AGUILERA: I feel no different. When I see him, I feel so full, I feel
    so proud of him. The manner in which you act with them, or they
    with you, doesn't have to change. Yes, they change, but he, I haven't
    seen that he has changed, such that he thinks he's more important.]

I similarly urged Junior's mother to contemplate whether she felt uncomfortable when her son spoke for her. She responded:

Fíjate casi no. ¿Será por la confianza? Sí, será por la confianza que hay
entre nosotros. Yo no siento, no, o sea, que pues, claro, sería
muchísimo mejor que yo supiera [inglés], verdad, que yo supiera
[inglés] y que yo por mí misma me valiera y todo, pero como yo digo,
pues con él no me siento mal.

[Look, not really. Might it be because of the trust we have? Yes, it's because of the trust that exists between us. I don't feel, or rather, sure, it would be much better if I spoke [English], that's true; if I spoke [English] and I could take care of myself and all, but as I tell you, well, with him I don't feel bad.]

Jasmine's mother recognized not only differences in the demands on children in the United States and in Mexico but also commonalities, as she highlighted the proper role of a child—to help one's parents: "Me pusiera en su lugar, o sea que eso me quiso dar a entender, digo, pues como allá no. Pero si me hubiera tocado así pues, a lo mejor sí, le tendría que ayudar a mi mamá." [I put myself in her place, or rather, this helped me to understand, I tell you, that over there no. But if I had had to do it, well, sure, I would have to help my mother.]

The upper elementary and middle school children that I got to know through my research into the daily lives of children in Los Angeles and Engleville also viewed their translating work quite nonchalantly. Nova put it this way: "It's just something you do to help your family." Jessica wrote in a journal about a specific encounter: "I didn't feel anything because I am so used to it that sometimes I forget what I said for a couple of minutes." Jasmine similarly noted: "I'm getting used to translating. Sometimes I don't even notice or forget." It was not something kids thought much about. They seemed surprised to learn that anyone *studied* this practice.

When I asked them how they felt about translating, more often than not they said they liked it; sometimes they volunteered this perspective without prompting. In one journal entry, Katrina talked about translating in the context of other fun things she had done at an amusement park: "I was translating and helping people (and) it was fun." Most indicated that they felt needed and valued, not burdened, and not particularly powerful. They said they felt brave, good, helpful, and happy.

Children did feel annoyed when a request to translate interrupted an activity they were engaged in or when they had to break their own concentration to explain what was happening to others, such as while watching a movie. In some cases, as with Estela's family, conflicts in the household were expressed partly around translating tasks, but language brokering did not seem to be the cause of the tensions. Children did talk about feeling anxious, nervous, or worried when they interpreted for others, especially in certain circumstances, such as talking on the phone, in public, in emotionally heightened situations, or when dealing with matters of importance to their families. They worried about the effects their words could have. For example, Monique mentioned being "kind of worried because I thought I would make a mistake about a bill." Jasmine talked of being "so, so nervous" when she spoke at the hospital for her brother. Adriana complained of a stomachache when she had to call the Social Security office for her mother. These more emotionally burdensome sorts of translation situations need consideration, but they were not the dominant kinds of translation experiences.

As children grew older, however, I found that sometimes their perspectives on translation shifted. This shift was also evident when I compared the viewpoints offered by younger children (those who were just beginning to take on active roles as family translators), and those of older youth and adult children of immigrants, like Luz, when they reflected on their past and present work as translators. The views of the older youth usually lay somewhat in between the perspectives held by most "American" audiences and immigrant parents. These young people still seemed to view translating as a normal part of their lives. But over time they had come to realize that their childhoods had been quite different from those of "mainstream" Americans, and they were more aware that some people might view their experiences as unusual (including, perhaps, researchers). They seemed to be reevaluating their own experiences through what Karen Pyke terms a "normal American family" monolithic cultural frame—one that constructed their own experiences as deficient.[5] They may also have been reevaluating their lives in the manner that many of us do as we grow older by acknowledging both positive and negative aspects of our own upbringing.[6] These young adults seemed a little more unsettled by their own experiences and talked about them in more ambivalent terms.

These different takes on children's translation work lend insight into normative constructions of childhood and of relations between adults and children. They suggest the importance of understanding varied and shifting vantage points on childhoods. We may see things differently when we contemplate childhoods in retrospect rather than as they unfold. We may judge others' experiences differently than our own. Conversely, we may assume that others feel what we have felt or what we imagine we might feel in their situations. Views may change as circumstances change and as awareness of alternatives grow.

The same facts can take on very different meanings depending on how they are framed and on points of comparison. In the case of child language brokers, it matters if their childhoods are compared with those of youth from dominant groups, nontranslator immigrant youth, the childhoods the brokers experienced in their home countries, observers' childhoods, or those of the children's parents. Further, one can ask: in understanding our own and others' stories, what do we foreground, background, emphasize, and leave out? What is most salient to us, and what misses our attention completely?

I remember talking with a colleague about my grandmother. I told her how my grandmother used to cut napkins in half to avoid waste. I attributed this to "culture"—to the fact that my grandmother was German and Catholic, which I associated with being thrifty and averse to self-indulgence. "Waste not, want not." "Don't take more than you need." And possibly an underlying message: "You don't deserve any more." My colleague resonated with my story and told me about her own grandmother, who also cut napkins in half to use sparingly. She attributed this not to her grandmother's "culture," however, but to the social context in which she lived—the era of the Great Depression in the United States—and to her social class positioning within that context. Through our conversation I came to realize that my grandmother also lived during the Depression and that I had no way of knowing to what extent her daily life habits were the product of "cultural" beliefs or shaped by economic circumstances. There was really no way to disentangle culture from the contexts in which cultural practices took form. What one may ascribe to values and beliefs is at least partly shaped by circumstances; and practices developed in particular circumstances may get rationalized in a set of beliefs and then reified as "cultural."

Social science frameworks may seem rather different than the everyday, informal theories that informed these contemplations on the thriftiness of grandparents, but these interpretive frames work in the same way; they give coherence to particular understandings of the social world. And just as different everyday theories can lend distinct meaning to the same set of events, so too can different social science frames alter interpretations of social phenomena. Theoretical frameworks influence both what is attended to and how these things are understood. These cultural tools both facilitate and constrain meaning-making.

Framing Children

For many years children in the social sciences were framed in limited ways. Scholars studied them mostly in the domains of families and schools and treated them as objects of adults' actions, in particular their efforts to socialize and teach them. Viewed as persons-in-the-making more than actors and agents in their own right, children were "becomings" rather than "beings." In institutions other than homes and schools, they were largely invisible.[7]

In research on immigration, children continue to be mostly invisible outside of families[8] and schools.[9] They are often addressed as baggage: "brought along," "sent for," or "left behind" by sojourning parents. Their participation in decisions to migrate and in processes of settlement has been little considered.

Attention has gone to English language acquisition,[10] school achievement, educational attainment, assimilation, acculturation and identity formation, and other measures of development along pathways to adult success.[11] Children's actions, perceptions, feelings, and experiences, especially outside homes and schools, have been less explored.[12] When language issues are considered, the focus is usually on how rapidly or well immigrant children are acquiring English.[13] Language brokering remains largely unseen.[14]

But over the last few decades a body of literature has been evolving as a corrective to these ways of seeing (or not seeing) children. Historians, anthropologists, sociologists, and cultural geographers have explicitly challenged the teleological or future-oriented developmental bent of much research with children. Variously called the "new sociology (or anthropology) of childhoods," "critical studies of childhood," and the "critical social science of childhood,"[15] this framework calls for explorations of children's actions, contributions, social relationships, and cultures, and for seeing these as worthy of study in their own right, not only in relation to adult concerns. In this line of theorizing and empirical research, importance is given to what children say, think, and feel, and what they *are*, as full participants in social processes, not just what they are becoming. Estela, for example, was at ten not just a preteenager (that is, a girl moving toward adolescence); she was "la mano derecha" [the right hand] of her family. Even as she was developing her own language skills, she was using language as a tool to do things in the larger social world.[16]

The critical social science of childhoods also highlights the socially constructed nature of the category of childhood itself. Childhood is an interpretive frame for understanding the early years of human life, and its meanings have varied over time and across cultures. Just as feminists distinguish between gender (as a social construct) and biological sex, critical childhood scholars differentiate the social phenomenon of childhood from the fact of biological immaturity; they study what Barry Mayall refers to as the "generationing" of the social world:[17] "the relational processes whereby people come to be known as children, and whereby children and childhood acquire certain characteristics, linked to local contexts, and changing as the factors brought to bear change."[18] Childhood is treated as a unit of social analysis, rather than a "natural" and universalized stage, or a given of biological age.

In this chapter I consider what this interpretive frame offers for the study of immigrant childhoods in general and the experiences of child language brokers in particular. I also explore what the study of immigrant child language brokering offers for theorizing about childhoods. The critical social science of childhoods is the first of two major social science frameworks that facilitates my sense-making about children's experiences and guides my representations of their work in this book; I present the second, that of sociocultural theory, in chapter 6.

CHILDHOOD AS A SOCIAL CONSTRUCTION

Phillipe Aries,[19] the first scholar to document the social construction of child-hood in historical time, posited that the very concept of childhood, as a time distinct from adulthood, emerged at the end of the Middle Ages in Europe, tied to the formation of bourgeois notions of family.[20] Childhood was in a sense a luxury that only the upper classes could afford to indulge. Viviana A. Zelizer,[21] following in this manner to examine changing views of and attitudes toward children in the twentieth century United States, traced the shift from viewing children as "useful"—active contributors to household economies—to economically "useless" but sentimentally "priceless." There is now a grow-ing historical literature documenting variations in the meanings and understandings of childhood over time.[22]

Paula Fass's substantive contributions to this literature have brought attention to the place of immigrant childhoods within the larger project of nation-building and "American" cultural identity formation.[23] Fass has exam-ined struggles to define what counts as a proper childhood, especially as these took form between immigrant parents and schools in the early part of the twentieth century. Carrying this forward to the end of the century, she has also brought children into view in contemporary studies of globalization, as the growing movement of people around the world raises new questions about the meanings and values assigned to childhood.

Similar to historical research, studies of children's experiences in varied cultural contexts have illuminated the socially constructed nature of child-hoods, and challenged presumptions of normative child development in the West.[24] Immigrant childhoods are particularly useful for illuminating the socially constructed nature of childhoods because changes are often hastened through families' movement across cultural and geopolitical borders as well as through their interface with institutions like schools. Immigrants' beliefs and practices can also help to denaturalize what is taken for granted in the domi-nant culture.

Partly based on the juxtapositions of discrepant beliefs and practices that are made visible by the movement of people around the world, some theorists argue that we are entering a new historical period in which the meaning of childhood is again being reconstituted, much as it was at the turn of the cen-tury in the United States. Barrie Thorne points to changes in the political economies that shape childhoods:[25] global economic restructuring, the speedup of changes in household compositions and divisions of labor within households, widening social class divides, the decline of the public sector, and the expansion of market forces that structure children's lives. Safe spaces for children to play in have been considerably eroded in many communities, as support for the public sector (schools, playgrounds, parks and recreation) has been cut back in the United States. (However, as I discuss in chapter 2, this also varies across communities because some cities and states have felt the impact of these changes much more than others due to differential tax bases.) Free time for children to play has seemingly diminished, owing to both increased worklike demands of schooling and the increased consumption of extracurricular "work."[26] Other changes are evident, such as more explicit sexualization of children in advertisements and on television, through the Internet, and in new technologies such as music videos.

But the juxtapositions of diverse forms of childhood make clear that changes are not homogeneous and unifying; childhood experiences are not undergoing transformation in the same way for all children.[27] Rather, what childhood means for different kinds of children and families may be under contestation in different ways. Now, as within any given historical period or cultural context, there are many types of children: girls and boys, two-year-olds and twelve-year-olds, rich and poor, documented and undocumented, to name a few dimensions that matter for experiences and perceptions of daily life as well as access to resources and pathways to the future. But some differences—such as those based on family income—may be more consequential now than they were a few decades ago; the growing gap between the rich and eroding poor and public sector supports wreak particular effects on children. (In California, for example, child poverty has increased by 10 percent since 1979, while government supports for children and families have been cut back.)[28]

IMMIGRANT CHILDHOODS

Immigrant families differ from those who have resided in the United States for generations on dimensions that certainly matter for children's experiences of growing up. For one, these families operate with an overt point of comparison— what life was like "back home." This may be an explicit reference point for children and an ongoing one for families who are able to travel back and forth between the two countries; but even if children do not visit their homeland, these places can hold an important space in their imaginations,[29] and "home" is often represented in talk to which children are exposed. Differences between childhoods "here" and "there" may be quite marked to families, and immigrant parents are often keenly aware of the trade-offs involved in their moves. Alma Martínez was the mother of a seven-year-old boy who was left in Guatemala with his grandmother when Alma came to Los Angeles, where her daughter was born the following year. Although she wanted to bring her son with her, she worried, because he was accustomed to "freedom" in the countryside in Guatemala. In Los Angeles, he would be "shut up inside with me, nothing more. He might get sick, or not be able to stand being here." She compared the situations of her two children:

> Él allá goza un poquito más de lo que ella no goza aquí. Y ella goza un poquito más de lo que él no puede tener aquí. Los que están allá no tienen lo material, pero tienen la libertad. Por ejemplo el mío, el niño goza de que tiene a sus abuelos, sus primos, sus tíos, todo. Y mi niña aquí sola encerrada en el apartamento lleno de juguetes se tiene que estar. Aunque tiene un closet lleno de juguetes, se tiene que estar encerrada.

> [He enjoys a little of what she doesn't enjoy here. And she enjoys a little more of what he can't have over there. The ones that are over there don't have material things, but they have freedom. For example, my son enjoys having his grandparents, his cousins, his uncles and aunts and all. And my daughter has to be here alone, closed up in an apartment filled with toys. Even if she has a closet overflowing with toys, she has to be stuck inside.]

Immigrant families also bring distinct cultural practices and traditions to their lives here, ones that may not be recognized or acknowledged by the larger society. Children have to negotiate their families' ways along with dominant culture norms, and these beliefs shape their childhoods. This includes beliefs about the proper relationship of children and adults, the place of children in society, appropriate domains for their activities, and what counts as successful pathways through childhood.

Of course, many immigrants speak a language other than English, which makes the home language environment distinct from "mainstream" English-speaking households; the language milieu and subsequent demand for language brokering constitute a major difference between childhood experiences in families' communities of origin and childhoods in a new land. Language brokering is a cultural practice, and, like all practices, it is shaped by beliefs about intergenerational relations. But this cultural practice is shared across groups from different national, ethnic/racial, and cultural origins; it is not specific to the experiences of people from any given nation or cultural origin. My own work was centered on immigrants from Spanish-speaking countries, and most of the children represented in this book were of Mexican or Central

American origin, but language brokering is not a "Mexican" cultural tradition; it is shaped by the needs and circumstances of being an immigrant. Cindy, the fourteen-year-old in the opening vignette, immigrated with her family from Hong Kong, and I included her here to remind readers that many young people like her, from countries all around the world—and in countries all around the world—do this same kind of work. This is especially true today given how global economic restructuring has created massive flows of migration around the planet, but it has been true throughout history as well.

CHILDHOODS IN "CONTACT ZONES"

Much research on children and childhoods has been situated within a single central cultural context and often in a single domain (such as home or school). It is aimed at understanding how children become members of a given social group or how childhoods are constructed in that setting. But immigrant children live in what Mary Pratt calls "contact zones"—social spaces where "cultures meet, clash, and grapple with each other."[30] The act of language brokering brings speakers of different languages into direct contact, with language brokers standing literally and figuratively "in the middle" between cultural worlds. When María negotiated between her mother and her teacher (as I describe in chapter 5), she had to manage these adults' divergent expectations for her own socialization, including their beliefs about how she should speak and act at such parent conferences. When Briana talked with a doctor and her mother about her sister's cold symptoms (presented in chapter 4), she similarly navigated between potentially variant perspectives on how to promote children's health and well-being. In crosscultural encounters, differences in beliefs, values, and practices may become more visible and heightened to participants as well as to onlookers. The juxtaposition of distinct beliefs about how children should behave and how adults should interact with them makes immigrant childhoods particularly useful for theorizing about historical and cultural change.

At the same time, just as immigrant childhoods differ in important ways from native childhoods (in either the home or host country), differences emerge in childhood experiences within and across immigrant families. Household composition, the age of arrival of different family members, and the nature and extent of prior schooling matter. Some nuclear families may be split across national borders, as Alma Martínez's was. In the same family some children may have citizenship rights (those born in the United States) while others may have different kinds of legal status, differences that are now more consequential than ever, given increased surveillance over immigrants and changing laws stipulating their access to public services. Older and younger children may grow up in very different contexts, including their language milieu, because more English enters the household once older siblings are in school and as adults acquire English over time. Indeed, contact zones exist within families as well as between families and the outside world.

CHILDREN AS ACTORS AND AGENTS

As translators, children make things happen for themselves and their families; they forge connections and open up lines of communication. They make it possible for adults to do things that they could not otherwise accomplish. I show many examples of children's direct actions—answering phone calls, setting up appointments, making purchases, soliciting services, and more—in the next few chapters. Schools and homes are not surprisingly the sites for many of the children's actions (because in modern Western society children's participation in other spheres is curtailed), but language brokering also takes youth into public spaces. Even within the home, children act in relation to an array of institutions by taking on financial, political, medical, legal and other matters where children's actions have been little studied. Moreover, language brokering takes place in public spaces that include a wide array of institutional domains. (See Appendix C for a summary of this study's reported and observed children's language brokering activities, organized by domains.)

Children's actions also open up space and time for other people in less direct ways. When Junior read to his younger siblings, his mother's time was freed for housework. When Luz helped her sister fill out college applications, the college counselor was spared that task. When Nova spoke for his father at the hospital, the hospital was released from finding a suitable translator—or as more often happens—the paraprofessionals and custodians who doubled as informal interpreters in many such settings were able to concentrate on the work that they were paid to do and not their informal, rarely compensated translation work.

The indirect nature of some of children's contributions to family processes is especially important for considerations of immigrants' contributions to society. In many ways, the children of immigrants support and sustain their parents as workers in the United States and allow them to engage in productive work. But children's labor—like that of homemakers—is largely invisible and often not counted as part of the labor cost equation, except by critical childhoods scholars.[31] The critical social science of childhood thus helps us to think about children's contributions to household economies within a much larger structural frame, and we see the relationship between everyday life and larger institutions and social structures. In any given household, children's actions may be small, but when they are added up across households they may represent a significant contribution to society. Children's efforts go well beyond the household, as we see in chapter 4.

Children also assert agency by resisting adults' efforts to socialize them, as María's mother perceived her to do when she complained that María didn't want to help her. And they are subjects as well as objects; the children take the lead and model expertise for adults, their siblings, and other children. When Cindy's mother fretted that she didn't know how to get to a location, she said, "We don't know how to get there, we haven't been there before." Cindy replied: "But that doesn't mean we can't."

AGENTS OF SOCIAL TRANSFORMATION. Children's actions as translators may also shape social structures by pushing at and sometimes transforming intergenerational social boundaries. By looking at intergenerational relationships on the ground, in the context of specific activities such as translation, one can then contemplate historical changes in the constructions of childhoods, identifying the contributions of children's work to either reproduce or change the status quo. This may include what children do directly through their own activities, as well as what children's presence and agency allow others to do.

Children's translation work is a discursive practice, but it has material outcomes for families; children use language to access concrete opportunities and material resources for their families. Through this practice they may transform childhood itself. The generational structuring of social processes shapes translation work (for example, the presumed "natural" role for children in social interactions); in turn, it may change those structures.[32] Beliefs about children's rights, needs, and responsibilities give form to this practice (for example, children should defer to adults, not interrupt or challenge adults' viewpoints), even as the practice may influence those beliefs. Translation work is implicated in the translation of childhood itself—in what comes to be seen as "normal" or appropriate for children.[33]

CONSTRAINTS ON CHILDREN'S ACTIONS. There are, of course, constraints on children's actions in any society. In the modern United States these include laws that are designed to protect children but that may restrict them as well, including currently proposed laws that prohibit children from translating in public hospitals and clinics;[34] institutional regulations; local practices; and cultural, moral, religious and ethical strictures that delimit children's actions. Physical or biological limitations may also pertain, due to height, weight, strength, and brain or bodily development. On average, children are smaller and shorter than adults, and this may pose limitations for them in particular activities, just as it may make possible their engagement in other practices. (Limitations always go both ways.) Further, any such constraints do not cut cleanly by age, which is why categorical labels are so problematic. Some adults are shorter than some children; some children are stronger than some adults; some children have a capacity for abstract thinking that some adults lack; and so on. But even with these limits on their actions, children always exercise agency; they act within and sometimes against constraints.

SEEING CHILDREN'S ACTIONS. Children's actions may be noticed most when they step outside the bounds of what is considered appropriate for children, based on moral, cultural, or legal guidelines. Reactions to such moments of rupture to the status quo can reveal a great deal about a social group's beliefs and normative practices. Child language brokering practices involve many such disruptions, which is what makes this work unsettling to some people, and studying the practice particularly useful for understanding the socially constructed nature of childhoods. The strong emotions that are sometimes evoked, either in participants or in those viewing the practice—feelings of discomfort, elation, pride, embarrassment or fear—are useful lenses into changing notions of childhood because intense feelings may indicate the transgression of entrenched social norms. In recognition of this I continually asked children how they felt about their work as language brokers in different settings, contexts, tasks, and relationships; I asked them what felt "just normal" and what did not.

Naming and Framing

NAMING AND FRAMING CHILDREN

In naming children's work as translators, several questions arise: What to call this labor? How to label the people who do it? Are these *immigrant child* language brokers or just language brokers? When participants are not given labels based on their membership in particular social groups (for example, those based on race/ethnicity, gender, social class, or age), there is a risk of misrepresenting them. There are unmarked assumptions, for example, that doctors are male, secretaries are female, and people are white unless they are identified as people of color. Similarly, "translators" may be presumed to be adults unless they are specifically named "child translators."

But age-based categories can also trivialize the work. The youth I introduce to you in this book are translators: they engage in more translation work than do many bilingual adults. In modifying the term translator with an age-based adjective ("child") my aim is to expose common assumptions about who is generally authorized to speak for whom—much as the terms "child soldier" and "teen mother" reveal beliefs about who should or should not go to war or have children.[35] Yet, marking the term *child* translator (like *child* soldier) reveals an assumption that this isn't normal; that is, translators and soldiers should be adults. And doing this may also diminish children's authority, power, and skills in the eyes of the reader.

Naming based on age categories is in some ways more troublesome than naming based on other somewhat more stable social groupings (such as gender and race/ethnicity) because the boundaries between age categories are blurred, and their content is continuously shifting. The eight- to eighteen-year-olds that I worked with are located in the borderlands between what is considered childhood and adulthood in modern Western society. They may be variously labeled, viewed, and treated as children, adolescents, preadolescents, teens, preteens, "tweens," or young adults. In this book, I mostly refer to these people as "children," but I sometimes use the term "youth." Across the years in which I worked with these young people, I found my own descriptions shift; when María was ten I was comfortable calling her a child, but less so when she was fifteen. Whether these people are viewed (and view themselves) as *children, youth, teens,* or *young adults* may well matter in how they engage in these activities or how others engage them. It may matter as well for what they take away from the experiences. And how I label them also certainly shapes how readers will understand their experiences.

Names define both by inclusion and exclusion. In taking lessons from feminists, critical childhood scholars note that childhood, like gender, is a relational category, constituted through opposition. A child is a child because she is not an adult. And one is always a child in relation to one's parents no matter how old one may be. Relationships between adults and children, particularly between parents and kids, are especially pertinent to language brokering because the children of immigrants, like Luz, may remain "child translators" long into adulthood. The needs and competencies of different family members may shift over time, and the nature of parent-child relationships may also transmogrify, but brokering activities will still be embraced in some form of parent-child relations.

Who counts in a particular version of "child" also varies across situations, tasks, and activities. Sometimes the designation may appear to be based on seemingly arbitrary distinctions, as every parent who has sought discount fees at museums and amusement parks knows. And sometimes these distinctions seem contradictory; for example, eighteen-year-old U.S. citizens can join the army but cannot purchase beer. Children may be seen as capable of translating in some situations and for some tasks, but not others. Mary Bucholtz points out that these age-defining terms shift meaning when used in different sociopolitical circumstances;[36] for example, children might be classified as adults in the U.S. legal system, yet older young adults might be called children in child labor discussions. I call on readers to question your own such assumptions—to notice your own reactions to my reports on children's activities.

NAMING AND FRAMING TRANSLATION

The labels given to the work of translating and interpreting also bear consideration. The various terms that have been used each capture aspects of the practice even as they misrepresent other dimensions, and each should be considered for the assumptions it embeds both about language and about the practice of children speaking to and for adults.

LANGUAGE BROKERING. "Language brokering," the most utilized term, captures the mediational work that children do as they advocate for their families and negotiate between monolingual speakers. These negotiations were captured nicely by Olga Vásquez, Lucinda Pease-Alvarez, and Sheila Shannon, in their foundational work on the practice.[37] Children use language as a *tool* of negotiation; they do not passively transmit words from one person to another in the manner that the dictionary definition of the word "translation" ("to bear, convey, or remove from one person, place or condition to another; to transfer, transport")[38] might suggest. Sara Chu uses a similar term: "immigrant child mediators";[39] others emphasize the cultural dimensions of the work with the term "culture brokering."[40] However, these labels obscure the power imbalances between participants in most translation events; after all, children are not neutral or powerful "brokers" when they speak to and for adults and represent their immigrant families to institutions of the dominant society.

FAMILY INTERPRETING. "Family interpreting," a term introduced by Guadalupe Valdés in her study of translation work as a form of giftedness,[41] extends the notion of "informal interpreting" by emphasizing the collaborations among family members (see chapter 3).[42] This term captures the ways in which children align with their families in this work, as they represent their families to the larger social world. Valdés follows the commonly endorsed stance that "interpreting" refers to oral transactions, whereas "translation" involves the transposition of written text. Indeed, in informal conversations, many people have pointed out that they see this work as interpretation, not translation.

NATURAL TRANSLATION. A distinction between orality and literacy is not made by Brian Sherwood, the author of the earliest term used to reference this phenomenon, that of "Natural Translation,"[43] nor does the dictionary definition of the word "translation" suggest that translation pertains only to the movement of words from written texts. I have elected to use the terms "translate" and "interpret" interchangeably because I follow sociocultural theorists who work with an all-encompassing notion of text and who argue that the oral/written divide is more illusory than real.[44] At the same time, adding "natural" in front of the word translation to describe the work that bilingual children do seems to presume that bilinguals "naturally" acquire a capacity to move between languages. Although many bilinguals do seem to offer spontaneous, "natural" translations, other translation situations that immigrant youth find themselves in are more contrived; this term may misrepresent the challenges they present. Gideon Toury suggests referring to the work of "native translators" rather than the act of "natural translation."[45]

PARA-PHRASING. To capture aspects of this phenomenon that may be obscured by other labels, I've sometimes used another term, *para*-phrasing, to refer to both interpreter-mediated-encounters and text-mediated interactions.[46] This coined term invokes a play on the Spanish word *para*, to emphasize how translation work is used *for* real purposes and *in order to* accomplish social goals. (This label, like all others, does not do justice to the full complexity of the practice.) Children do not simply move words and ideas or explicate concepts; they take action in the world. The prefix *para* also indexes the disparity of power between what these children do and what is seen as "real" translating. Like other kinds of "para-professionals," child "*para*-phrasers" act in capacities for which they have little or no formal training and in which their qualifications are open to question and critique. Indeed, largely because they are children, they are subjected to adult coparticipants' evaluations of their linguistic, communicative, and social performances (see explicit explanation in chapter 5).

TRANSCULTURAL AND INTERGENERATIONAL WORK. Children are particularly vulnerable to such critique when they speak for adults in public spaces (see chapter 4). Public *para*-phrasing activities have received considerable attention in the media—while everyday home translations go largely unrecognized—precisely because in these situations children appear "out of place." When children speak for adults in public spaces that are normally the domain of adults, they overstep generational boundaries in U.S. mainstream notions of childhood, and their actions become marked and visible. Indeed, to be "out in the world" is to *be* an adult; Cindy commented on this explicitly: "I've been out in the world more. I feel I'm an adult as much as anybody."

Adult public space in the United States is also *white* public space,[47] a place where immigrants, like children, are expected to be "seen but not heard" and where alternatives to English and to white, middle-class interactional styles appear as deviant from the unmarked norm. Thus, language brokering is also transcultural work,[48] and the children of immigrants stand at the borders of both intergenerational and cultural/social class borders when they speak to and for adults in most public spaces, and those borders are imbricated with power relations. Spanish and English are accorded different symbolic capital in public interactions, and children's words—as well as the families they represent—may be interpreted through the lens of racializing discourses as well as discourses about appropriate tasks for children of different ages.[49]

The presumed dangers of overstepping generational and cultural borders are evinced in popular representations of child language brokering. In an episode of the TV show "ER," a Spanish-speaking mother died because her child mistranslated the dosage of medicine that was prescribed to her. The instructions read "Take once a day"; the child read "once" as the Spanish word "once" [eleven], and so the mother overdosed on the medicine. Leaving aside the ways in which this account stretches reason (that "take once a day" would be misread and interpreted as "take eleven a day" rather than the more logical "take one a day," that a child would presume a Spanish word to be embedded in an English sentence—something that never happened in any of the translations we recorded—or that mothers would comply without questioning such a dosage, especially when dispensed from a small vial), this popular representation of translation work strikes a chord of danger: children should not be entrusted to provide information to adults. Adult community translators have been shown to make many medical mistranslations,[50] but such mistakes are not attributed to the age or social competencies of the translator; indeed, they may go unnoticed, and to my knowledge, no popular television show has dramatized translation mistakes made by adults.

The Value of Multiple Frames

The critical childhoods framework focuses attention on children's perspectives on their translation experiences and illuminates how their activities are shaped by their own and others' beliefs about what children should or should not do, as well as the generational dimensions of institutional structures. It foregrounds how children's work as translators matters for their households, schools, and communities and for larger social processes. This framework guides my representations of children's activities as *work*, and my explorations of how this work shapes children's experiences of childhood. In this meaning of the term "translating immigrant childhoods" I address childhoods as social phenomena, not property of individual children.

But even as I focus on children as actors and agents who contribute to social processes, I also recognize that children *are* continuously growing and changing—as indeed we all are, across our life spans. We all learn from the practices we engage in and the experiences that we garner, and our participation in those practices changes over time. The complex social, cognitive, and linguistic nature of language brokering suggests this to be a particularly powerful vehicle for learning and development. Not to consider the role that language brokering plays in children's learning and development would be to overlook an important dimension of these experiences. And so, in chapter 6, I sketch a second theoretical framework that has been important for my analyses—sociocultural theory. This developmental framework offers ways of understanding what children learn and how they develop from their work as translators and interpreters. It provides a lens for zooming in on the growth processes of children who engage actively in practices of translation.

Junior, María, Nova, and Estela

With these thoughts on how to name, frame, and report on children's experiences in mind, I present three more child translators to you and provide more background on Estela and Nova, two of the young people I introduced at the opening of this chapter. Estela, Junior, Nova, and María are the four children whose translation experiences I documented most closely, in thousands of pages of transcripts and field notes gathered from 2001 to 2007; and their experiences figure prominently in this book. The portraits I sketch here are based principally on my earliest field notes, when these children were ten to twelve years old. In chapter 6 I offer a second portrait of these youth when they were fifteen to seventeen years.

In representing these young people, I face the same sorts of challenges that youth translators face when they take complex ideas and concepts, or "whole" realities, and summarize them in words to audiences that lack access to the original material. I wish that I could spark the same sense of each person that I feel when I reach into my memory to construct these representations. Junior, Nova, María, and Estela are so much more than either "participants" in my studies or "subjects" of my research; each has a very special place in my heart, and they cannot be fully represented in two-dimensional portraits through words on paper.

JUNIOR

Junior immigrated with his parents from a small farming community in Guanajuato, Mexico, when he was two. The family went first to Phoenix, Arizona, and then to Chicago a few years later. When Junior was four, the family moved out of the city to the suburb I call "Engleville," as Junior says, "because there were too many 'gangas' in Chicago." Junior's sister, Natalia, was born when he was six, and his brother, Roberto, when he was seven.

When I met Junior he lived with his family in a one-bedroom apartment on the second floor of an apartment row house on a main street in town, a block from my own home. When I returned to visit them two years later they lived on the first floor of a house on a tree-lined street in what seemed like a quiet, suburban neighborhood. The upstairs neighbors included twin girls that were Natalia's age, and on the hot summer day that I visited them the children had created a doll's house out of scraps of cardboard in a backyard that boasted dozens of tall, lush tomato plants cultivated by their parents.

For his first four years of school, Junior was bussed to a school that housed the district's bilingual program on the far end of town. In the fourth grade, Junior officially "exited" from this program, which meant that he was no longer eligible to attend the school. He was sent back to his neighborhood school, a transition that he and his mother both found difficult. Sra. Flores regretted that she could no longer easily communicate with teachers and office personnel. This placed Junior in the role of home-school language broker by interpreting for his own parent-teacher conferences, deciphering information that was sent home from school (because no official translations were provided), and sending messages back and forth between his mother and his teacher.

Junior's father worked six days a week during the spring, summer, and fall doing yard work. Sometimes Junior accompanied him, which could involve him in brokering language between the clients and his father. Sra. Fernández did occasional house cleaning and childcare outside the home and later took in a neighbor's child to care for in her own home while the child's mother worked. Junior spent most of his out-of-school time in the company of his mother and his younger siblings and used his English skills with them in many ways, including reading stories, reading and deciphering the mail, and speaking for his mother in shops, the public library, medical appointments, and on the phone. He consistently wrote that he "felt good" about helping his family by translating.

When Junior was in sixth grade, his mother complained to me that her son sometimes mumbled too much. She claimed his teachers said the same. Sometimes I found it hard to understand Junior, both in person and on tape,

as he blended his words together and inserted the word "asina" into his talk. (This literally means "in this way." It is an archaic version of the word "así" that is used by Mexican rancheros more or less the way young people use "you know" in English.)[51] But other times I heard a lilting voice on tape, as when Junior read to his younger brother and sister, his Midwest-nasal-Spanish-inflected vowels rising and falling with marked expressiveness as he read the English text and then rendered his own translation. In one such reading, he paused only slightly in his search for the words for ribbons and bows (opting for a reasonable translation: bows and more bows), and self-correcting his English transliteration of "Cinderella's friends" as "Sinderela's amigos" into the proper Spanish grammatical form ("los amigos de Cinderella"):

> But Cinderella's friends, Jack and Gus, and the birds sewed ribbons and bows to one of her dresses. Oh! said Cinderella. It looks so priiiitty. Thank you, mah liddle frinds.

> Pero Sinderela's amigos, los amigos de Sinderela, Jack y Gus, y los pájaros, cosieron, cosieron moños y, más moños, en su vestido. ¡O! dijo Sinderela. Se mira bien:: maravilloso. Gracias, mis, amigos chiquitos.

> [But Cinderella's friends, the friends of Cinderella,[52] Jack and Gus, and the birds, sewed, they sewed bows, and more bows, on her dress. Oh! Said Cinderella. It looks really:: marvelous. Thanks, my little friends.]

NOVA

Nova was born in a small farming town in Guanajuato, Mexico, that is just a mile or so from Junior's hometown. He moved to Engleville with his family when he was eleven. He described the move in a school essay written in eighth grade:

> The first time I came to America was in a Greyhound-like bus called "El Conejo" [the rabbit], and it took us two nights and one day to arrive in Engleville. I think it was spring in the U.S.A. on May 13. It was kind of cold. The things that impressed me about the U.S.A. were: the big city that Engleville was, the restaurants the buildings, and the people because they were white, with "gold" hair. The familiar things from the U.S.A. and Mexico were all the Mexican people I met, and my uncles.

Whereas Junior, after five years, exited from their school district's bilingual program in fourth grade, Nova, who entered U.S. schools in fifth grade,

continued to receive bilingual supports through middle school. In the same school essay, he claimed he had "problems" with English: "I used to mix some English words with Spanish words. I used to make up some words that I didn't even know." But even as Nova was learning English, he was expected to help his parents in translation tasks. Nova used the tape recorder that we gave him to voice-record commentaries on his translation activities, and his hesitation with English vocabulary, grammar, and pronunciation was evident on these tapes he made when he was in sixth grade, even as he carefully self-corrected:

> Friday, July Twenty-Seven. Two Thousand and One. Today we were at the restaurant, and then::, my dad wanted to get some ag-, some more water. And he told me to tell the guy 'cause there wasn't no, almost nobody who speak Spanish on there. IN there. So I asked the guy. He was, uh, American. And my dad told me to tell him, and I di= I told him. And then my dad, he said thanks. For telling the guy. And I felt proud of it.

When I first met them, Nova's family lived in a two-flat next door to Junior. A few years later they moved to freshly-painted duplex on a quiet residential street, sharing the house and the mortgage with extended family (Sr. Aguilera's brother, wife, and three children). Nova had his own room, and the computer that he helped his family to purchase was located there. The family managed to purchase this home and computer despite their limited incomes from unstable, low-wage jobs. They did this in part by forgoing trips home to Mexico, although they continued sending money to family living there. Nova's father worked in landscaping, supplemented by snow removal in the winter. Nova's mother also contributed to the mortgage with income from her job as a maid in the guesthouse of the nearby university. Her work hours varied, depending on guesthouse bookings; her work hours decreased dramatically right after September 11, 2001, which created considerable hardship for the family.

MARÍA

María was ten years old when I met her, but she had a feisty spirit that made me think she was so much older. In our project focus groups, or what we came to call "Junior Ethnographer Meetings," María always held back at first, watching from afar with eyes politely, but not shyly, averted, her mouth pulling up slightly into a smile, quietly attending. But given an opening there she was, in the center of the action, commanding attention, holding the stage. "Don't you see you can't just stand there? You've got to act!" she told Nova and Tony, boys from another school that she barely knew, two years and a head taller than she. "Her mom thinks she's going to jail, and I think she's going to Yale," reported her teacher. "It's cause I talk a lot," María conceded.

María, who selected this pseudonym in an apparent display of identification with a fieldworker on this project (María Meza), was born in Engleville, a few years after her parents had moved from the same small farming community in the state of Guanajuato, Mexico, where Junior was born. (Indeed, Sra. Gutiérrez and Sra. Flores are cousins). Her parents spent a year in Chicago before moving to Engleville just before María was born. Her mother maintained active ties with family in Mexico; María and her brothers spent several summers there with their mother.[53]

When I first met them, the Gutiérrez family lived in a basement apartment on a main street in Engleville. María was in the fourth grade at Jefferson Elementary School, walking distance from her home. A few years later, her parents purchased a home in a section of town that had historically been an African American neighborhood; now it was populated with a mix of Mexican families and African Americans. The small three-bedroom house had a large backyard complete with a swing-set and jungle gym. It was a few blocks from the high school that María attended. María's mother was proud of their new home, though meeting the mortgage payments demanded sacrifices of the family, one of which was to forego trips back to Guanajuato; and in the year 2003 the family struggled because employment was cut back, and their car needed significant repairs. Sra. Gutiérrez also took on part-time work as a lunchroom aide at Jefferson.

María's work at home included extensive translating; in her journal entries she reported on translating letters, phone calls, school information, television shows, as well as interactions in stores, doctors' offices, and at school. María used her English skills to provide homework help to many people: her siblings, her neighbors, and even her mother, who was studying English at night. She translated mostly for her mother; her father could usually get his boss to help him with translating complex texts, but María helped him with smaller day-to-day things. But María's life was not all work by any means. She enjoyed riding her bike, reading, watching Disney movies, listening to Mexican ranchera music, and playing computer games.

In general, María was very aware of and attentive to her family's financial status. She frequently asked questions about how much various things cost—from movies to sodas to computers to college. She asked to see our receipts when we mentioned having bought something at a local store. Once when her mother said something about wearing a coat because they couldn't afford to see the doctor if she were to get sick, María responded, "Yeah, I know, the money, the money." She also displayed an awareness of the intersection of race/ethnicity and social class when she commented: "Casi todos los mexicanos no tienen mucho dinero" [Most Mexicans don't have much money]. And she took much interest in the topic of ethnic labels. When we gave her the consent forms to participate in this research, she asked what the word "Latino" meant in our title ("Latino children as family translators"). María Meza, a fieldworker on the project, explained that the term referred to people from Latin America. María replied, "Then I can't be Latino because I'm from here." María Meza explained that because her parents were from Mexico, she could call herself Latina. María responded, "Can't I just be Mexican?"

ESTELA

Estela came to the United States with her parents from a small town located just outside the ranchos where Junior, María, and Nova's families lived in the state of Guanajuato, Mexico. Here are Estela's own words, unedited, in her fourth-grade essay, "All About Me":

> I am going to tell you about myself. I have two sisters one is fore and the other one is one month old and I am the only one ho can cary her except for my mom and dad she eats a lot and my mom lets me berp her some taems she thros up on me.
>
> I was borne in Mexico in Mexico is so fun but hear is more in Mexico you can go out in the night and no one will rob you. There is no cars in Mexico well there is some but not were I live there is a lot of stores ofer hear and in December there is a fest and you can go on lot of raeds. That is all about me for raet naw.

When I first met them, Estela's family rented a small apartment on the second floor of a house on a busy street, two doors down from the house that Maria's parents had just recently purchased. When I visited after my move to Los Angeles in 2001, the family had purchased a home, located on a quiet, residential street with a huge park that extended from their back yard. And as described in the opening vignette, Estela's work increased as she took care of her younger sisters while her mother worked the night shift at Burger King. Her father worked several jobs and also played in a band made of fellow migrants from this town (and indeed, they had played together back home).

Of all the children with whom I worked, Estela was perhaps the most prototypical child translator, one whose experiences may give support to the idea that children can be burdened by this work. Like María, she also spent many hours in play activities. She liked to dress up, dance, play with Barbie dolls, and sing. Her childhood was shaped by all of these experiences and more.

Each portrait I have painted here is, of course, partial. Families, like the communities described in chapter 2, are dynamic; they can be photographed from many angles and in many shades of light, all of which render different effects. Portraits fix dynamic and continuously changing situations into the ethnographic present. They freeze the frame, douse the image in fixative, and then sear it into our consciousness, while life in each family and community moves on. (I have, however, tried to avoid this by using the past tense, rather than the "ethnographic present," to make clear that I am depicting the family and children at specific points in time.[54] I do the same when I detail specific translation events in the following chapters.) I face this same problem in chapter 2 when I present three of the communities in which I worked, especially because I worked in each during different points of historical time. I'll try to give some sense of these changes that communities, individuals, and families go through, especially in chapter 6, but these cannot fully capture the experiences any family has in the process of raising children and of growing up. This is one of the many challenges of "translating" these children's experiences in this book.

Chapter 2 Landscapes of Childhood

Hᴏᴛ ꜱᴜᴍᴍᴇʀ nights in New England, circa 1970. I was ten years old, and school was out, so I got to play outside after supper until dark. Most of my siblings and the rest of the neighborhood kids were there. We sorted ourselves at times in pairs matched by age and gender; across these Irish- and German-Catholic families of five, six, eight, and ten kids, we could always find some age-mates. Other times we collapsed into mixed groups with girls and boys of different ages to play games like Kickball, Spud, and Kick the Can.[1] Kick the Can was my favorite, because you got to run hard and disappear somewhere out of view. Places to hide were plentiful, and my memories of childhood summers are those of being unconstrained by either time or space. There was freedom, too, from the eyes of adults: this was our territory, and we negotiated our own rules, solved our own problems, and forged our own memories, at least on those hot summer nights.

My thoughts shift from my childhood in New England to a classroom in the inner city of Los Angeles some fifteen years later, on another hot summer day. I was a teacher now, and school was in session because this was a multi-track, year-round school in which instruction proceeded with two months on and one month off, leaving us in sweltering classrooms on days when other kids were at the beach. I was leading my class in one of their favorite games, that of "Head's Up, Seven Up." Here, constraints were everywhere; this game was played in their seats by kids, with heads down, moving no more than an arm or a thumb, and in silence. My students loved this game, and the school coaches often led the class in rounds of it in the name of Physical Education on "Smog Alert" days when classes couldn't be held outside. When we did go out, it was to a fenced area no bigger than a football field that accommodated eighteen hundred children's bodies in the course of a day. Fifth-grade students patrolled this yard, wearing yellow traffic control vests and wielding hand-held STOP signs to remind kids that they couldn't run here because it was too crowded, all asphalt, and there weren't enough band-aides in the nurse's office to cover all the scraped knees that could result. Yet this was the one place in this neighborhood with more than a few feet of unconstrained space—one of the only outdoor places where kids could play.

Flashback again to a farming town in central Mexico where Nova and Junior were born, a place I found my way to by bus from Mexico City in the summer of 2000. The quiet was what I found most palpable here: the slight hum of the summer air, broken by the occasional sound of crickets, a bird chirping over head, or a rooster braying from someone's backyard. It seemed to me to be an idyllic world for children in so many ways—with almost limitless space to roam, few of the dangers imposed by modern technology (from traffic to smog to pesticides to the junk food that's so readily available on most city corners), and many watchful-yet-unobtrusive eyes of adults. There was a daily menu of beans, rice, hand-picked fruits and vegetables, fresh eggs, and cow's milk. Time seemed to exert no pressures; here life seemed to watch itself go by. Indeed, that was the problem. This may be a place for idyllic childhoods, but futures are limited. Everyone knew this fact so few young adults were left in town.

Views of Childhoods

The children that play on the schoolyard in central Los Angeles, some of whom you meet in this book, come from rural areas like this one in Mexico and Central America. Their parents talk about life "back home" much the way I remember my childhood "back then" in mid-twentieth-century New England—nostalgic musings about the freedom of movement that some associate with childhood, value for their children, and see missing in city life. Children living in global urban centers like Los Angeles experience very different rhythms of daily life than their parents did as children in Mexico and Central America. These differences shape the meanings that childhood takes on here and there and suggest how those meanings may be "translated" through the movement of people across geopolitical borders and sociocultural spaces. The points of comparison that are used to understand experiences shape interpretations.

Urban Los Angeles, as a context for childhoods,[2] is a far cry from rural areas of Mexico and Central America, and immigrants who move to this global city experience many discordances with the way things were done back home. When immigrants move to other places—such as the rural and suburban areas that are increasingly becoming new receiving contexts for immigrants[3]—some of those transitions are not as vast, while other differences may be more pronounced. Immigrants may be seen by native-born residents in different ways, based on their social positions within the "fields of difference" in different locales. Children's work as translators both shapes and is shaped by how immigrants are seen within the constellation of local groups.

In this chapter, I develop comparative portraits of three communities in which I studied children's daily lives between 1983 and 2003. These landscapes shape the structuring of immigrant childhoods in many ways, including in the needs and opportunities for children to serve as translators and in how their work is viewed by others. Local contexts serve as backdrops against which children's translation work is seen; they shape the available discourses for understanding this practice; and they structure families' access to information, material goods, and resources as well as the available resources for doing so.

The first portrait is of the neighborhood around a school that I call Madison, in central Los Angeles, where I both lived when I first moved to Los Angeles and worked for more than ten years. As I detail in Appendix A, I observed the daily experiences of children in and out of school during a period of three years as part of a comparative study of childhoods in three California communities.[4] In studying children's daily life experiences my attention was drawn to children's work as language brokers because translation work was part of everyday life. In this community I interviewed dozens of child translators, whose voices appear throughout this text.

When I moved to Chicago in 1998, I concentrated my research on the linguistic, cultural, and social demands of language brokering and the relationship between everyday translation work and school language practices. I began by surveying fifth and sixth graders at a Chicago public school about their ways of using language, which included their translation experiences. I then led a team of researchers in conducting interviews and observations with students who indicated that they were active translators for their families. We worked closely with thirteen children, visiting them in their homes and classrooms throughout a period of two years. The work took place is a relatively "settled" immigrant community on the northwest side of Chicago, where immigrants from Mexico were filling in around a previous and continuing wave of immigrants from Poland.

The third site is a small city that I call "Engleville," just outside of Chicago, where María, Estela, Nova, and Miguel lived with their families. In this community I most closely observed children translators in action, and I report on these four children's translation experiences more than on other children throughout this book. As I detail in Appendix A, I spent a great deal of time hanging out with these families, talking to the children about their daily lives in general, and their translation experiences in particular, and audiotaping them in a variety of translation encounters. In all three communities, children also wrote about their translation experiences in journals.

The three communities represent a range of receiving contexts for immigrants and distinct grounds for the construction of childhoods. A contrastive analysis is useful for exposing dimensions of social contexts that matter for children's experiences of living, growing, and being raised. This includes the resources, opportunities, supports, and barriers that they encounter in their work as translators. Children can experience very different sorts of "translating childhoods" even if practices of translation are similar across sites because the ways in which others see practices shape their meanings.

Madison

I look from my memory's eye at the corner of a busy intersection toward the entrance to the school that I call Madison—my everyday workplace from 1983 to 1993. I first recall fences, gates, and barricades. Tall iron bars blocked the entrance, flanked by signs warning against transporting weapons onto campus and instructing all visitors to check in at the office and secure a badge. (The gates were presumably there to protect children from intruders, but I remember being locked *inside* that gated area when I and a fellow first-year teacher stayed into the evening; we had to shimmy the fence in order to get out.)

On the other side of the school, a chained link fence enclosed an asphalt yard the size of a football field. Additional wire fences were added after I moved from Los Angeles; on a return visit I saw that the lunch area had been enclosed in what looked to me like a cage. A yellow police barricade blocked traffic from turning in front of the school, reminiscent of the concrete barricades that were erected a few streets away to control the flow of drug sale traffic in that neighborhood. I remember coils of barbed wire atop the fence of the car repair shop, beyond which loomed the skyscrapers of downtown. A gas station, liquor store, 99-cent store, and brick apartment building with boarded up windows lined the corners. Looking past the school in the other direction, there were rows of three- and four-story apartment buildings interspersed with a few 1920s-era houses that had now been subdivided into multiple living units. A few thin trees lined the sidewalk—planted during a city-sponsored tree-planting campaign—and there was one very lush plot of land that constituted a community garden, but what I remember most is concrete, brick, and asphalt.

Madison, located just a few miles west of downtown Los Angeles, was almost literally under the shadow of the Hollywood sign. Census blocks, political divisions, police precincts, and school intake areas all used different boundaries to carve up this community; from the perspective of children, the block or apartment building was perhaps the most meaningful sense of "neighborhood," and the school intake area put the clearest bounds on the area to structure families' daily lives. For the purposes of my research, I defined this community as the intake area to Madison, which was one of more than a dozen elementary schools located within the larger section of the city that was loosely known as Pico Union, Central Los Angeles, or, sometimes, Little Central America, and that bordered on the city-demarked area called "Koreatown."

At the time that I taught there, Madison had a population of 2,700 children in grades kindergarten to five.[5] The families of these children lived within ten square blocks around the school. Many families doubled and sometimes tripled up in one- and two-bedroom apartments to afford the rent. In a home that I visited one family shared a bedroom, while the living room was partitioned into two spaces, shared between an uncle and an unrelated family of five. More recently, the high cost of living, aggravated by gentrification in the central Los Angeles corridor, has had the effect of driving down the school age population. Enrollment has dropped, reaching a low of 1,650 in 2006, as families moved to outlying areas of Los Angeles, as well as to many other places around the United States, including new immigrant receiving contexts like Engleville.

According to school records in 1998, 94 percent of the student population was "Hispanic;" 4 percent was "Asian;" and the remaining 1.8 percent encompassed Filipinos, African Americans, Native Americans, and whites. The school did not record the national origin of residents, lumping all Latino immigrants under the rubric "Hispanic," but figures for the larger area suggested that the greatest number of residents were Mexican, followed by Salvadorean, Guatemalan, and Nicaraguan.[6] The population undoubtedly included members of indigenous communities from Mexico and Central America, for whom Spanish was a second language; there were some ten thousand Mayans living in Los Angeles in that time period, though this was obscured by the racial and linguistic classification systems in place in the school, as well as by parents' reporting practices.[7] Of the students 86 percent were considered "limited" in their English proficiency,[8] and virtually all qualified for free or reduced lunch. Census figures for the area around the school indicated that 54 percent of residents under the age of seventeen lived below the poverty line at that time. Only 23 percent of families, however, received public assistance.

A stranger coming through the Madison area would not necessarily have sensed the presence of children, despite the fact that some nine hundred children were on vacation in this community every month, as they rotated through a multitrack, year-round school. There were few overtly child-friendly spaces in the public domain; the local parks were known as places where hypodermic needles and used condoms could be found,[9] and most parents kept their children away from parks. Instead, children played in either the corridors and parking lots of their buildings or in their apartments.

THE POLITICS OF TIME

To accommodate the student population in this community Madison—like most of the other schools in the central Los Angeles area—adopted an alternative school schedule. The driving force behind the multi-track program was the shortage of classroom space, and despite the misnomer of "year-round," there was no greater time investment in teaching here than in schools that ran on the traditional school calendar. Madison was set up on a three-track system that demanded considerable temporal coordination; two tracks of students were enrolled at any given time; each track was "on" for two months followed by one month of vacation, and three classes shared two classroom spaces. To accommodate the three tracks, children attended school for forty additional minutes each day but thirteen fewer days in the year.

The tracking system had the effect of partially segregating students from different immigrant backgrounds at the school; the cultural and linguistic fields of difference across the three tracks were distinct. The Korean bilingual program was housed on one track, along with classes that were run in English for "gifted" students and for speakers of diverse other languages. Spanish-English bilingual programs were housed on the other two tracks. In some ways, these divisions mirrored the larger community, where there was relatively little contact between Spanish and Korean speakers, except when Spanish-speakers shopped in Korean-owned stores.

Another effect of the multitrack system was that children were "off track" or on vacation every third month. This shaped their daily lives in many ways.[10] For some, it mattered for the experiences they garnered as translators. Some children accompanied their parents to work during their vacation time; these situations put them in contact with English speakers, such as in factories run by "American" or Korean bosses or in private homes where their parents served as house cleaners, gardeners, or nannies to English-speaking children. Some helped their parents to prepare and sell food and other goods in the informal economy. Most of the clientele for street vendors were coethnic

Spanish speakers, but thirteen-year-old Yandara helped to negotiate a deal with a local Korean shop owner, in which she and her family members did piecework at home placing tiny plastic flowers into vials that were sold at the store. Hundreds of other children volunteered their services as helpers at the school,[11] and in this role they sometimes used their bilingual skills to interpret for teachers as well as to teach and tutor younger children.

In the Madison community the demands on children to serve as language brokers depended greatly on the specific activities in which families engaged. Much of the regular work of daily life could take place without the need for translation, but specialized situations required brokering between English speakers and their parents. Occasionally, these involved multiparty exchanges in which children of Korean speakers and children of Spanish speakers used their collective knowledge of English, Spanish and Korean to communicate.

THE POLITICS OF HISTORY

Before turning to the next community, I want to place my work at Madison within a historical context as well as a geographical one. I served as a teacher at Madison from 1983 to 1993, during the height of the civil wars in Central America, and most of my students were economic or political refugees—though not officially recognized as such by the U.S. government.[12] Families came fleeing poverty and devastation, and they had had minimal access to formal schooling. Many families lived in extreme poverty and without legal status. The research at Madison was also done around the time of the passage of Proposition 187 in California. This anti-immigrant legislation aimed to deny public services to undocumented immigrants in schools and clinics. Proposition 187 was followed by the passage of Proposition 227, which mandated that California children must be taught in English, another indication of the anti-immigrant sentiments that were prevalent during this time.[13] Although Proposition 187 was eventually overturned in court and some forms of bilingual education managed to persist following the passage of Proposition 227, the fact that these bills mustered popular approval reveals the xenophobic and antibilingual context in which immigrant children did their work of language brokering.

Regan

Just as my memory of the Madison community centers on bars and gates, when I recall my days at the school I call "Regan" I think of dark, crowded halls and classrooms. I remember students waiting in long lines to descend the stairs and

maneuver through the lunch line, then sitting in patrolled silence in long rows
of picnic style benches for fifteen minutes before being granted five minutes to
talk. I recall chipping, peeling paint and very old, tattered textbooks. When I
think about the "cages" at Madison and the toilet paper that was either hung
on rolls suspended from the walls outside the bathrooms at Regan or else doled
out by teachers, I find myself recoiling at the insults that are waged against
children in some communities in the name of doing school. Although these
are only partial glimpses into life at Regan and Madison—there were many
vibrant learning spaces as well, with teachers who really cared about their
students—both schools were large, underfunded public institutions, and it is
hard to report dispassionately on these contexts because I believe children
deserve so much more.[14]

Regan was located in what had been a predominantly Polish immigrant
community until the 1980s, when immigrants from Mexico began moving in.
Polish immigration retains a mark in the area, as evidenced by Polish-run bak-
eries and shops and Polish names on the local Catholic Church and school
building. A number of the teachers at Regan were the children of Polish immigrants, and a small bilingual program has remained at the school to this day.

The school's enrollment of 1,689 includes kindergarten through eighth
grade students, grouped in three buildings on the school grounds. Fifth and
sixth graders were housed in a building that was owned by the Catholic
Diocese, formerly a parochial school named for a Polish saint. Seventh- and
eighth-grade classes were held in another church building. In between, a new
building had been erected to house kindergarten to fourth grade students; this
contrasted with the older buildings because it was light and bright, but its
placement on the school grounds eliminated all play areas. Fifth- through
eighth-grade students had no recreation time scheduled in their days; they ate
lunch in a crowded room and then returned to their classrooms for study.[15]

The school population was categorized as 41.3 percent "Limited English"
speakers; 92.2 percent was low income. Of the school population 75 percent
was classified as "Hispanic," an indicator of the youthful nature of the
Hispanic population because in the census track surrounding the school only
47 percent checked this box. Of the 23 percent of the school population listed
as "White" most were immigrants or the children of immigrants from Poland.
Less than one percent identified as "Black," and only 1.2 percent identified as
"Asian" (compared with 1.6 percent and 3.8 percent, respectively, in the census track).

My work in and around this community was conducted during what,
arguably, was the height of xenophobia in recent years—around the time of
the attacks on the World Trade Center in 2001. This historical moment is an

important backdrop to children's activities as language brokers, which marked families as immigrants in the gaze of a public that had grown suspicious of "alien others." Many of the children I worked with proclaimed overtly pro-American positions during the post-9/11 days—participating in the waving of American flags. One boy talked with us at length about all he learned watching CNN about Al Quaida, the Anthrax scare, and terrorism. At the same time, families were ambiguously positioned because as nonwhite immigrants they knew they could be viewed as potential terrorists themselves.

Many Regan parents worked at the Chicago airport and were severely affected by the post-9/11 reduction in air traffic, as some were laid off or had their hours reduced. Others worked in factories, generally for long hours; a common family strategy involved staggering work shifts so that an adult was usually home to supervise children. Most families had lived in the area for fifteen years or more, and a number owned their own homes (often two-flats shared with extended family members), but they maintained close ties to their Mexican states of origin: Guanajuato, Guerrero, Jalisco, and Durango. Unlike Central Americans in Los Angeles, who were separated by greater distances, multiple borders, and the instability imposed by war, there was extensive movement of family members back and forth between Mexico and Chicago. This movement mattered for children's experiences of growing up—the points of comparison that they had for their own lives—as well as for the translation experiences they garnered. With the frequent arrival of new family members, children found themselves translating for aunts, uncles, and cousins as well as for their parents and siblings.

Fields of Difference

As these descriptions suggest, the fields of difference in the Regan community were distinct from those around Madison. At Madison, Spanish-speakers were the majority, and teachers and others often made group comparisons with the second largest immigrant population of Koreans. At Regan, the marked line of difference was between the categories of "Mexican" and "Polish." The small number of Central and South Americans and Puerto Ricans who lived in the area were generally presumed to be Mexican (as Tony, whose parents were from Ecuador and El Salvador, complained). Comparisons between Mexican and Polish students were made often, especially by teachers at Regan. For example, in an interview, a Regan teacher and daughter of Polish immigrants stated how she believed immigrant Polish families differed from Mexicans. After a long pause, she declared that in Mexican households there was a "less of an emphasis on education," adding that this made it difficult for Mexican students to read or to remember what they had read: "These kids have a hard enough time just reading a sentence with all the words in it and telling, and retelling it . . . They forget; it's like a sieve." As we see in chapter 5, such deficit-laden assumptions may be encoded both explicitly and implicitly in conversations that children are asked to translate, and so understanding the local ideological context is important for grasping the psychological and emotional toll of translation work.

Engleville

The city I called Engleville was a very different sort of receiving context for new immigrants than the ones represented by either the Regan or Madison communities. At the turn of this century, it was a good example of a contact zone, in Mary Pratt's sense of that term.[16] The demographic trends seen in Engleville can also be seen in countless small cities and towns around the United States, as migration changes the face of the nation.

Engleville is an urban/suburban area just outside Chicago, with a population of about seventy-four thousand. In the 2000 census, the majority (64 percent) identified as "white;" 22 percent as "African American," 6 percent as "Hispanic," 6 percent as "Asian," and 3 percent as "Other." An additional 3 percent of the population identified as biracial or multiracial. These demographics reflected a slight change over the previous decade, with the "Hispanic" population increasing by 91 percent from 2,379 to 4,539. The proportion of Hispanic children in the public schools was greater than that among adults; it reached 9 percent (while the white population dropped to 45 percent, presumably owing to private school enrollment).[17] As we approach the 2010 census, these figures appear to be shifting even further in the same direction.

Engleville's population varied on more than racial/ethnic diversity; it was also home to families from a wide range of incomes and social class backgrounds. In 1998, the per capita income was $34,000; the median income was $63,000. Still, almost 12 percent of households had incomes below the poverty line. Of the school-age population 30 percent was considered low-income, and most Mexican immigrants were included in that figure; but many of these, including the families of Maria, Estela, and Nova, still managed to purchase their own homes by pooling resources with extended family. The four Engleville census tracts that had a Latino population greater than 10 percent were the four lowest-income census tracts in the city, and the wealthiest census tract was less than one percent Hispanic, and so there was little diversity of income within the town by neighborhood; but school intake areas were set up to ensure that no school exceeds 40 percent of either "minority" or "white" students, which also secured some socioeconomic mixing. (To establish this mix, school lines were continuously redrawn across neighborhoods, and many African American and Latino students—and only rarely whites—were bussed to other schools.)

The Mexican immigrant population in Engleville goes back about fifty years.[18] One of María's uncles was one of the first Mexican migrants to move here, in the 1970s. Most families—including the Aguilera, Balderas, Flores, and Gutiérrez families—were from one of two small ranchos or old frontier settlements in the state of Guanajuato—small farming communities that are less than a mile from each other and a few miles from the nearest small town. The Flores and Gutiérrez families were from one of these ranchos, and the Aguilera family from the other, which was separated by about a mile. Estela's parents had lived a small town that was a short bus ride away from these ranchos. (The capital of the state of Guanajuato, the city of Guanajuato, was a four-hour bus ride away, and few families that I talked with had ever been there.) These ranchos have a particular history within Mexico and a sub-culture of their own, one that Marcia Farr characterizes as an ideology of rugged individualism coupled with a deep sense of loyalty to family.[19]

Adult migrants worked for the most part in the service sector and in factories. Many men, including Srs. Gutiérrez and Aguilera, were hired as gardeners and landscapers, lending expertise garnered from farm work in Mexico to the benefit of Engleville gardens. Snow removal during the winter offered some supplement to this seasonal work; for those who had the means—and for those young men who left women and children behind—winter could also be a good time for return visits to Mexico. Women worked in factories, fast food restaurants (as Estela's mother did), the service sector (Nova's mother cleaned hotel rooms), or part-time jobs such as in school cafeterias (as María's mother did). Others were principally homemakers, sometimes providing childcare to fellow migrants for a small fee, as Junior's mother did, and sometimes finding work with "American" families.

The school I call "Jefferson" is in many ways the heart of the Latino community in this midwestern town. The city's first Spanish-English bilingual education program was launched here in the 1970s, and most of the city's bilingual personnel worked here. The building was flanked by broad swatches of grass that border open play areas complete with sandbox, monkey bars, and a climbing structure over a protective floor of woodchips. Until recently, the playground was also adorned with a large wooden wagon and iron canon that was pointed directly at a wire climbing structure in the form of a teepee. (These structures, holdovers from days when white western supremacy over native populations was flaunted, were finally dismantled when the playground was remodeled in 2004.) Beyond the play area lay an open field, dotted with trees, a space that was filled each weekend with the brightly colored uniforms of youth soccer players; multiple simultaneous games were played in this broad expanse. The kindergarten classrooms looked out onto the field through full-length, open panels of windows; these windows also allowed outsiders a peek into a brightly-colored environment that was well stocked with books and toys. On the far side of the field were tree-lined streets with mixed housing stock, including one-hundred-year-old Victorian "painted ladies," a smattering of Chicago brick bungalows, and "two flats." The school and its surrounding neighborhood echoed the feel of the larger city, at least to my urban-based comparative frame: expansive, resource-rich, and filled with spaces of green.

The Politics of Diversity

To illuminate the social context in which children's work as translators took place, I want to summarize some issues that were debated at Jefferson at the turn of this century, as the town responded to changing demographics. The political maneuvers that I sketch reveal some complexities of life in this contact zone.[20] They show how people who were differently positioned within the landscape of differences in this town reacted to the population increase in Mexican immigrants. These complexities sometimes played out in translation encounters because children had to negotiate who they and their families were seen to be within the particular mix of social groups in this town. Engleville was a particular kind of contact zone; new immigrants mixed with a well-established and economically stratified population of African Americans and whites, and the nature of contact between people from different social classes, cultural backgrounds, and racialized ethnicities mattered greatly for children's experiences of childhood, as well as for how their work as translators was seen and understood.

Jefferson Elementary School first began providing bilingual services to the children of Mexican migrants in the 1970s, through "pull-out" ESL classes, in which Spanish speakers left their homeroom classrooms for English instruction and thus were separated from English speakers for a good portion of the day. In the 1990s, as the population of English Learners grew, a second school began providing ESL services, and English Learners were divided between the two schools. The second school was on the far end of town, in a wealthy neighborhood; the decision to house the bilingual program there was part of the district's effort to maintain its commitment to desegregation, by assuring that there would be more than 60 percent of either white or nonwhite groups at any school. The bussed-in Latino children helped to "balance" the school, or as some expressed it, to "provide diversity." Indeed, diversity was highly celebrated in this city's public rhetoric; the city's web page, for example, proclaimed: "Engleville prides itself on its diversity. Evident in the multi-cultural and socio-economic roles of Engleville's many citizens and visitors alike, people of all walks of life, live, work and play in Engleville."

In 2000, Jefferson became the site of a contentious battle when attempts were made to transform it to a dual-language school.[21] Spearheading these efforts were a group of English-speaking parents who wanted their children to have the opportunity to learn Spanish in school; they gained support from teachers who wanted to reform the problematic pull-out program, a program that bilingual educators consider to be the least effective form of bilingual instruction.[22] They met with considerable opposition from both neighborhood parents who wanted the school to remain a "neighborhood school" and English-speaking families who did not opt into the dual-language program. Some of these parents invoked a celebratory multicultural rhetoric in their calls to maintain the "natural diversity" of the school—a diversity that they presumed would be upset by the formation of a dual-language classroom, perhaps because few African Americans had enrolled in the program at that time. The implication was that these parents valued having an even mix of white, black, and Latino students at the school. However, some countered that the real concern beneath this argument was that the racial balance within *individual classrooms* would be skewed, as the dual-language classrooms would draw white and Latino children and few African Americans; thus, white children who did not enroll in the dual-language classrooms would be left in classrooms that were predominantly comprised of African American students. Further, class size for English speakers would effectively increase, once English learners were not pulled out for instruction. This is important for considering the place that Latino immigrants took up in this town; in some ways they served as buffers between African Americans and whites, with their positions evaluated by different forces in relation to an historically tense black-white color divide.

Eventually the decision was made to house a single track of a dual-language program at Jefferson, giving English-speaking neighborhood parents the option of choosing either this program or a regular English program for their children. Junior, María, and Estela's younger siblings all signed up for the dual-language program. Among other things, this affected the language demands in their households; Estela noted that she couldn't really help her younger sister with her math homework because it was in Spanish.

This brief description of Engleville illustrates some contradictions this city afforded as a space for the immigrant childhoods, including tensions around the place of Spanish speakers in the educational system and the town. These things mattered for how immigrant children's translation work was viewed. Spanish was a highly marked language at the time—valued by some (for example, English-speaking parents who supported dual-language education), and condemned by others (for example, those who were upset by the dual-language discussion). In subtle and not-so-subtle ways, public debates about bilingual education encoded messages about immigrants, language, and culture that influenced how child translators were seen.

Comparative Views of Childhoods

Looking across the three communities, one can sense how local contexts shaped children's daily life experiences, including their opportunities for learning and development. Local contexts also shaped the experiences that children garnered as translators and interpreters: in the needs and demands for children's translation services; in the availability of other bilingual supports; and in the manner in which children's actions as translators were seen and understood by others, as conditioned by the local social context and the available fields of difference.

First, the language resources in each community were at variance. Families in the Madison community, and to a somewhat lesser extent, those living in the Regan community, could secure most of their basic needs and live their everyday lives without the need to communicate with English speakers. Children's work as translators took place mostly during excursions out of the immediate area, through printed media (including signs in the urban space), and in particular kinds of encounters, such as with monolingual teachers in the school, landlords, or parents' employers. In contrast, children in Engleville were called on to translate for everyday tasks making purchases at local markets as well as in more specialized encounters.

Second, communities differed in terms of the demands for translation work. More bilingual resources, in the form of older children and bilingual adults, existed in the Madison and Regan communities than in Engleville. Most clinics, schools, stores, and restaurants in these metropolitan areas employed Spanish-speaking employees. Children in urban immigrant communities still served as translators for their families, but not to the same extent as did the children of non-English-speaking adults in Engleville. The tasks got distributed across the available population of bilinguals.

A third, ironic difference between the sites lies in the nature of bilingual supports. Although bilingual resources were far more abundant in Los Angeles than in Engleville (there was for example a fairly large cadre of bilingual teachers at the school, a product of twenty-five years of bilingual program capacity building), there was more institutional support for the development of bilingualism in Engleville, given the dual-language program that was established there around the same time in which bilingual education was dismantled in California, under Proposition 227. Both policies (the establishment of the dual-language program and the demise of bilingual education) were arguably direct responses to the presence of immigrants in these "contact zones." The former, however, represented an *embracing* of diversity and a claim on the part of English-speaking parents to some of the "bilingual goods," while the latter, like national movements for "English Only," represented a rejection of linguistic and cultural diversity.

Finally, the fields of difference in each community influenced how children's actions as translators were seen and understood by others. Although it's difficult to make broad generalizations across the three sites, Engleville stands out as the context in which immigrant children were most visible, against a backdrop of suburban English speakers. Immigrants were warmly received by many in the town, in an embrace of linguistic and cultural difference, while to others they represented threats to the status quo.

The landscapes that I have sketched here in rather broad strokes shape children's daily lives and experiences in countless ways. In chapter 3, I move further into these landscapes to describe what happens in households across the three sites, as children engage in the everyday work of home-based translations.

Chapter 3   Home Work

Sra. Balderas got out the insurance letter that she had carefully set aside for her daughter to look at after school. When Estela walked in the door, Sra. Balderas greeted her with: "M'ija, me ayudas con esta carta." (My daughter, help me with this letter.] Estela set down her backpack and walked over to the couch. She peered intently at the text as her mother looked on nervously. She read aloud in English, hesitantly at first, then confidently, switching seamlessly to Spanish after short stretches to explxain the letter's meaning to her mother: "Ok, mira. Dice: [Ok, look. It says.] 'It is important that you give pro- pro— miss attention to, attention to this notice. Dice que, uh, le pongas atencion?" [It says that you need to pay attention?] A bit later she asked her mother if she was paying attention to her. "It's important," she emphasized.

Junior was reading a book to his brother, a Disney story that they had received from their pediatrician (as part of a program aimed at distributing books to low-income homes in Engleville—one of many such social service programs this town offered). The book was written in English, and Junior's three-year-old sister spoke mostly Spanish. So Junior pointed to the pictures, read the text silently, and translated the story aloud, page by page. He was interrupted at one point by the telephone. His mother, who was preparing food in the nearby kitchen, motioned to him to answer it. Later that evening Junior's family rented the movie *Independence Day*. Junior wrote in his journal:

> Today I translated a part that a guy said in a movie to my dad it was Independence Day a black guy told the president that he could ride the spaceship because he knows how to ride almost anything.

Places and types of translating seemed to have gendered dimensions as well: about 6 percent more girls than boys reported translating at doctors' and dentists' appointments, and significantly more circled that they translated "conversations" (45 percent of girls versus 31 percent of boys). When we analyzed the survey results regarding how often children claimed to translate, another gendered pattern was evident; a higher percentage of boys marked that they translated "everyday" and "once/week" for the various people we inquired about (mothers, fathers, grandparents, teachers, friends, younger siblings, older siblings, and other family members), while girls were more likely to mark "sometimes." Looking at the survey results of case study participants, we began to suspect that there was a tendency for some boys to inflate and some girls to diminish their reported scopes of translating.

Children are not the only ones to change over time, as they develop competencies, lose or gain interest in particular tasks, or shift the nature of their relationships within the family. Families also change as a dynamic whole. Older siblings may move out of the house, get jobs that keep them busy, or go to college. These things affect the availability of translators and their willingness to do the work. When new siblings are born, new demands are introduced into the household. Younger siblings may acquire English more rapidly than older ones because of the greater presence of English in the household; and, as we have found, they may *lose* or not fully develop their home language.[5] This was the case in Estela's house; her younger sister began to regain Spanish when she enrolled in Engleville's dual-language program. Reduced home language development meant that younger siblings were ill prepared to take over translating tasks, even as it potentially introduced the need for another kind of translating—between Spanish and English speakers in the same family. Of the surveyed children 32 percent said they sometimes translated for their younger siblings (while only 15 percent said they did so for an older sibling). This may have included translations between younger siblings and grandparents (or even parents) and translations provided in the service of helping younger siblings with homework.

Although some things were set aside for the "designated translator" to deal with, circumstances sometimes propelled other members of the family to step up to the plate. There were also changes over time, across contexts, and in relation to distinct relationships within the family. When María grew older, for example, she became busier with schoolwork, and her younger brother often became the translator who accompanied their mother on errands. (María noted that this made her feel kind of left out.) Children in the same family often experienced different kinds of childhoods, and their own experiences also changed over time.

I felt kind of good because my dad was really paying attention not just watching the killing.

It was five o'clock, and María was working on her homework. She had just begun middle school, and the burden of homework had increased substantively since fifth grade. Next to her, her brother worked on his homework, turning periodically to María to ask for help. On her other side, María's mother did her own work for an ESL class she would attend the next day. María wrote a journal entry about helping her mom with that task:

On Tuesday I helped my mom write a story. The story that I helped my mom was about going to a market and buying food. She got the food from papers. I helped my mom write the book. Words that she didn't know how to spell I helped her spell. I felt happy because I like to help my mom and write stories. I had to help my mom because tomorrow she had to go to classes to learn English. When it was tomorrow and my mom went to English class at my school. My mom gave her teacher the book. She said it was a very good book. She liked it. Then it was over and we went home.

Sometime between three and ten P.M. on school days, in homes all across the United States, children can be found hunched over their kitchen tables, seated in front of computer screens, spread out with papers across the floors of their bedrooms or living rooms, or otherwise absorbed in doing homework. Homework is a powerful artifact, one of the few items that regularly crosses the divide between home and school. Homework brings school into homes and shapes households rhythms.

Homework is *schoolwork* that is done at home, an activity that imposes itself on children's daily lives and family life, often inflexibly and inexorably. But families' experiences with homework are little known in part because homework, like other labor performed in the domestic sphere, is an "invisible" sort of work. Like *house*work, it is generally unremunerated (except indirectly by teachers' rewards, praise, or classroom grades), and it sometimes causes considerable stress and strife in homes.[1]

In addition to school-supplied homework, immigrant children also regularly do a different kind of home-based work. Some of this looks surprisingly like school assignments; children like Estela, Junior, and María bent over papers with furrowed brows, filling out forms, reading books, and writing stories. This kind of homework is also *house*work—labor done in the domestic sphere—and it is consequential to families, yet largely invisible to the public eye.

Everyday, at-home interpretation of English texts was the most common kind of translation work that immigrant children engaged in across all three communities. In this chapter, I want to bring greater visibility to this hidden labor and explore the assorted kinds of translation work that children did in everyday ways at home for their families—as both household contribution[2] and activities with at least as much potential for fostering children's language and literacy development as offered by school homework exercises.[3]

Distribution of Translation Work within the Family

In any household, tasks generally take on some degree of person-specificity, by either design or habit. This is true for translation work as well. In most cases in immigrant households, the "designated translator" is one of the oldest children. María was ten when I first met her; her younger brothers were five and two. Estela was eleven; she had three sisters, all younger than five. Junior was eleven, with two siblings, also younger than five. Nova was twelve, and his younger sister was seven. In these families, the linguistic, literate, and cognitive capacities of the oldest children were considerably more advanced than those of the youngest, so it was quite clear who would be called in to translate in almost all circumstances.

Our survey of 280 fifth- and sixth-graders at Regan bore out these general patterns of the family positioning of translators. Using children's responses to an array of questions about translation experiences, Lisa Dorner, Christine Li-Grining, and I differentiated children based on the depth and breadth of their translation experiences.[4] We classified students as either "active" or "partial" language brokers: 41 percent of language brokers were the eldest children still living at home. Although the most active family translators tended to be the eldest, younger children sometimes took up this role, depending on a variety of circumstances.

When we asked Nova about his work as a translator, he spoke more generally about his responsibilities to the household, as the eldest child with working parents:

> Well sometimes I uh, yeah my mom gets like I said frustrated about it, but sometimes she's kind of hard on me you know because I'm the oldest and I'm supposed to this and I'm supposed do that, you know. And if I don't do something or something is not clean, it's always me, I'm always the person that gets blamed, even though she knows that my sister has to do it or something like that, I'm the oldest, I'm supposed to do it. I must say it's one of those typical things that you know every family goes through. You know, I'm not going to say our

family is perfect or it's that bad . . . But, before that, 'cause you know my mom gets here at 4:30 or sometimes five. And so I clean the house, I keep it clean, sometimes I make food for my sister or something like that . . . I wouldn't call it work 'cause, you know, it's one of those things that you do to help the family.

In contrast with Nova's attitude, María complained to us abou responsibilities she had as the oldest child in her family. María's tasks inc cleaning, helping her younger brothers, and sometimes cooking; she sho snow in the winter and raked leaves in the fall. She was expected to ave siblings from dangers—to watch them so they wouldn't run out to the . She told us that she preferred shoveling to minding her brothers.

When oldest siblings were close in age, other factors weighed in to mine who was the most commonly designated translator. This includ perceived dispositions of the children (their willingness to engage ir tasks), their perceived abilities (shaped by their dispositions), and their ability. Ten-year-old Jenny noted that her sister usually translated, but, she was not around, Jenny would take her place. Eleven-year-old described her sister's response to translation requests: "She'll get aggra because they sometimes still don't understand, so then she leaves and I have to do it." She added, "And they won't ask my brother no more, b he'll just be like, 'I don't know, you live here, you should know.' So they me and I'll just translate." Jasmine explained why her parents no longer her brother: "I don't argue. I just do it." Adalia, who was older tha brother Andrés by only two years, said that she was the language broker f parents because she was the oldest and also "not shy;" but sometimes he ents ask her brother, "just to see, because he is shy."

When brothers and sisters were close in age a gendered division of sometimes took hold. This gendering seemed partly shaped by girls' g general willingness with household chores, and perhaps by parents' g expectation for their daughters than for their sons to do such chores. But also *relational*; children translated for their mothers more than for any adult, and girls often spent more time with their mothers than with fathers. Relationship patterns were also evident in that more girls tha surveyed (50 percent) than boys (39 percent) indicated that they tran for their grandparents; and girls (38 percent of them) were more likely boys (26 percent) to translate for younger siblings. Few other such differ were evident in the survey results, but our observations suggested tha dered patterns took a stronger hold as children moved through adoles because of the gendered nature of family relationships and different straints on boys' and girls' movements outside of the home.

Parents' language abilities also did not remain static. Despite popular opinion to the contrary, adult immigrants enroll in ESL classes in large numbers, and over time many develop competency in English.[6] Three of the four Engleville mothers studied English in formal classes. Most Regan parents we worked with also had basic competency in English. Parents in Pico Union varied in their English skills, as this was a community with many new immigrants, but adult ESL classes in this community were always full. Although some parents continued to depend on their children for translations even after they acquired basic competencies in English—either out of habit, lack of confidence in their own abilities, or concern for how their nonnative English would be received—others began to speak for themselves, especially when their growing children became less available or willing. Nova gradually stopped translating for his mother as he grew older and got busier with school activities, but his younger sister did not fill in because his mother's confidence in English had grown. Thus the combination of needs, abilities, and availabilities may force changes in the distribution of translating tasks, just as it does the distribution of other forms of household labor.

Often children do not perform "solo" as translators.[7] The whole family often works together to make sense of information, such as letters, forms, applications, and bills; they figure out what is required to respond. Family members sometimes mutually support each others' understanding of the tasks at hand; for example, parents may explain what they know about the topic, task, or context, and kids help decipher the actual texts. As Nova's mother acquired more English, she began to read documents herself and then sometimes asked Nova to go over them with her to see if she had understood them properly.

Even when parents did not speak much English, they supported children in translation tasks. They did this by supplying background information and Spanish vocabulary and negotiating meaning with them. Briana explained how she and her family would "figure things out together"; she said that she attempted "different ways" and that "they figured it out too." María's mother put it simply: "Nosotras nos ayudamos" [We help each other]. Ashley told of working in collaboration with her brother and her parents:

> Well, they [my parents] just want to know, what kind of benefits were in it, what would they help with, like what does it cover, and stuff like that. And I would just tell them what it said in the booklets and stuff like that . . . Well, sometimes I couldn't figure out how to translate some of the stuff. Like, one part would be that he would get a benefit, from, I'm not sure what it was, but something, from his work, and I couldn't translate it. I couldn't figure out how to explain it to them.

So I tried different ways, but they didn't understand it . . . 'Cause
they're like: are you sure that's what it says? And I'm like, 'Yay.'
And I was thinking like, well, what if I say it this way, they might
understand it better. But at the end, we figured it out . . . I just did it
different ways. Then I figured it out; then I remembered a few things;
then I would just put them all together, [and] they would figure it
out, too.

Whether and how parents scaffolded their children's translation work mattered for what children learned from their translation work, a point I return to
in chapter 6.

TASKS

Like home-making work, home-based language brokering involves discrete
kinds of tasks. The most common were making and taking phone calls, translating written texts, especially materials from school and the daily mail,
and helping siblings[8] and other family members with homework. Children
served as information conduits as well as teachers and tutors to others; their
work demanded a complex set of interpersonal, language, literacy, and social
skills.

TUTORING AND TEACHING. Most of the youth who were the eldest in their
families took on extensive roles as teachers and tutors to their younger siblings. Estela and Junior read often to their younger siblings and translated stories into Spanish. They also helped their siblings with homework, though they
found this more challenging after the formation of the dual language program
in Engleville because their homework was often in Spanish and the older
youths' educational experiences had occurred in English.

Homework help extended beyond the immediate family. María often
helped a younger neighbor with school assignments. Twelve-year-old Jacqueline
described helping her cousins with their homework in a journal entry:

Today I was helping my two cousins with their homework. One goes
(is) in 2nd and the other goes (is) in pre-kinder. First I helped my
cousin. He had this homework that they put (give) you a drawing and
you have to put the name of that drawing down (on) the picture.
He had some difficulties in his homework but I helped him so then
he got it. Then my other cousin didn't know how to read the colors
in English, so I helped him (with) the colors and (to write) the
numbers to 1–20.

And children were not the only recipients of tutoring services. María wrote a second journal entry about helping her mother with her English homework:

> *February 13, 2002*
> On Tuesday I helped my mom read a book. My mom knew some of the things on the book. So the words that my mom didn't know I helped her on. It was a short book, but it was fun. The book I read to my mom was about people that moved. The title was, "*Why People Move.*" I had to read it to my mom because on Wednesday, that's tomorrow she went to classes to learn English, and at classes the teacher gave her homework. That was why I had to help my mom read the book, "*Why People Move.*"

Children helping *parents* with homework may strike some readers as a clear case of role reversal. It's further worth noting that María's mother did not typically help María with her school assignments. Sra. Gutiérrez knew that she couldn't provide much help, and so she had made arrangements for María to secure homework help at a nearby tutoring center. Maria completed her homework with the available household and community supports.

ENABLING COMMUNICATION. In many households, not just immigrant homes, children serve as information conduits. In my own home, when the telephone rings, I often ask my son to answer because he likes to do so and he's usually more willing than I am to stop what he's doing and answer the phone. Children in many households also take and relay messages; they are easily deployable sources of labor for such activities. But in immigrant households, children's contributions are more needed than in homes where parents speak English because, when the phone rings, the caller may be an English speaker.

The children I talked with were sometimes expected to do much more than just answer the phone; they might be asked to decide what information should and should not be given out to strangers. Before "Caller ID" services became available, children would often be asked to screen the household from calls from English speakers—and more specifically, from sales pitches. Once Caller ID service became available, many families purchased this service and used it to check for potential English calls so they could either avoid answering the phone or make sure their children answered those calls. In a small group interview Marco declared: "I take the English calls." His friend echoed him: "I take all the calls." Nova recounted a time when he had answered a telephone survey on behalf of his mother:

> Yesterday I translated something to my mom in the phone they called to ask what radio stations we listened to, I just told the lady that my

mom listened to Spanish stations, she asked me if I was older than
sixteen years then they told me that they would call back but they
never did. I felt really proud of my self to help other people especially
some one in my family.

The query about Nova's age suggests the ironic fact that Nova may not have
been considered old enough to answer the survey on his own; it is unclear
whether his response on behalf of his mother was utilized in the survey.

Children do not just help their own immediate families, and parents do
not only rely on their own children for such help. Alma Martínez, whose
daughter was only six, recounted animatedly how she would run to get her
neighbor's fourteen-year-old daughter to answer her telephone when an
English speaker called to talk with her husband:

> Yo tengo una mi vecina que mucho me ayuda. Hay veces que me
> llama, porque mi esposo sí sabe inglés. Entonces a veces él le llaman, y
> le digo, "Hold on." Porque yo puedo por poquito, no mucho. Por eso?
> estoy yendo a la escuela. Y rapidito, voy a llamar a la niña y le digo,
> vente, vente, corrale, me están hablando inglés.

> [I have my neighbor who helps me a lot. There are times that I get a call,
> because my husband does know English. And so then sometimes they
> call him, and I say, "Hold on." Because I can (speak English) just a little,
> not much. That's why I'm going to school. And quickly, I go and call the
> girl and I tell her, come, come, run, they are talking to me in English.]

Alma's daughter was only six, and her mother did *not* expect her to answer
the phone; instead, she solicited her neighbor's help. Across households, if
parents had access to older youth they did not rely on their own younger children for certain tasks. But it felt more onerous to ask outsiders for help than to
deploy their own children. Junior's mother told me that she felt better now
that Junior was older and could help her; when he was younger she had had to
ask favors of relatives and neighbors.

Telephone translations were some of the hardest kinds of translation
activities that children engaged in and some of the most discomforting to kids.
Making and taking telephone calls required procedural knowledge, an understanding of the issues that were the substance of the calls, and the negotiation
of three parties' words in a situation that is designed for two parties. This was
made more challenging by the absence of paralinguistic cues. As twelve-year-old
Rosario made explicit, the problem is that "you don't know who you're talking
to." The complexities of phone translations were not well understood by
coparticipants.

I translated what the guy was trying to say, but she didn't get it as much as I did." These kinds of translations could also be annoying, as Jacqueline noted:

Today we went to Hollywood to rent a movie. We rented a scary movie. So we started watching the movie and eating popcorn with our soda. So I was into the movie 'cause it was interesting, so my mom and dad started saying what did they say, what does that mean? But I tell them, "Let me watch the movie please, and when it's finished I'll tell you a summary of the movie." I like to translate but if it's a movie that I really like I get mad and then I don't even know what I am saying.

Jasmine similarly complained:

It kind of bothers me when I'm watching TV and my mom's sitting right next to me, and I'm trying to pay attention, like what they're saying—a movie and something, when it's really hard to understand, like what's building up into the action. And then my mom's like, "¿Qué dijo?" What did they say? "¿Qué está pasando? ¿Qué están haciendo?" [What's happening? What are they doing?] I'll be like, 'Mom, please let me listen and I'll tell you.' She's like "ay, yo ya me voy a dormir porque tú no me explicas. Yo aquí estoy bien aburrida y no le entiendo nada." [Well, I'm going to go sleep because you won't explain it to me. I'm here totally bored, and I don't understand anything.]
    She'll get frustrated. She's like, "you guys want me to wait, 'cause you guys understand everything." It's kind of funny. I'm trying to pay attention to the movie, but it's kind of funny.

Jasmine's report suggests she felt pressured by her mother. This is important to keep in mind; even if children feel good about helping others (as Junior said he did when translating a movie for his father), they may also experience some level of stress. The stress may derive in part from striving to be "good children" as they face tasks that are far more challenging than they may appear to be to monolingual speakers.

FOSTERING CONNECTIONS. There were other home-based translation tasks that seemed more pleasurable than stressful. Briana reported on helping her mother to select greeting cards for her father:

I translated for my mom on July 13, 2001. It was my father's B-day so me and my mom went to Osco. My mom wanted to buy a birthday card for my dad so she picked the card and I read the card in English, then she told me what did it mean in Spanish. Well I don't really

In the summer of 2006, I walked into María's house to find María
telephone, trying to get a refund on a mail-order purchase her motł
made.[9] María ended up making three phone calls on this matter becau
time when she hung up her mother was dissatisfied with the results. T
reminiscent of a phone call we recorded five years earlier, when María
years old. In the earlier case, Sra. Gutiérrez objected when María pas
telephone to her, after having taken the strategic action of asking, in l
for a Spanish-speaking "doctor" to talk with her mother. (The call was
on the results of a tuberculosis test.) Sra. Gutiérrez seemed to interpret
action as a reluctance to help her when she said, "Ay María, por qué me
el teléfono, si te dije que tú lo hicieras." [Ay, María, why did you give thí
to me, if I told you to do it.] María, in response, named the paradox of l
ation: that she was expected to speak for her mother but she didn't knc
to say: "Porque, tú, yo no sabía que tenía que decir y tú sí." [Because, yo
n't know what to say and you did.] Turning to the researcher, Sra. C
said: "Ya ves, que ella no me quiere ayudar?" [Now do you see, that she
want to help me?]

In this incident, Sra. Gutiérrez may seem unyielding and unsuppc
her daughter. In other contexts Sra. Gutiérrez scaffolded María's tra
work to a greater degree than she did in this encounter. This may be
the challenges of phone translation were not patently obvious—jus
challenges of managing three-party conversations are not always rec
when people interrupt others when they speak on the phone. Further,
that a researcher was observing may have heightened Sra. Gutiérrez' aí
to María's behavior rather than to the complexities of the task she wa
María to do.[10]

In situations like these I felt particularly torn about my role as res
I wanted to step in to help, but the research goal was to see how thesí
transpired when I was not present. Generally, I offered to assist after tl
lies had gotten as far as they could on their own. But when people aske
help, as indeed they did, I talked with families about what they woul
were not there, asked them to show me, and then contributed what I

ENTERTAINMENT. Translating television shows also involved rapid,
processing, often about things that are hard to explain, and kids di(
explaining things to others while they were watching. Nova told of a tir
he was watching a movie with his mother and saw that she wasn't l
at a joke. He tried to explain the joke to her, but he knew that "it's
same, you know, translating a joke either in Spanish or English into tl
language, because it just loses the whole, you know, funny thing. Aı

remember what it said on the card but my mom picked it. I think I'm
really helping my mom in something. I've helped her in other
moments like this. Well, I really like it so I hope I help more.

Briana also told of writing a greeting on a card from her mother to her
father. Her mother wanted to write in English; Briana noted that she had
"translated to my mom like this every Father's Day since I was nine." Briana
felt especially proud to participate in this exchange, as she was instrumental in
helping her mother to tell her father "how much she loved him."

INFORMATION MANAGEMENT. A regular activity that many children
engaged in involved reading, interpreting, and responding to the daily mail
and providing oral translations of many other kinds of written texts. Jasmine
found this kind of translation easier than oral language brokering:

If I read it I understand it better and if I don't I read it again and when
I translating and listening it's hard because if the person says
something I don't understand the first time I feel embarrassed telling
that person to repeat what they said again. So that's why I translate
better by reading something.

At the same time, the texts that children read at home were often complex
ones, not easy things to translate at all. They covered a wide range of domains,
topics, and genres, including letters from school (about school programs, policies, and special events), report cards, interim grade reports, consent and field
trip forms, instructions for medicine and vitamins, manuals for small machin-
ery, greeting cards, medical forms, jury summons, email, storybooks, homework,
product labels, receipts, library card application forms, information solicited
from the Internet (usually with the children taking the lead in the search for
this information), letters from insurance companies, receipts, and advertisements. This was a much wider genre of texts than children read in school or for
their school-based homework assignments.[11] School texts also offered more
explicit supports, in the form of instructions, definitions of key vocabulary, and
clear contextualization within a predictable topic of study. The myriad of texts
that children encounter in their home-based translation work had far fewer
explicit supports. For example, fifteen-year-old Adriana translated a jury summons for her mother.[12]

Several features of this text made it especially challenging to decipher. It
was written in various fonts, with capital letters serving to reinforce its authoritative tone. The language of the text was similarly authoritative, as it began,
"BY ORDER OF THE CIRCUIT COURT OF COOK COUNTY, ILLINOIS,
YOU ARE HEREBY DESIGNATED AS A STANDBY JUROR." It includes

a threat of punishment for disobedience: "FAILURE TO OBEY THIS SUM-
MONS MAY BE PUNISHABLE BY A FINE." The text delineated complicated instructions about what jurors needed to do and how to respond to the
summons. It had a form that was to be filled out (that among other things
questioned the respondent's criminal history). It made assumptions about the
respondent, including that s/he would understand what a "One Day/One
Trial" jury system is; that s/he would know what counts as "appropriate dress"
(only shorts were singled out as inappropriate); that s/he would realize why
these particular questions were posed, and what they would be used for; and
that s/he would want to read a book while waiting.

On the top of the back page of the summons, three questions were posed.
One asked (in English) if the respondent spoke English; another asked if s/he
was a U.S. citizen. Anyone answering no to either of these questions was
directed to a call a number on the form (again, without information about
what would then happen). Adriana's job might have been so much easier if
she encountered those questions at the *start* of the summons, before she
worked her way through the first page of bureaucratic text.

FEELINGS

How do children feel about their contributions as translators to their households? As I have noted, the most common response to queries about how children felt about translating, across communities and over time, was that it was
just normal and not a big deal. The second most common response was that it
felt "good"; kids said they were happy to help others, especially their families.
Junior wrote in a journal: "I feel really proud of myself to help other people,
especially someone in my family." Estela said: "The part that I like is helping
my dad, or anyone which actually needs it. I mean, I feel great when they're
like 'oh, thank you!' You've really helped me out." (She contrasted this "good
part" with the frustration she felt with herself when she couldn't find the right
words while translating.)

Monique wrote in her journal:

> I do translating to my parents mostly about bills. I'm going to be
> honest, most of the time it's boring but sometimes it's cool because
> you know something that people don't know. I'm not making fun of
> other people, but it feels good because you could help those people.
> I have to do all the translating because I'm an only child.

Everyday translations at home for family members did not generally evoke
strong emotions, beyond the "annoyance" I noted above. A few did evoke more

markedly positive or negative emotions, and these offer insight into intergenerational and intercultural dynamics of power, especially when we contrast these situations with ones that felt "just normal." The most uncomfortable tasks involved situations that brought them into contact with strangers and authority figures outside the home, such as making and handling certain kinds of phone calls. Many of the markedly positive feelings that children named centered on the sense of accomplishment that they got from either translating well or demonstrating their abilities to others. These feelings of pride seemed to emerge from a sense of growth or change in their positions in either family or society. Ten-year-old Jenna spoke proudly: "I feel that I am a big girl now and I could help the family a little bit." Children seemed aware that translating allowed them to assume a more active presence in the social world than might otherwise be accorded to them. It allowed them to "gain respect, be appreciated"; "feel bigger, smarter, (like I'm) taking over mother's place"; and "feel like a mature person, especially if you're a kid." Cindy explained: "They value your opinion more, because you are the one who knows English here . . . Translating makes me feel good, wanted, and noticed." María wrote that she felt "excited" when she translated, because "every time I translate I feel like I'm talking to somebody." In a family portrait Maria drew herself looking quite like her mother's equal (in terms of size, dress, and hair), as she refreshed the authoritative voice of a school dress code letter in her description.

Language brokers may feel paradoxically both subordinated and elevated in their relationships with their parents. Cindy told how her mother "summoned her" to translate but then "listened to her a lot"; translating served to build relationships and open lines of communication within the family. Sammy said he translated for his mother because she expected him to and might otherwise "get mad"—but also because he enjoyed the feeling of importance he gained through this work. As I have argued already, the only times that families seemed to see children having too much power was when children were reluctant to translate or when they didn't respond quickly enough when they were "summoned." No "role reversal" was evident to parents as long as children acted obediently by lending their skills to the family.

But when children felt they had overstepped the bounds of what was considered appropriate for children, or assumed *too* powerful a voice, feelings of guilt or anxiety were sometimes evoked. Beatríz, the adult child of immigrants, remembered having manipulated her mother's goodwill by claiming the local church had called requesting support; when her mother offered ten dollars, Beatríz pocketed the donation. None of the children we worked with confessed to such maneuvers (though we might not expect them to admit such things to us), nor did we witness anything that suggested this took place. As I show in chapter 5, however, children tended to heighten their own sense of personal responsibility for less than positive behaviors, and they did not seem to take advantage of their language broker positions to inflate themselves in any way. The guilty feelings that Beatríz was left with many years after this incident suggest the strength of the psychosocial forces mitigating youths' abuse of this kind of power.

Not all children felt the same about their work, of course, and not all said that it always "felt good." Brianna and Jasmine expressed less enthusiasm about helping than did most of the other children, especially when this involved supervising their younger siblings. Brianna said she helped her sister with homework "if her dad tells her" but didn't like to because her sister sometimes didn't listen to her. Katie laughed as she talked about helping her sometimes "impatient" mother find information on the Internet, and Josh said it annoyed him when his uncle (who shared his bedroom) asked him questions as he was trying to fall asleep. Moreover, kids felt annoyed by disruptions to their activities, especially when watching television. Still, they described these as minor inconveniences and gave little suggestion that such occurrences led to "role reversal" or marked parent-child conflict. This does not mean that there was an absence of conflict in these households, but we did not see evidence that translation work was a direct cause of any tensions.

Children also saw their translation work as part of a *reciprocal* set of relationships. As twelve-year-old Randy put it: "Sometimes I feel like I owe them . . . They take care of me, like help me to grow up and stuff. They just gave me life." Only three of sixty-six children whom I interviewed said they received any compensation for their work.[13] Danny said his father once gave him twenty dollars for translating. Mario got paid but didn't know exactly how much. Alan said he knew someone whose parents "give him like a dollar or two," but he presented this as unusual. In a small group interview Marlen said, "I get rewards"; Jolyn responded to this, "I get a smile." Some, like Nova, expressed a sense of indebtedness and obligation to their parents. And there may be other, less tangible rewards for translating, including feelings of pride and satisfaction.

Looking across Communities and Households

Across communities, there was less variation in home-based translation work than in translations outside the home because all households were "infiltrated" to some extent by the English-speaking world. Differences across communities in children's translation work was mostly a matter of degree. Central Los Angeles is widely known to be a "Spanish-speaking" area, and households there receive many telemarketing calls and mailed advertisements in Spanish.

Schools in Los Angeles and Chicago routinely sent home materials in Spanish, while schools in Engleville did not. Because of these norms, children in Engleville were called upon for greater amounts of home-based translation work than were children in Chicago or Los Angeles. But in all three communities home-based translation was one way that children helped out at home.

Perhaps more important for children's understandings of their own experiences, what seemed to vary considerably as we look across communities was the extent to which children's daily life practices fit with the local norm. Less than 10 percent of Engleville families spoke a language other than English at home, while more than 90 percent of Madison families did, and so childhood for immigrant children in Engleville looked quite different than that of their local peers. That sense of *a-typicality* may most mark children's experiences of "translating childhoods." These differences became even more marked when children stepped out of the domestic sphere and into the public, as detailed in chapters 4 and 5.

Chapter 4   Public *Para*-Phrasing

LIKE HOME-BASED translation work, public *para*-phrasing involved a myriad of activities involving an array of institutional domains, set in distinct relationships, and directed toward assorted problems. Children developed and used a wide array of what Luis Moll calls "funds of knowledge,"[1] as they engaged in tasks that ranged from relatively simple things such as asking where items were located in a store or for directions on the street to much more complex negotiations with doctors, lawyers, and social service providers. Translations were provided mostly for family members, as when children read signs, labels, maps, and directions; often, public *para*-phrasing acts involved the most challenging kinds of mediating work in which children spoke to and for authority figures representing educational, legal, medical, and financial institutions, negotiating between these people and their families in multiparty interactions. In many of these situations children were positioned both literally and figuratively in between people who moved in different social worlds. Children were uniquely positioned to make communication happen. As Cindy said, "I'm the main key in the conversation. If they were just out there talking and nodding their heads, they wouldn't know what they were talking about." In this work "in the middle" children mediated between people from different social classes, cultural backgrounds, and racialized identities, and they were sometimes expected to translate racist, xenophobic, or otherwise deficit-laden views of their families.

Supports for these encounters varied greatly. Sometimes, children were sent alone to make purchases, solicit information, and negotiate transactions. Other times, adults carried on the activity with only a little support from child translators, who were expected to track the conversations, correct misunderstandings, and supply occasional words and phrases. Occasionally, translation happened in carefully parceled ways, when adult coparticipants left space for the child to translate each chunk. But more often, people rattled on at great length and then turned to the child to say, "tell your mother what I said." As I'll show through a close look at parent-teacher conferences in chapter 5, some adults supported children's translation work, checked their understanding, and approached the communication task in a positive light or treated it as a learning opportunity. In other encounters children dealt with people who did not want to assume the burden of communication across linguistic borders and who viewed their families in less than benevolent ways.[2] All of these things mattered for how kids experienced and understood their work as translators.

Public *para*-phrasing, a form of housework outside the home and instrumental for household reproduction, benefits families directly by securing resources, goods, and materials as well as access to information and services. Beyond benefiting families and households, this labor also represents a social contribution. Children provide services that arguably could or should be provided by the state or other institutions; children served their families as well as societal institutions and the larger public good.

Connecting Families and Schools: Teaching and Tutoring

In Engleville, one of the most regular forms of public *para*-phrasing involved interactions between parents and teachers in relation to their own education or that of their siblings. This included extended, complex mediating work that took place in parent-teacher conferences, an activity setting that I examine in chapter 5. In central Los Angeles, in contrast, because most schools had bilingual personnel, children might only be called upon to translate brief, everyday exchanges between parents and teachers, but children remained important for facilitating dialogue between home and school.

Children also played a role in educational decisions made by their families. Jasmine, in helping her mother select a preschool for her brother, served both directly as language broker when her mother visited the schools and indirectly as consultant when her mother decided on the best program. She also was active in making sense of the options available to her for her own high school education in the Chicago public schools.

Some schools, like most in the Los Angeles area, had teaching assistants and other bilingual support staff who played important roles in making instruction accessible for students, even in the post-Proposition 227 era in which many classrooms functioned entirely in English. But children provided additional language support to their peers in these classrooms, as they did, to a greater extent, in contexts like Engleville where there were fewer bilingual personnel. As with home-based work, children's small, everyday translation efforts form an unrecognized, undervalued, and unremunerated form of labor. In fact, children sometimes got in trouble with teachers for offering help to their fellow students because of the ruling ethos of "doing one's own work" in school. Some situations in which they were asked to translate also got them in trouble with their peers. Tony detailed such a case in his journal:

> On an ordinary school day I was walking with my friends when Ms. Day was with someone who could not speak English. So she told if any of us knew Spanish. I was the only one. The lady told me that at the other side of the building a group of kids were doing something weird that was not appropriate. So I translated to Ms. Day what she said. Ms. Day told me to tell her what did they look like, so I told her me puedes describir estos niños [if I could describe those kids]. She told me kids with black shirts. Ms. Day told me to tell her thank you that she will go tell Mr. Rork to give them suspensions. The translating felt good because I helped the school to stop something bad. The kids were caught and given suspensions so Ms. Day and the lady told me thank you.

Sammy similarly described how his translation skills were part of a larger set of services that he provided at his school:

> Today was parent open house at my school. They need people to help with directing traffic so I helped. A mother came up to me and asked me if I knew where one of her child's classes was. I walked to the class and just then the teacher who was Mr. Gregorio bumped into us. She asked him how her son was doing but in Spanish. I helped her translate and translate back. It was all right, but weird, because Mr. Gregorio was one of my teachers. I guess that I didn't really want to mess up in front of Mr. G. After I saw both Mr. G and Mrs. Ramírez (I think her name was) smile it was a lot easier. They both thanked me and I walked away. This made me feel good about myself.

Sammy and Tony each claimed to "feel good" about their efforts. They felt some sense of performance anxiety, as when Sammy had to speak in front of his teacher, but the act of providing services to others consistently emerged as something that the children felt positive about, both at home and in the outside world. Feeling good about helping others also helped them to feel good about themselves.

Facilitating Civic Engagement

Civic engagement is often assumed to be the domain of adults and is often narrowly defined as participation in electoral politics or volunteering for public services. But notions of what counts as civic engagement can be expanded by considering children's translation work as a contribution to the public good, as in the school examples noted above. Often other adult immigrants were the recipients of these services, as when Ashley gave directions to someone at a bus stop, or when Jasmine read signs in the laundromat for an immigrant neighbor. In other cases, even when the direct recipient of the translation was an immigrant—for example, when a librarian asked Junior, in Junior's words, to "tell a guy about a book"—the services that children provided benefited institutions. Immigrants were also not the only direct recipients. When at a Mexican bakery in the city, María's mother noticed an English speaker having trouble communicating with the Mexican clerk. She asked María to help him, and she did.

As in the case of Tony's reporting on misbehavior at school, translation skills may be utilized in the service of keeping the public peace. Several children told of translating for police. In her journal ten-year-old Bella recorded a time she reported to police on suspicious activity in her Los Angeles neighborhood, in a situation that made her feel nervous:

> I forgot to tell you that I have talked for my aunt in a very important
> talk with Police officers. My cousins saw a man in the second floor.
> The man tried to follow my two cousins. I was telling them what color
> his blouse was. And every information they needed to know. I felt
> nervous. The police officer asked me a lot of questions.

Sra. Aguilera also recounted another, rather different form of civic engagement in which Nova spoke for her to public officials. This was soon after September 11, and Sra. Aguilera took it upon herself to organize a thank-you note to local firefighters for their contributions to public safety. Sra. Aguilera wrote the words, and Nova translated them; they then went with a group of families to the local fire station to present the note to the firefighters. Nova wrote about this in his journal, a display of patriotic sentiment that was echoed by many children we worked with in the days following 9/11:

> 9-13-01
> Today we went to the fire fighter's station and I did two translations
> one from one paper to a another and then at the fire fighter's station
> I felt really really *proud*.
>
> God bless America.

Other ways that we saw immigrant children using their language skills to facilitate civic engagement included reading election brochures to their parents, translating letters from school soliciting donations (socks for firefighters, money for homeless children, and holiday gifts for "the poor" —in actuality, people like themselves, as their families were among the lowest income in Engleville), and helping their parents to study for citizenship tests. Thus, in small and larger ways, children facilitated families' involvement in "the public" and their development as public citizens. In doing these things, the children displayed a loyalty to the United States, which takes on greater meaning when considering the racist, classist, and xenophobic treatment that many of these children and their families received.

Enabling Consumption

In everyday commercial transactions, children sometimes interpreted for their parents when they spoke; other times, they were sent by parents to make inquiries or complete sales transactions on their own. They also assisted their families by reading labels and signs, filling out credit applications, checking receipts, crosschecking sales advertisements with prices in the store, and registering complaints about merchandise. They facilitated their parents' ventures into the consumer world; as Beatríz put it: "My mother has never gone anywhere alone." This was especially true in communities like Engleville, where even the most basic items could not easily be secured without interacting with English speakers. But even in communities like central Los Angeles, certain goods and services were not available for purchase from local Spanish-speaking vendors. Children's interpretation efforts may have made a difference in families' willingness to seek out specialized goods.

There is perhaps some irony to the fact that the commercial domain was the one where more children reported on tension-filled encounters than in any other domain: moments of embarrassment, humiliation, and shame. In commercial transactions, families are consumers, and child translators support the commercial establishments by facilitating their parents' abilities to purchase items; arguably the onus of communication should fall on the party that stands to profit from the transaction. Yet in commercial transactions, social class position, inferred through symbols of social distinction including clothing, interactional style, language forms, phenotype, and general comportment,[3] may impact social interactions, as judgments are made about families' ability to pay. Marina voiced her understanding of how her parents were infantilized in such encounters: "I felt embarrassed, because there I was, a child translating for adults. I felt that people would think bad of my parents because they did not know the language. I did not want them to be stereotyped. At times I felt that they would be looked at like little kids. I did not want that." Sixteen-year-old Josh talked about the overt and covert racism he perceived when he went with his family to purchase a car, displaying this through his articulation of the salesperson's thought processes:

> I don't think like he really wanted someone to, I don't know, translate or whatever. Maybe like, "'oh this person doesn't know English, catch him right here with these different prices," you know. "By the end of the day, I'll have a sale," you know, "this guy doesn't know what he's doing," you know . . . we were there, and then my sister said that she heard that guy talking about how us Mexicans can't buy a car.

The children of immigrants may be exposed to similar expressions of racism and xenophobia in everyday ways that do not involve translation, but in translation situations they were positioned not only to hear and respond to such comments but also to navigate these environments for their parents. Often, the hostility they experienced was subtle and indirect, encoded in assumptions that were made about them and their families, and revealed in emotions that flared in such encounters—emotions that the children then had to manage. In an excursion to a music store where her father attempted to rent a musical instrument, only to be denied credit, Estela repeatedly turned the tape recorder on and off—as she told us later, because her father started saying bad words.[4] Luz similarly talked about "cleaning up" her father's language in public interactions. Sociologist Arlie Hochschild discusses the *work* that is involved in emotion management—the kinds of skills required of airline personnel and other service providers.[5] This is a hidden dimension of the services that child translators provide. This work is particularly difficult when children sense that they or their families are being scrutinized.

Beatríz recalled a commercial transaction, the humor of which is predicated on Beatríz's sense that her ethnicity was being surveyed during a seemingly benign commercial transaction, in which she was sent by her mother to purchase cheese:

> I was about seven years old. My mother and I were at Jewels. My mother told me to stand in line and order a pound of American cheese from the deli while she shopped for other items. After about fifteen minutes of waiting my turn, the woman behind the counter asked for my order and I told her that I wanted a pound of cheese. The woman then asked, "American, Italian, Swiss . . ." I thought she was asking for my nationality. I responded by saying, "Mexican." In a frustrated tone of voice, she told me that they did not have any Mexican cheese.

Even when their racialized identities were not salient to the children, as in Beatríz's deli purchase, public commercial transactions had other potential dangers. Beatriz similarly talked about being embarrassed when shopping with her mother for gloves because she thought her mother was being too picky, and she was concerned that the salesperson would think badly about her: "I thought she was being a nuisance, and I thought, 'I don't want this lady to think this way about my mom.' It's okay if I think this way, but . . . I saw it as protecting her image." Beatríz reported she chose to modify her mother's comments; for example, she said that they "didn't fit" rather than that they were "too rough." Commercial encounters in white public space seem especially ripe for the marking of social class and racialized identities because social class is displayed in terms of taste as well as in other ways. Children may also be embarrassed simply by their parents' public behavior, as children of all social standings sometimes are.

When racialized judgments were made, as in Josh's experience, they were not usually explicitly marked or directly interrogated (as Beatríz believed she was being interrogated when she was sent to buy cheese). Children might be asked to mediate messages that were subtly laced with assumptions about them and their families. These involve what Daniel Solorzano, Miguel Ceja, and Tara Yosso refer to as "racial micro-aggressions."[6] For example, in the music store incident with Estela and her father, the store clerk repeatedly emphasized the price of the instruments. At one point, Estela faithfully rendered a literal translation of her father's comment that his friend had "taken out" instruments from the store, leaving ambiguous in English as in the original Spanish, just how the instruments were "taken out." The salesperson responded by emphasizing that those customers had *paid* for them:

ESTELA: He says he wants credit like=
SALESMAN: A payment plan?
ESTELA: Yeah
SALESMAN: Ok, uh::
MR. BALDERAS: Dile que hemos sacado muchos instrumentos aquí [Tell him that we have taken out many instruments from here].
ESTELA: He says that his band has taken out a lot of instruments from here?
SALESMAN: They've *paid* for them.

In responding in this way, the clerk did not take up the substance of the statement—that Sr. Balderas played in the band and that the store had a history with this band. Instead of aligning with Mr. Balderas, the clerk framed Mr. Balderas as someone who might not pay for the instrument. As this micro-interaction suggests, assumptions about families—in particular their social class standings, as imputed by racialized ethnicity and language—could shape translation encounters. This happened especially in terms of what got picked up or ignored even when child translators stayed very close to the original wording.

Many commercial encounters reported by children evoked uncomfortable feelings, rather than the "feel good" responses reported for most other engagements. But when commercial transactions went smoothly, these incidents were "no big deal"; and when the child translator was not the object of racializing discourses, she or he might feel good about providing services to others. Sammy wrote about a time when he went out of his way to help a Spanish-speaking stranger even when the paid service representative would not, and felt pleased with the service he provided for a person who was like his own mother:

> Today after school I went to Toys R' Us. I was looking around and I heard a lady asking someone if they knew where an item was. I looked over and I noticed that they had no idea what the other was saying. So I walked over and helped. The lady was wondering where a toy soldier that was in the paper was. The other lady said there wasn't any. I felt bad because the lady that was working looked like she didn't want to look. I told the lady sorry and she went on her way. That is what usually happens to the people that I help. I will help them and never see them again. It leaves me wondering what happens to them. Most of the time they leave me with a smile also. Which makes it all worthwhile.

Sammy's words offer further evidence of the pride children felt when they offered services to people in public spaces, especially when well received. They also reveal the emotion management that is integral to translation work, a further contribution to the public good. Sammy helped this woman to feel better about the way she was received in the store—perhaps making her a more satisfied customer—and in the process he felt good about himself.

Soliciting Services

Social services offered another domain in which families' positions as working-class immigrants were marked and also elicited uncomfortable feelings. Perhaps because of their relatively young age, only a few of the children I worked with reported on translation experiences in this arena. When seeking social services parents of young children would often solicit help from older, more distant relatives, neighbors, or friends. (Families often asked the research team for assistance.) The young adults who had helped their families in such matters presented these as emotionally loaded encounters. Luz had rather extensive experience talking with social service providers because her father was intermittently unemployed and her mother disabled. She told of translating when her mother filed for welfare benefits:

> I just remembered that it wasn't "how much do you need this time?" but instead they would always ask, "'Have you had any changes in your income or situation? Are you receiving any other sources of income? Do you have a job now?" They would always insist on asking these questions in an interrogating way that was meant to put pressure on my mom, as if they were seeking her to confess or something. It was really bad, especially because I would sense it and I would have to be the one to respond to these sorts of accusations.

Luz articulated a clear sense of surveillance by the state and awareness that her words could be used against her mother. Cecilia Wadensjö's work with community interpreters underscores the point that interpretation for state and legal institutions always involves elements of both service and surveillance.[7] Language brokers are *not* neutral parties in these exchanges, and helping their families in these encounters required careful navigation.

Promoting Health

The final domain that I examine is medical. When translating for medical personnel, children directly served their parents, but they also provided a service to doctors, nurses, receptionists, and clinics—a service that, in some states, the medical establishment is legally bound to provide. In these encounters, as in parent-teacher conversations and most other multiparty encounters, children did not simply move words between speakers. They were active participants in the presentation of health information and in families' health-related decisions; their families trusted them perhaps more than they might have trusted an outside interpreter. Luz remembered:

> I used to have to translate for my mom at the doctor's office so much that it came to the point where the doctor would only talk to me. He wouldn't even look at my mom. Instead he would ask me for updates and symptoms. Afterwards he would give me his recommendations and had me choose what the best options would be for my mom. Often I had to interrupt him to explain what had been going on with my mom and to ask her what she thought, but I must admit that sometimes I made choices for her without asking her first.

This is evident in the following scenario, important because it shows a different side of medical translations than has been publicized in public reports on children's translation work. This was not a particularly onerous interpretation task, as there was no grave illness involved, and Briana did not hold full responsibility for the health and well-being of others. Rather, she assumed a position as a team member in family care processes. This encounter also offers a useful illustration of the multifaceted nature of translation work.

In this event, twelve-year-old Briana participated in a multiparty exchange involving a doctor, Briana's mother, brother Gerardo, and sister Jasper. Both siblings presented as patients: Gerardo, because of an apparent infection on his hand where he had received stitches the week before, and Jasper, because of a cold. The doctor initiated the conversation directly with his first patient, Gerardo, and accommodated him by speaking in short phrases and seemingly simplified language, as well as by revoicing much of what was said:

DOCTOR: Let's start with him. Let's start with Gerardo. Uh::, how are you? Good? The nurse wrote that your legs hurt?

GERARDO: Mhm. Got cut.

DOCTOR: Yeah, like that hurt. You got, like, got cut. Ok, when did it happen?

GERARDO: Um:, like ( ).

DOCTOR: Ok, tell me ( ).

GERARDO: Um:, I um, kicked door? And it had glass.

DOCTOR: Oh! Ok, so you kicked the door, there was glass. Did the glass break?

GERARDO: Yeah.

DOCTOR: What'd you do then?

At this point, Brianna took up a caregiver's position and responded directly to the doctor's queries. She continued to do so throughout the rest of the interaction by posing questions that she had pre-prepared with her mother:

BRIANA: He went to the doc-, the emergency room and got stitches.

DOCTOR: [ok] where?

BRIANA: Here. So::, my mom wants to know, cause when they check-, when we: put?, they get-, the doctor gave us Neosporin.

DOCTOR: Uhuh.

BRIANA: So that makes like the::, the skin fresh? So, it's not like closing.

DOCTOR: Oh, ok.

BRIANA: So we leave it, we took it off and he sleeps with it on.

DOCTOR: I'm sorry, when was this?

BRIANA: Like:, a week and a half ago.

In all of this, Briana did not strictly interpret or mediate language between speakers; she used her knowledge of English to speak on behalf of her family. She spoke from the position of a knowledgeable caretaker and presented herself as an informed consumer of medical products like Neosporin. Not only was she aware of the details of Gerardo's skin condition, but she also assumed responsibility for his care when she included herself with her family as part of the "we" who took care of the bandage at night.

In the next segment of the exchange, Briana sometimes overlapped in her speech with her mother, who was also clearly tracking the conversation. Throughout the encounter, when Briana's mother spoke in Spanish, Briana translated without hesitation, and when she spoke in English Briana often revoiced and/or extended her mother's words, as here:

DOCTOR: Where, which emergency room did he go to?

BRIANA: Ma::: =

MOTHER: =Era el Masonic.

DOCTOR: Masonic. Good. Did you see a doctor after the emergency room, before today?

MOTHER: Yes, he got back uh::: =

DOCTOR: ((to Gerardo)) [Let's take a look ok?]

BRIANA: =when, he got it uh, Monday, Wen-, then he went Wednesday back.

DOCTOR: Ok, so a week and a half and then came back, oh ok. How does it feel? Same as yesterday? Same as two days ago? Same as five days ago?

BRIANA: Yeah, cause we wash it out everyday.

I wondered about why Briana made a point of saying that "we wash it every day."[8] Was she signaling to the doctor that she and her family were good care providers, that they are clean and had complied with the emergency room instructions? In light of the fact that the cut had become infected, it seems Briana may have felt responsible for representing her family as particular kinds of clients. Perhaps she worried about the doctor's opinion of the care her family had provided.

When the doctor turned to treat her sister, Briana similarly demonstrated her awareness of family health issues, as she responded directly to the doctor's queries and posited a question that her mother had wanted to ask:

DOCTOR: Sure. Ok, what's going on with Jasper?

BRIANA: She has had fever for three days.

DOCTOR: Ok. Does anybody else have a fever?

BRIANA: No, only her.

DOCTOR: Ok, um:, anything else in addition to the fever?

BRIANA: No. She wanted to know if it's ear infection.

Throughout, Briana was a coparticipant in the exchanges, as she and her mother collaboratively engaged with the doctors in the care of the two younger children. Some of the work for this endeavor had taken place before hand, as Briana was prepared with questions her mother wanted to ask. Briana presented these questions as coming from her mother, but consistently copositioned herself with her mother, using the pronoun "we" in references to the care of the children.

In this case, the situation was not life-threatening, and the doctor seemed experienced at communicating clearly with families. He also seemed comfortable working with a translator—a "child" translator at that—and he responded respectfully to Briana throughout the exchange, even as he also directed his words and his gaze to Briana's mother. This is an example of how certain kinds of medical encounters can be managed in ways that are not overly burdensome to child translators and that respect family processes.

Although children may be the only people capable of representing other people in medical and legal encounters, it is ironic that they are generally deemed incapable of representing themselves under the law. In another medical encounter, Sammy presented a nurse receptionist with his family's proof of insurance, social security information, and other medical information, which he knew by heart, a reflection of his accumulated expertise in navigating these encounters. But when it came time to sign the paperwork, the nurse receptionist told Sammy, "No, you don't sign. You're not old enough to sign anything."

Paradoxes of Power

In their positions as public *para*-phrasers, immigrant children are powerful social actors. They have more power to shape the flow of conversations and to make things happen in the social world than is often possible for young people to assume. These children had tremendous influence on the flow of information and successfully deployed their skills to secure information, goods, and services for their families, as well as to make things happen in the social world. When transactions went smoothly and their work was appreciated, these young people felt good about having something to contribute to others.

The service work, however, opens them and their families to surveillance in white, adult-centric, English-speaking public space. These are institutional domains where children are not usually seen or heard, and where immigrants may be marked as alien and infantilized. As well, adults, including their parents, sometimes evaluated their behavior and skills in ways that they would not judge other adults. Any power that children acquired was still circumscribed within larger, unequal power relations in society. Translation work took place on the borders of relations between children and adults, immigrants and native-born, and English and non-English speakers, and in transgressing those borders, children were subjected to multiple critiques. Again, children's emotions illuminate intergenerational and intercultural power relations, especially in situations where presumed generational borders were crossed. Ten-year-old Jenny first talked proudly about her delight when she ordered pizza for her parents and heard *her* name called out when the order was ready; then she began to worry that she might be expected to *pay* for the order. But Sammy took delight in showing adults what kids can do:

> If it is an adult they think that younger people don't really know how to translate. They just look down on them and by showing them that a kid translates it kind of raises up my spirits a bit. It kind of gets back at them. . . . What I think is that older people, they look down on a younger person and the little person is trying to, trying to translate, and the older person does not really think that he is translating pretty good. . . . He will look down on him and he will be like, "ha, ha, ha," and he will start laughing at the little kid. And if the little kid does show him he can translate it kind of raises up the kid's spirits. It gives them (him) more encouragement for the next time.

Here, Sammy seemed to be talking about "outsider" or "generic" adults— not his parents, who presumably knew that he could translate and who may in fact have taken his skills for granted. This feeling intimated his awareness that adults held different assumptions about what children can or should do, an awareness that influenced how he understood his own translation work. In chapter 5, I describe children's mediational work in parent-teacher conferences and probe some of the challenges that arise from being in the middle of contrasting cultural perspectives and dissimilar beliefs about children and childhoods.

Chapter 5   Transculturations

Because PARENT-TEACHER conferences offer particularly rich insights into the complexities of child language brokering on social, psychological, cultural, cognitive, and linguistic dimensions, I examine this activity setting in detail. The transactions also reveal adults' assumptions about children and childhood, learning and development, and suggest how these beliefs influence children's pathways.[1] They illuminate some challenges that interpreters face when they engage in interactions that would normally involve only two people. Cecilia Wadensjö,[2] in her extension of Erving Goffman's concepts of participant frameworks,[3] points out that the presence of translators makes dyadic exchanges into multiparty ones, but participants often continue to act as if interactions are guided by the principles of two-party conversations. She further notes that translators have to be good listeners as well as good speakers of both languages.

But in parent-teacher conferences these multiparty exchanges were even more complex than the kinds of interpreter-mediated interactions to which Wadensjö refers. In these encounters, interpreters were multiply positioned. They were children whose social, linguistic, moral, and academic trajectories were being evaluated by their parents and teachers; they were both the objects of those evaluations and the vehicles for transmitting them. Not only were they expected to relay words between adult participants, but they were also sometimes treated by teachers and parents as conversational participants. The transcripts that follow show how both parent and teacher sometimes directed their words to the children and sometimes treated them as the conduits of information to the other party, speaking about them, using the third person.

The skills of listening that were demanded of them took on additional dimensions as language brokers had to be prepared to respond appropriately from the various positions into which they were placed.

Finally, as objects of adults' evaluations, children could be judged on conflicting criteria, when their parents and their teachers held anomalous beliefs about children's developmental processes and about what children should be allowed or expected to do. Children had to mediate between adults who brought their own values, beliefs, and assumptions to the communicative exchange and who held distinct kinds of authority over them. Parent-teacher conferences thus provide windows into intergenerational relationships (between children and different kinds of adults) as well as into beliefs about children, childhoods, development, and learning. These relationships and beliefs shaped the nature of translation encounters as well as how they were experienced by children.

María's Fall Parent-Teacher Conference

It was a cold November day when I met María and her mother at Jefferson School in Engleville. The presence of María's three-year-old brother added "older sister" to the multiple positions María held in this setting. María vigilantly watched her younger brother's movements around the room throughout the conference; in the middle of the session she cautioned him about something that could fall. I had prearranged consent to record the conference with María, her mother, and her teacher, Ms. Salinger, and so after speaking briefly with Ms. Salinger, I positioned the tape recorder on the table and sat nearby to watch.

Ms. Salinger initiated the conference by giving María a few items (a bookmark and some pamphlets); she prompted María to translate by saying "tell your mom about this." Throughout the conference, Ms. Salinger made careful efforts to contextualize information, explain it in several ways, prompt María to translate, and check for her understanding. When she used specialized school vocabulary, sometimes she explained the terms to María; other times she queried to see if María understood. María, in turn, alerted Ms. Salinger to things she wasn't sure she understood, an indication of María's comfort level with her teacher. For example, when Ms. Salinger referred to "the specials teachers," María checked by asking "like drama teachers and?=" In María's translation to her mother, she spelled the meaning out, using the English terms: "drama, art, music y library," then again queried her teacher: "y gym, too?"

Ms. Salinger began the conference by reporting on María's work habits and citizenship, which she explained as "how she does her schoolwork, how she acts in class, what she does with the other students." These school values reflect larger cultural values of using time constructively, being cooperative, practicing self-control, being consistent, and participating in class discussions. (Participating in class discussions was the school-sanctioned way of talking in class, in contrast with "talking too much," which was considered problematic—a distinction that could be unclear to immigrant parents because how much adults allow or expect children to talk varies considerably across cultural and institutional contexts.) In reporting to María's mother, Ms. Salinger spoke about María in the third person, but she directed her gaze mostly to María as translator. She interspersed this report *on* María with a comment directly to her (underscored here), and then directed her to speak at the end:

> These are the worksheets, work habits, and citizenship. How María,
> you know, does her schoolwork, how she acts in class, what she does
> with the other students, and she's always consistently very, very good.
> She uses her time constructively, she's very cooperative with other
> students. Um, always does her homework and her classwork. Um,
> practicing self control. She's been very good. *I know you're excited to
> hear that, aren't you?* She does a really great job. Her, uh, she
> completes her homework with quality and her, uh, her classwork with
> quality. But there's one area where she's not as consistent. And that's
> her tests. All her homework, she does very well and she participates in
> class discussions very well, but she doesn't seem to get the marks on
> her tests that I would expect from, from what she shows me in class.
> *Now you have to tell her.*

In response to Ms. Salinger's directive to tell her mother all of this, María protested: "I don't know how to say all that!" This comment likely indexed her recognition of the difficulty of translating these culturally loaded terms as well the sheer length of the utterance. It also suggests María's comfort with her teacher, in that she was willing to resist the command. In response, Ms. Salinger recapitulated her points, chunking them in smaller pieces, which made the task easier for María.

Ms. Salinger had only glowing things to say about María throughout the conference. But in María's translation of this segment, we see an example of a pattern that occurred consistently across all the parent-teacher conferences that we recorded:[4] the children consistently diminished and downplayed their performances and assumed greater responsibility for problems than their teachers accorded to them. Much praise simply was not translated. Other praise was downgraded through syntactical transformations. The children generally assumed direct, personal responsibility for any problems that were identified and gave disproportionate attention to those problems; here María claimed that she needed to practice more to do well on the tests, something that her teacher did not in fact say:

> Dice que, um, todo asina muy bien en todo asina, bien mi tarea, o sea todo el trabajo de la escuela en la clase tengo bien, um, pero, dice que, um en las tests? Necesito más práctica.

> [She says that, um, everything like is very good in everything? like, (I do) well on my homework, or like all my work in school in class I do well, um, but she says, on the tests? I need more practice.]

In glossing the positive detail into a simple "She says I do well," María took up a socially appropriate position as a child speaking to adult authority figures: she diminished her ego and assumed a self-effacing stance. This inversion may also be considered a transcultural move, an implicit recognition that the kinds of things valued in school (for example, participating in class discussions) might not be valued by her mother and an awareness that her mother was fundamentally concerned with the teacher's evaluation of her behavior and schoolwork—that is, was she doing well and being good or not. María's previous teacher had told me, "I think she's going to Yale, and her parents think she's going to jail"; María's parents were concerned that María talked too much, while her teacher saw her contributions as a sign of her intelligence.

A similar sort of transcultural move took place later in the conference, when Ms. Salinger invited Sra. Gutiérrez to ask any questions she might have. María translated this for her mother, and Sra. Gutiérrez spoke to María in this way: "Yo quería decir, preguntarle a ella, si te portas bien aquí" [I wanted to say, to ask her, if you behave well here]. When María translated this to her teacher, she did not just ask if she had "behaved well"; rather she inserted the possibility that she had been *bad* (something she also did at two other points in this conference): "She said that if like, how like, um::, am I being good in here like, um, like acting good or bad?" In response, Ms. Salinger took up a child-centered discourse and authorized María to evaluate her own behavior; Ms. Salinger asked her: "What do you think?" María's reply ("I don't know") suggests her implicit understanding that her mother was interested not in her self-evaluation but rather her teacher's evaluation. In this case, Ms. Salinger helped María out of this awkward position by replying directly to Sra. Gutiérrez: "Very good. Yeah, wonderful. She's delightful. I mean, just great." (María did not translate this praise, but Sra. Gutiérrez's immediate response of a smile and a laugh suggested that she understood the gist of the message.)

When María mentioned "tests," Ms. Salinger, who had been tracking the translation, asked María what she had just had told her mother. María back-translated faithfully by reporting that she told her mother "that I need more practice. Like, um, I need to learn more." By checking for understanding in this way, Ms. Salinger had an opportunity to clarify to María that that was not quite what she had meant. She spoke directly to María to further elaborate her theory of the discrepancy between María's test scores and her schoolwork:

MS. SALINGER: Well, not quite learn more. It seems like you know what, what you're, what we do when we do your, when you do your home-work, and when you are in class and you're doing your work, like the beautiful job you did on the presentation?

MARÍA: Mhm.

MS. SALINGER: Right. But then when you take the tests, it doesn't show me how much you've shown me in class or in your homework. It, it doesn't quite, look the same. You miss a lot more questions on the tests than you do on your homework or the work that you do.

This turn constituted a dyadic exchange; Ms Salinger had spoken to María in the first person and looked directly at her as she spoke. María seemed to recognize the ambiguity of her position (as translator and dyadic partner) when she asked her teacher if she should explain this to her mother. Ms Salinger replied that yes, she thought so, that "that's the important part about it." María again struggled with the challenges of transculturation, settling for: "En mi tarea hago asina, enseño lo que hago en mi tarea, ¿verdad? Pero en, en los exámenes, casi no, no enseño asina como el trabajo" [In my homework I do, like, I show what I do on my homework, right? But on, on the tests, I don't really, I don't show like on the (other) work].

In the next segment much positive detail was again lost as María focused on a problem identified by her teacher: her English work was "not quite there." Again, too, María took up personal responsibility for this by claiming that she had to practice more. This was the interpretation that her mother picked up on, as she revoiced "practice, practice:"

MS. SALINGER: This is her accuracy in reading English. OK, um, the two on here, María. You know that you got a two on accuracy with your, with your reading English. And that's just because you're working towards that. You're not quite there with the English, but you're doing a great job, you're working towards it . . . Can you tell her that?

MARÍA: Dice que allí me dió dos porque, um, cuando estoy leyendo que, estoy practicando más y más, tengo que practicar más. Porque a veces hay unas cosas que no me sé? Y tengo que, asina, what did you say? Tengo que= [She says that there she gave me two because, um, when I am reading, that I am practicing more and more, I have to practice more. Because sometimes there are things that I don't know? And I have to, you know, what did she say? I have to=]

SRA. GUTIÉRREZ: =Practicar, practicar [Practice, practice].

In the next segment of the transcript, María faithfully assumed her translator position and relayed her mother's words back to the teacher, but Maria introduced them as a question, marked by upward inflection. In doing this, she seemed to be checking the accuracy of her own interpretation, as well as the one that her mother had taken up. She may have intuited that she had transformed the message by emphasizing practice and that her teacher held a different theory about how to make academic progress. This offered Ms. Salinger the opportunity to explicitly reframe this within a developmental discourse in which María's English abilities would unfold naturally over time, not as abilities that must be developed through practice.

MARÍA: To like, practice more?

MS. SALINGER: No, no, no, not practice more. This would be, how the difference between your reading in Spanish and in English. You know, you're learning to read English better. So you're not at the same level as a lot of the other kids in the class because you're still, you're still learning your English too.

María struggled to explain this developmental perspective to her mother, but again fell back on the more familiar notion of "practicing": "Dice que um, que yo no estoy en el:: en el grado como los otros niños porque yo apenas estoy aprend-, em, um, practic=" [She says that um, that I am not in the:: on grade (level) like the other kids because I am barely learn-, em, um, practic=]. Sra. Gutiérrez had been tracking the conversation, however, as indeed most of the parents we observed did; parents did not rely solely on their child's interpretations to make meaning, and as we saw in chapter 3, they often coconstructed meaning with them. (Sra. Gutiérrez confirmed this after the conference, when she explained to me that she understood a little of what the teacher said and attended to nonverbal cues in the interaction as well.) Sra. Gutiérrez made evident that she was tracking the conversation when she cut María off with a gentle correction: "Empezando, hija" [Beginning, my child], effectively taking up the teacher's developmental framing. María's revoiced this: "Uhuh, empezando a leer asina en inglés" [Uhuh, beginning to read like in English] and provided additional contextual information for her mother; it suggested that she was different from the other students because she was still learning English.

The distinction that Ms. Salinger seemed to be making between abilities that develop through practice and those that naturally unfold by engaging in the work itself (without assuming personal responsibility for practicing) was not an easy one to put into words, even in the original English. It reflects particular cultural perspectives, beliefs about learning and development, and nuances that might be hard for a child to comprehend and convey. In several further attempts to elaborate her theory, Ms. Salinger used the present participle forms of the verbs "to learn" and "to work" ("You're learning more English grammar, so you're working on that") to signify this as an ongoing process, but María continued to convert this into an active first person verb: "Necesito practicar" [I need to practice].

The conference continued in this same vein. Ms. Salinger bestowed great praise upon María; María downgraded the praise and took up responsibility for improvement. María also continued to manage a complex interaction in which she was sometimes engaged in a dyadic exchange with either her teacher or her mother and sometimes positioned as the message-bearer between speakers. She distinguished between information that she was expected to translate, from information that she provided, of her own accord, to each party. For example, she provided her mother with contextual information to understand the work they were doing in class, and she told her teacher about talking with a classmate for twenty-three minutes on the phone one night to complete a project. [When Ms. Salinger responded, "You were on the phone for twenty-three minutes?" María did not translate her teacher's words to her back to her mother; instead she told her teacher, "She (her mother) doesn't know that, I was in my room."]

At the end of the conference, Ms. Salinger and I engaged in our own dyadic exchange about María, with María positioned as a third party and further object of evaluation. Ms. Salinger wrapped up her conversation with me: "She's just really, she's just a wonderful little girl."

María's Spring Parent-Teacher Conference

The next conference, later the same year, again involves María, her mother, and teacher. But this meeting added an interim administrator, Ms. Jonas, who took over María's position as translator when she walked into the conference at a midway point.

The same pattern is evident here as in the first conference: Ms. Salinger spoke glowingly about María's schoolwork, using the current academic jargon of "standards" and judging her performance by the cultural value of "consistency." María downgraded this to a mere "doing well" and emphasized the problem that her teacher named: she didn't do as well on tests as she did on classwork. This was the reason for her grade of "I" for "inconsistent (consistency in performance being a school value). In doing this, María explained the *meaning* of "inconsistent" but didn't attempt a verbatim translation of the term.

> MS. SALINGER: María's report card is really good. She, she's really doing a great job in fifth grade. All of her marks are meeting grade level standards. She's done much better on most of her tests this, this quarter. Social Studies tests. The only reason that I put an inconsistent, is sometimes María's math tests aren't, they don't show me as much as what I know that she knows. Can you translate that for me?
>
> MARÍA: Dice que voy bien en las clases, que estoy bien, hago bien. En las tests, um, what did you say on this one? [She says that I am doing well in my classes, that I am well, I do well. On the tests, um, what did you say on this one?]
>
> MS. SALINGER: Um, this "I" Inconsistent means that=
>
> MARÍA: =Dice que cuando tomo las, tengo una "I" porque cuando tomo las, las tests, no hago bien como le hago en, cuando, cuando tengo tests, como cuando hago en Social Studies? Le hago más bien que en el test [She says that when I take the, I have an "I" because when I take the, the tests, I don't do well as when I do, when, when I have tests, as when I do in Social Studies? I do better than on the test].

At about this point in time Ms. Jonas entered the room. Ms. Salinger and I acknowledged her presence by explaining that María had been translating and that we had been recording the conference for research. Ms. Jonas was familiar with the project. On her own initiative, Ms. Jonas stepped into the translator position. This offers an interesting comparative frame for understanding María's work as translator in these transcultural situations.

Ms. Jonas did something similar to what María had done throughout these conferences—she downgraded the praise and emphasized María's responsibility for improvement. Arguably, however, she did so for different reasons, and certainly, given her position, with different effect. Most of the superlatives that Ms. Salinger used (marvelous, wonderful), and much specific detail was glossed by Ms. Jonas as simply "doing well":

> MS. SALINGER: In every other way, María has been, doing marvelous. Her writing is, is just wonderful. I mean, she uses a lot of detail. And she's

got really good vocabulary. Um, she's doing great on her spelling. And, um, her reading. And she's keeping up with all her homework, so I'm really, really pleased with her progress.

MS. JONAS: está haciendo muy bien, está um, escribiendo, y tiene muchas ideas, y puede expresarse y ella está satisfecha con su progreso [She is doing very well, she is, um, writing, and she has a lot of ideas, and she can express herself, and she is very satisfied with her progress]. Anything else that I missed, that you want me to tell her?

The specific details that Ms. Jonas did translate were "she has a lot of ideas and can express herself"—important school values, but ones they may not hold the same meaning to Mrs. Gutiérrez and were easily lost in translation. This emphasis could perhaps have reinvigorated a concern that Ms. Gutiérrez has had, that her daughter talked too much in school.

In the next move, Ms. Jonas moved well beyond a "verbatim" translation and stated her own views of what María needed to do. Just as María did, Ms. Jonas added on in a way that exaggerated María's responsibility:

Ella está haciendo muy bien, está, um, escribiendo, y tiene muchas ideas, y puede expresarse, y ella está satisfecha con su progreso. Depende de si, de si trabaja mucho y estudia mucho? Entonces sale bien, pero cuando no pone atención a lo que estudia, no sale bien. Es evidente que para sacar buenas notas en el examen tiene que estudiar.

[She is doing very well, she is, um, writing, and she has a lot of ideas, and she can express herself, and she is very satisfied with her progress. It depends on if, she works a lot and studies a lot? Then she does well, but when she doesn't pay attention to what she has to study, she doesn't do well. It's evident that to get good grades on the exams, she has to study.]

This message—that María had to study—was picked up and echoed by Sra. Gutiérrez, who said, "Tiene que estudiar" [She has to study].

In the next turn, Ms. Salinger attempted to take back control and re-authorized María to translate. Once again, María presented the gist of the message faithfully but reduced and glossed over the precise praise.

MS. SALINGER: And the other thing is, María is just, you know, she's just really a wonderful classmate, um, student in class. She's very very helpful with the other students. She's always enthusiastic. She asks a lot of questions, um, you know, she's just very delightful to have in class. It's been really enjoyable to, have her as part of our, our group. You want to try this one, María?

MARÍA: Dice que voy bien en todo? Y que participo y decir preguntas a los niños y ayudarles. Y, that's all [She says that I'm doing well in everything? And that I participate and ask questions to the kids and help them. And, that's all].

Once again Ms. Jonas stepped in to add her own viewpoint. Here she introduced a new concern—that María had to do her homework:

Que ella está haciendo muy bien. Estamos satisfechos, bastante satisfechos con el progreso de ella. Y que, tiene que estudiar. Tiene que trabajar. Tiene que estudiar en la casa, trabajar, y Ud. puede asegurar que haga su tarea y todo. Eso sí estaría bueno.

[That she is doing very well. We are satisfied, very satisfied with her progress. And that, she has to study. She has to work. She has to study at home, work, and you can make sure she does her homework and everything. Yes, that would be good.]

In doing this, Ms. Jonas effectively ascribed moral responsibility to Sra. Gutiérrez for making sure that María did her homework. She did not know that Sra. Gutiérrez had worked out an effective arrangement for María to attend an afterschool program that provided homework assistance. Ms. Salinger was aware of this arrangement and had stated in both this conference and the earlier one that María always did a wonderful job on her homework.

We might ask what drove Ms. Jonas to gloss over the positive detail and elaborate in these ways. Could assumptions about María's family in particular, or about immigrant families in general have framed this thinking? By considering such implicit framings we can begin to grasp the complexities of the transcultural work that kids like María do every day because they must translate not just ideas but also underlying ideologies and world views that include the interlocutors' assumptions about them and their families.

Estela's Parent-Teacher Conference

The final transcript excerpts involve eleven-year-old Estela, who, like María, was positioned in multiple ways in this transcultural exchange, which involved her teacher, Mr. Vick, and her mother, Sra. Balderas, in the middle of her fourth-grade year. I'll pick up the transcript in the middle, when Sra. Balderas raised a concern of her own about Estela's homework: Estela gets desperate sometimes when she has an assignment that she can't complete in time.

She specifically connected this problem with the families' lack of access to computers and books:

> Cuando tú tienes una tarea, y no la pudiste hacer por cuestión de que, la computadora no te funcionó, que te tienes que escribir, o porque no encontraste el libro o algo en la biblioteca, y tienes que entregarla para el otro día la tarea? Tú te me pones, este, a llorar, desesperada. "Mami pero tengo que entregar esta tarea." Hija, pero si no se pudo, 'ira le explicas al maestro. Eso no es para que tú llores hija. Yo te lo digo. No hagas eso, no te pongas así, hija. Tú explícale al maestro porque no la llevaste.

> [When you have homework, and you couldn't do it because the computer didn't work, and you have to write, or because you didn't find the book or something in the library, and you have to turn the homework in the next day? You start to, um, cry, you get desperate. "Mami, but I have to turn the homework in tomorrow." My daughter, but if you can't, look, you explain it to your teacher. That's not a reason to cry, daughter. I tell you. Don't do that, don't get like that. Explain to your teacher why you didn't bring it.]

In her rendition, Estela did not translate this detail. She merely stated, with repeated upward inflection, "She says that sometimes? When like, you give us homework? And it's due the next day? I, I'm disappointed and I cry." This contrasts with most of Estela's translations; generally she always attempted very close or "verbatim," line-by-line translations. Perhaps she glossed the information here because of the way her mother chunked the information in a long stretch of speech; her approach may also have been influenced by her position in this transcultural space, as the object of evaluation of both parent and teacher. In her words, Estela did not transmit the reasons for her upset at home; she simply took up responsibility for her behavior (being disappointed and crying). And indeed, her voice trembled when she said this, which suggested that she was on the verge of tears here as well.

Without the information that Sra. Balderas had offered for why Estela sometimes wasn't able to do her homework on time, Mr. Vick responded to this concern based on his own beliefs. In doing this, he framed it as a problem that Estela had and that other (Latino) kids have had too—a problem of language—that their parents don't speak English (his language)—and that they don't have help at home.

> I am, tell Mom I understand, and you and I, when we've had, when we've had projects, you've come to me and said, like with that country report when you had to hold it up, you said you couldn't do it

at home, because Mom or Dad couldn't bring you to the library? if you didn't have the Internet? and I understand, you know what? Flora's had the same problem, if you don't know this. Uh, Mario has the same problem. Their parents don't speak, my language. Ok. And if they can't get that done, do I ever get angry or upset with you? No never, ok? If you can't get things done because you don't have the help at home? I'm okay with that, I understand it.

Here, as throughout the conference, the teacher presented himself as a kind and caring teacher who doesn't get angry or upset, and his response to Estela's "problem" clearly stemmed from his concern over her well-being. But he unwittingly set himself up in contrast with Estela's mother, who appeared upset at this point in the conference and continued to become more agitated as the conference went on. This may have further complicated Estela's sense of being "in the middle" of two authority figures who were quite differently aligned. If she accepted her teacher's sympathetic outreach to her, was she somehow being disloyal to her own mother? To what extent did she feel implicated, as translator, in her mother's growing sense of frustration?

As the conference progressed, Estela was placed more deeply into this awkward position between her mother and her teacher. In the next segment, Mr. Vick directed Estela to direct her mother to speak to her in particular ways. He did so with the same gentle voice that he used throughout the conference, even as he placed Estela in the position of having to tell her mother how she should parent. Here Estela's translation was almost exactly verbatim (again, like most of her translations); it was tempered only by signaling this as reported speech by using the words "he says."

> MR. VICK: And tell Mom she needs to remind you that, she needs to say "Estela relax!"
>
> ESTELA: Y dice que tú me tienes que acordar, de que me tienes que decir "Estela relájate" [And he says that you have to remind me, that you have to say, "Estela, relax"].

Following this, Sra. Balderas went on to express her frustrations with Estela directly to her, using the first person, in a long series of dyadic exchanges. Mr. Vick seemed to try to spare Estela the task of translating this to him, by telling her that he understood everything Sra. Balderas had said. He continued to frame the conference in a positive light, as Sra. Balderas continued to express her own frustrations with how Estela approaches her homework assignments. Sra. Balderas spoke louder than usual and with an agitated voice with raised pitch and rising intonation. She took up the position that Mr. Vick had given to her, as a parent who "couldn't help" her daughter, in contrast with a teacher who could, when she said:

¿Que cuando tengas ese problema? ¿Que no te podamos ayudar nosotros, tus padres? ¿Y al otra día tienes que entregar la tarea? ¿Y no lo puedes hacer por cuestión de que no pudimos nosotros, o equis cosa? Tú vengas y le explicas al maestro y él te va a entender. ¿Ok?

[When you have that problem? And we, your parents, can't help you? And you have to turn in the homework the next day? And you can't do it because we couldn't help you, or some such thing? You come and explain to the teacher and he will understand. Ok?]

In a final set of turns, a mistranslation of a single word further exacerbated the position Estela was in as the bearer of her teacher's directives to her mother, which served to infantilize her mother. Mr. Vick told Estela to tell her mother that she "has a lot to be proud of." Estela translated this as "You have to be grateful for me."

MR. VICK: Tell mom again she's got a lot to be proud of.
ESTELA: Dice que tú tienes que estar muy, um agradecida por mí [He says that you have to be very, um, grateful for me].

Sra. Balderas accepted the teacher's supposed mandate, but in a voice that signaled disgruntlement, even as she clearly tried to end the conference on a positive note:

OK, estoy agradecida. No más que, me desespero que tú te pongas así. no quiero verte ya así, yo te lo he dicho. Yo quiero que tú te relajes en tus cosas, en tu tarea, te concentres. Eso es lo único que yo quiero de ti.

[OK, I am grateful. It's just that, I get desperate when you get like that, I don't want to see you like that, I have told you. I want you to relax with things, with your homework, and concentrate. That's the only thing I want of you.]

Estela and Mr. Vick similarly made efforts to conclude this complex transcultural encounter on a positive note; Estela translated her mother's words simply as "She says that? she just wants me to concentrate and that she is proud of me." And Mr. Vick concluded with "Good. Wonderful."

Transcultural Skills

These transactions offer two revelations: translation is not a process of passively conducting information from one speaker to the other—what the linguist John B. Haviland refers to as the "verbatim" theory.[5] And attempts to provide verbatim translations can be especially problematic, given both the cultural nuances of utterances and their ideological framings and the lack of equivalence of syntactic and semantic fields across languages. When attempting verbatim translations there is always the risk of mistranslating words that can further skew the intended messages.

Estela and María each engaged a variety of strategies to deal with the challenges of transculturations,[6] as well as the awkward positions in which they were placed. They contextualized information, eliminated specific details, and paraphrased terms rather than attempting to find matching words in Spanish. As translators and as interlocutors, Estela, María, the teachers, *and* Ms. Jonas each seemed to shape their message for the audience they presumed themselves to be engaging. They struggled, in different ways, and to different degrees, with the cultural nuances of these messages, and they differed especially in the degree to which they remained faithful to the original words and the kinds of license they took in either expanding or eliminating detail. How they skewed the messages—what they said, how they said it, and what they left out—reveals much about their own positions in these encounters, their assumptions about their audiences, and their transcultural dexterity.

The words of the adult authority figures are particularly revealing of their assumptions about who these children and their families are and what they "need" or what "problems" they have. These seem to include some assumptions that led teachers at Regan to find Mexican youth lacking in comparison with Polish immigrants, as discussed in chapter 2. At times such assumptions were declared openly, as when an Engleville teacher proclaimed: "The fact is that they (Mexican students) don't read, and the reason their families don't read is because they don't know it's important or because they can't read very well." As many researchers have documented this kind of widespread deficit thinking about Mexican immigrants may overtly and covertly influence communicative exchanges.[7] It comes through in the information that speakers highlighted, elaborated, contextualized, and deleted; furthermore, deficit thinking appears especially in teachers' additions and assumptions when they did not have direct access to the other party's words. Such assumptions are important to contemplate because child language brokers face them every day.

When children are expected to relay these messages from institutional authority figures to their parents, they effectively act as agents of the institutions.

They are not neutral brokers in such contexts, and their ability to represent their families' interests is compromised. Like the medical interpreters that sociolinguist Brad Davidson studied or the court interpreters that Marco Jacquemet studied these children can become gatekeepers for the institutions in acts of surveillance or critique against their own families.[8]

The parent-teacher conferences I examined here involved adults who cared deeply about promoting these students' learning and development. Both Ms. Salinger and Mr. Vick were highly dedicated professionals who took their role as educators and advocates for children and families very seriously. Ms. Jonas's emphasis on the importance of studying and doing homework most certainly came from a place of good intention. Ms. Jonas was aware that immigrant children have odds against them, particularly in this mixed-income suburb in which upper-middle-class children had the benefits of social and cultural capital. Her translations were likely influenced by her ideas about what children like María needed to compete on an unequal playing field. She emphasized the importance of work and practice to get ahead—a perspective María and her family already fully endorsed. This was not, however, the message that Ms. Salinger wanted to convey.

Even well-intentioned, positively framed, and respectful assumptions about the children and their families complicated children's transcultural work. If child translators recognized the assumptions encoded in talk in both large and subtle ways, then they might not challenge them because they were children speaking to adults; they were children of immigrants operating in white, English-speaking public space.[9] Self-effacement is an appropriate stance for children to assume in front of adult authority figures, and they were unlikely to challenge inaccurate portrayals of themselves or their families.

Children also may have been aware of the multiple ways in which they could be evaluated by adults. When Estela reported on another conference in a journal entry, she highlighted the emotions she felt—not about her work as a translator per se, but about being judged as a student. She simultaneously revealed her awareness that we, the researchers, might also judge her performance. Indeed, readers of this text may judge her when I present her words to you, as she wrote them, in the way that adults tend to evaluate children when they speak and write. What leaps to your attention? What judgments do you make about Estela?[10]

Today of mi conferensia me senti muy nerviosa pense que lo iva a
agara malos grados pero cuando mi papi avlo con mi maestro el le dijo
que llo estaba asiendo mui bien entonses me deje de precupar proque

supe queseestaba asiendo mui bien. Es pero que agree todo mui bien y que si tengo unos problemas le digan a mi papa pero qureo que lo agare casi tod muy muy sbien ustedes piensan lo mismo si "o" no?

[Today of my conference I felt very nervous I thought that I was going to get bad grades but when my father spoke with the teacher he told him that I was doing very well and then I stopped worrying because I knew that I was doing very well. I hope that I get everything very well and if I have some problems that they tell my father but I believe I got everything almost all very very well do you think the same yes "osr" no?]

Chapter 6   Transformations

Nova

"Marjorie!" I looked up from my lunch in this restaurant frequented by university faculty on this first day of a return visit to the Midwest, startled to see "Nova" standing straight and tall in a waiter's white pressed shirt and red tie, looking and sounding professional, confident, mature, and at home in this position and setting. After I registered my surprise to see him here, Nova told me of his activities: working as a waiter; designing web pages for cyberspace clients who paid for his services (with a business partner from Mexico); playing on the volleyball team (despite his father's preference for him to play baseball); forming a Latino club at his school; teaching salsa lessons; and yes, still translating, especially for his dad. He talked about his college search and noted that he was researching art schools in Italy and hunting for scholarship money on the Internet, but he was also being recruited by the army (aggressively, from Nova's description) and was tempted to join because he'd like some day to be an astronaut and he knew that is one pathway to NASA. I remembered the shy boy that I first met in the park near my house six years ago, a boy who had moved to the Midwest from a rancho in Mexico the previous year, and who was just learning English. I wondered at his transformation into the outgoing, articulate, and worldly young man I saw in front of me.

Junior

Junior's family had moved twice—just like I did—in the time since I moved away from this town. His mother apologized for this new home: "es muy pequena" [it's really small]. But all I could think is that it was bigger than my apartment in Los Angeles and that small can be cozy and cozy can be nice. Photos, lining the room, allowed me in one fell swoop to see Junior at ages four, eight, eleven, twelve, and thirteen, as well as the three children in various constellations together and alone. The television show, "The O.C.," was playing, and I wondered what sense this family of Mexican immigrants living in the heartlands of the United States made of the opulence and decadence of the lives that the died-blond cast of characters lived under blue skies and brilliant sunshine along the shores of the Pacific—a show that I knew only through my daughter, who introduced me to its opening song when we moved back to California from Chicago: "California, here I come, right back where I started from. . . ."

When Junior entered the room I barely recognized him. His baggy clothes belied the thinned out frame, but his face had thinned out, and he was taller than his father by at least four inches. Junior was wearing a heavy silver chain with a metal cross, loose fitting jeans, and shiny white tennis shoes with laces undone. He spoke to me in both English and Spanish, as he told me that he wanted to be a car redesigner and that he was joining an after-school club at his high school where they fixed up and redesigned cars. He had already learned a lot from watching his father: "My dad fixes his car, so I kind of learn from the things he does to it, like when he does tune-ups to it. I'll go find the pieces he needs, change the oil, (see) what kind of oil it needs, where he puts it in."

Junior said that he translated more than he used to "because there's more stuff to do around the house." He told me about some recent translation work for his parents: calling the phone company to change their service; reading information about a new law on car emissions so his father could renew his car's license plate; researching information about digital cable on the Internet to help his family choose cable service; and translating at his own parent-teacher conferences.

It seemed that from their dress, talk, present activities, and future ambitions that Nova and Junior—neighbors and friends, whose families migrated from the same farming community to the same Chicago suburb at around the same time—had taken up very different kinds of teen identities and perhaps different trajectories of development. Nevertheless, for both, translation work continued to shape their daily lives, and both used their bilingual skills as well as their familiarity with modern technology to help their families in many ways.[1]

Estela

Estela's family had also moved twice since I left, first into a rented home and now into one that the family owned. Estela's mother worked from four P.M. to one A.M. five days a week at Burger King; her father had a factory job and worked as a gardener nights and weekends; and Estela's uncle pitched in to make the mortgage payments. Estela worked, too, as a babysitter for a young couple, and she was home with her younger sisters during the time that her mother worked: she helped her sisters with their homework, fed them supper, cleaned the house, and got the girls to bed. Estela complained that the girls didn't go to sleep easily, especially when they had napped that day, so sometimes she fell asleep with them.[2] She still translated, now for her aunt and a cousin who recently moved here from Mexico as well as for her mother. But she also complained about speaking Spanish with her mother; Estela felt she expressed herself much better in English. At the same time, her resistance to Spanish was not paired with a rejection of her cultural origins; to the contrary, she talked proudly of being a Mexican and a Chicana, and she showed me her MySpace page, decorated with the colors of the Mexican flag, where she reported on her participation in recent immigrant rights marches.

Tensions had mounted in the family, and Estela had had what she called a "panic attack" recently, after which she spent several days in the hospital. She was given medicine, which made her fall asleep in school, so she stopped taking it. She was now seeing a therapist, and her parents were participating in her care and adjusting their own routines to accommodate her needs. The stressors of life here seemed palpable–seemingly the price this family has paid in their struggle to attain the American Dream of living in a single-family home with freshly painted walls on this quiet suburban street in Engleville.

María

María's family had also purchased a home in this suburb, on a busy street in a part of town that historically been home to African Americans. The family was able to buy the house with a big backyard complete with a play structure for María's brothers because they decided to forgo trips to Mexico. Mr. Gutiérrez's boss also helped by cosigning on the mortgage.[3] Sra. Gutiérrez continued in her primary role as homemaker, although she also worked part-time in the cafeteria at the children's elementary school. Like Estela, María still held some responsibilities vis-à-vis her younger siblings, but because Sra. Gutiérrez was home with the children every day after school María was free to stay late for volleyball, gymnastics, and woodworking, as well as to go to the local youth center for homework assistance. María contrasted herself with the "girly girls" at her school who didn't like sports. Her favorite subjects were science and math; she complained that she got a lot of homework and felt the pressure between doing her homework and helping her mother around the house even more than when she was younger. María still translated, as she says, "everywhere we go, basically."

On this return visit to Engleville, I was seated at the kitchen table with Sra. Gutiérrez when María arrived home from volleyball practice on her bike; dressed in sweats and a T-shirt, she toted a backpack full of books. She brought her things upstairs and then joined us as her mother served us a plate of enchiladas mineras ("miner's enchiladas," a native food of Guanajuato, México). After eating I took out my laptop where I had a folder full of data files: field notes, drawings, transcripts of translations, interviews, video clips. I showed María a few of the transcripts and saw her eyes grow wider. "That's a lot of words!" she said, and I told her they were hers. As we were talking the phone rang. María's mother motioned for María to answer it; she signaled this with urgency after the third ring. María stepped into her role as family translator once again by answering the phone and fielding a sales pitch for her mother.

These glimpses into the lives of the four Engleville youth seven years after I had begun working with them give a sense of the varied pathways taken by not only the children of immigrants as they forge their ways through adolescence but also their families during their processes of settlement in the United States.[4] Thus far I have focused on how children's actions contribute to households and communities, especially in the years when I first observed them in their homes, when they were in upper elementary and middle school. In chapter 6 I leap forward to portray these same youth in high school and to study how their lives and experiences, and those of their families, have changed over time. I consider the role that translation work has played in their processes of learning and development, as well as in shaping their experiences of childhood, and I contemplate changes in children's forms of participation in households and communities, including their work as translators.

Because my approach to understanding child development is informed by sociocultural theory, I begin by discussing this theory and contrasting sociocultural perspectives with dominant ways of theorizing learning and development within Western developmental psychology. I then contemplate the changing nature of children's participation in language brokering practices through the accumulation of such experiences as children grow from childhood through their teen years. For the latter, I draw on interviews and observations of the children I first met when they were in fifth and sixth grades; they were now no longer really "children," but adolescents, or young adults.

Views of Development

Traditional theories of human development focus on what children of different ages can be expected to do or accomplish.[5] Often discussions are organized in terms of developmental stages, such as early childhood, middle childhood, and adolescence. (The boundaries of these categories may change over time and across contexts, and new categories may appear, such as the previously unmarked stage of "tweens.")[6] This stage-based approach to understanding children's transformations over time is centered largely on individual processes of learning and development, with attention to groups mostly in terms of categories of children (of different ages, genders, and abilities). The relationship between children's competencies and developmental processes is generally addressed from one direction: researchers ask what developmental competencies children should have before they engage in determinate activities. For example, children are assumed not to be "ready to read" until they have mastered skills like letter recognition and some level of phonemic awareness. (In the past, "reading readiness" was also measured by a wide battery of abilities, including fine motor skills like the ability to cut with a scissors and large motor skills such as those needed for riding tricycles.) Once children have achieved these competencies, they may be considered developmentally "ready" to take on new tasks.

Underlying this framework, and implicit in it, are assumptions about normative developmental processes. There is concern that children whose experiences violate some presumed norms of development—for example, those who take on "adult" responsibilities at too young an age—may be damaged. However, only some kinds of violations of developmental norms are viewed as problematic; for a child to be an "early reader," for example, is not considered detrimental to his or her well-being.[7] The assumption is that negative outcomes follow because specified developmental competencies were not in place when children took on these tasks. Much of the literature of language brokering assumes this.

Sociocultural Theory

Sociocultural theories about development differ from these approaches in some important ways. Rather than identifying universal developmental processes, these focus on the learning that happens through engagement in particular kinds of tasks, talk, tools, and relationships, in situated contexts in the social world. Learning and development happen through participation in what Jean Lave and Etienne Wenger call "communities of practice;"[8] Barbara Rogoff describes development as "transformation in forms of participation"—that is, changes in the way people participate in the practices.[9]

The theoretical anchor for sociocultural research can be found in Lev Vygotsky's profoundly social approach to the study of mind.[10] Working with the dialectical tension between psychological and sociological forces, the individual and society, emotions and intellect, and generalized culture and particular activity, Vygotskian psychology makes a central claim: humans transform themselves as they transform their social world. This transformation occurs through the use of tools. Language is one of the most important and pervasive tools that humans use for activity. The practice of translation makes clear how language functions as a tool that people use to do things in the social world.

VIEWS OF CULTURE IN SOCIOCULTURAL THEORY

In sociocultural theory, culture is viewed as practice—something that people *do*, rather than something they *have*. Culture is expressed in how people organize themselves, using cultural tools, in relation to other people, tasks, and talk—how they "live culturally."[11] Rather than viewing culture as a thing that people have (that is, traits of individuals), socioculturalists like Kris Gutiérrez and Barbara Rogoff look at culture as the repertoires of practice that people develop through their participation in the routine activities of daily life.[12] This contrasts with traditional ways of viewing culture in both fixed and group-bounded terms that obscure the heterogeneity in experience and practice within as well as across groups. Culture is never static; it changes just as the material and symbolic tools that give it form change over time, and, although regularities of practice are important to understand, it is also important to identify variations in "histories of engagement" in cultural practices by individuals and groups.[13]

Differences can be found among socioculturalists in the relative emphasis on cultural or historical processes and in the manner in which the relationships between culture, context, and history are teased out. This is evident even in the labels used in the field. The term "sociocultural," which privileges the *social* and *cultural*, has had the greatest uptake in the United States. But Lev S. Vygotsky referred to his work as "socio*historical*," and, though he examined cultural practices, he was influenced by Darwinian evolutionary theory and especially interested in cultural practices as instantiations of phylogenetic development or changes in the historical context of human interaction. This implicitly teleological view of human history sits in tension with the thrust of most sociocultural researchers today, who appreciate cultural practices in their own right, not situated on a continuum that can be ranked both within and across cultural settings. In examining the skills of translators, however, I indeed argue that this practice demands high-level cognitive skills and that acting as a translator may make a person smarter on some measures.

Socioculturalists face the challenge of exploring both cultural and historical changes without reducing one to the other or otherwise confusing the two. This offers a partial answer to the questions I posed about my grandmother in chapter 1; perhaps her actions are best understood as both "cultural" (in the sense of continuing practices of thrift that were valued in her family and community) and contextual/historical (in that they were useful and had particular take-up in the historical context of the Depression years). *All* cultural practices change over historical time, as conditions and the available forms of mediation change. Translation practices are a clear case in point.

VIEWS OF DEVELOPMENT IN SOCIOCULTURAL THEORY

Vygotsky was a psychologist, and, like most developmental psychologists, sociocultural theorists are interested in psychological and cognitive changes in people over time. But a Vygotskian approach to development is quite different from that taken by Western psychology. A teleological bent (the assumption that forward movement is inevitably a positive progression) is perhaps inescapable given the field's historical roots in turn-of-the-century Darwinism and Marxist theories of the historical development of human societies, as well as the questions of learning and development that the theory pursues, but sociocultural theorists do not attempt to lock development into predetermined stages (for example, "eight-year-old children do X"). Rather, they are interested in how competencies emerge from engagement in particular activity. They ask about the cognitive *consequences* of practices like translation, not the cognitive *requisites* for acquiring translation skills. What do children learn from their engagement in practices of translation? What cognitive consequences follow from the complex linguistic negotiations involved in translation work?[14]

Vygotskian theory considers four interactive levels of development: changes in thinking and behavior that occur within an individual's lifetime (ontogenetic development), changes that occur across the history of a species (phylogenetic development), changes in the social and cultural history of particular groups that modify the forms of mediation available to the individual members of that group (sociocultural development), and changes that occur in the learning or behavior of an individual within particular problem/learning situations (microgenetic development). These levels are inseparable; individuals can be understood apart from neither the society around them nor the historical conditions that gave rise to the present form of that society and its social groups.

To study the developmental consequences of language brokering, I focused mostly on the microgenetic and ontogenetic levels; I looked at how people learn from their engagement in the work and how that learning accumulates over time. The first involves learning through interactions in specific activity settings of translation—moment-to-moment transactions in which different kinds of relationships, supports, and artifacts mediate the learning process. In this chapter, I examine a few language brokering events to explore these as activity settings for learning. The ontogenetic level is a bit more elusive; this second approach refers to changes in thinking and behavior that occur over the lifespan—or in this case, over the course of children's development from about age ten to fifteen. In part we see this development through their changing forms of participation in translation activities, which I documented through interviews and observations. Other Vygotskian levels development are also implicated in language brokering; the practice is a product of both sociocultural changes (for example, the movement of people across linguistic and cultural borders) and phylogenetic changes (for example, the evolution of different languages and discursive practices over the course of human history).

Sociocultural research has examined how people learn through apprenticeship in cultural practices such as tailoring, weaving, reading, writing, and playing basketball.[15] Researchers have studied how novices gradually acquire skills from "experts" (those who are more competent than they in those skills) and how novices move from the periphery to the center of such activities. As people engage in all of these tasks, they acquire language.[16]

The work of child translating poses some interesting questions for sociocultural learning theory. How do bilingual children learn to become translators when there is no community of practice in which to apprentice? Are these children experts, novices, or something in between? Where should expertise be located when a child, who knows English, but nothing about how juries function, translates a jury summons for her mother, who reads little English, but has direct experience with juries? How do issues of social power enter into the expression, display and take-up of such expertise? In language brokering interactions, expertise is often distributed across participants, and both parent and child may facilitate each other's learning (of English, Spanish, and content matter) through these events. This arrangement challenges the traditional, unidirectional assumed apprenticeship model.

The standard apprenticeship model of cultural transmission offers little attention to how innovation arises. The model is based on the assumption that children's learning is scaffolded by more expert others, leading to some kind of known outcome—the development of relevant skills or expertise. But how can we understand the generation of new forms of cultural practice in relation to the take-up of ongoing ones? The study of child language brokering may help address relationships between cultural continuity and change because in this practice children not only take the lead but must also continually recreate the practice in new circumstances, on their own, with few models to follow. Many children I spoke with were not really aware that other kids did this work, and they did not recognize much of their own work as translating. In some ways they were engaging in a practice they were inventing themselves.

When people move across geopolitical and cultural spaces, they bring potentially different sets of practices into contact with each other, even as forms of practice and the available tools for engaging in them change. Immigrant childhoods allow us to examine the interrelationship between sociocultural changes and developmental processes and to see the confluence of multiple sorts of changing practices, contexts, relationships, tools, and technologies. For example, movement across linguistic borders means that adults can no longer use the tool of language as they would in their home country. This forces them to rely on other people's linguistic toolkits.

The developmental processes of different individuals are, in turn, interwoven in complex ways. The proclivities and activities of one family member may both shape and be shaped by how others' capacities unfold. Children's interpretation skills both emerge from and influence their parents' language abilities in potentially contradictory ways. The fact that Nova can speak English may diminish the need for his mother to speak English on her own, but his translation work also scaffolded his parents' engagement with English, facilitating their language acquisition. The need for children to serve as interpreters—and thus their growth in linguistic and social skills—may further fluctuate as parents acquire English themselves, or as new siblings are born, as in Estela's household. Additional sociocultural changes also weigh in, as families adopt practices fitted to their new contexts, and as the tools, technologies, and politics of the era change.

Learning at the Microgenetic Level

In sociocultural theory, learning is presumed to be cultivated best within "zones of proximal development."[17] In their idealized form, these are spaces in which learners, or "novices," collaborate with more competent people, or "experts," to accomplish tasks that the novices could not achieve alone. Learning is assumed to be most effective under two conditions: what is being taught is somewhat more difficult than what the learner could do on his or her own but not so difficult as to cause frustration, and there are sufficient supports in place to scaffold the process. This is important to keep in mind when considering the potential of translation events for activating zones of proximal development. Experts scaffold learning by modeling, facilitating discussions, and providing prompts, clues, explanations, encouragement, leading questions and efforts to focus the learner's attention. They may engage jointly with novices in these tasks.

Most discussions of the zone of proximal development and scaffolding presume experts to be adults, older than novices, and novices to be younger than experts. This may reveal an implicit assumption of universal developmental trends—that people develop along similar trajectories, so those who are older are necessarily more advanced in any given skill—an assumption that bears reconsideration. Children may well be more expert than adults in many domains, for example, new technologies, popular culture, or skateboarding. Children's expertise may be obscured because of a lack of interest on the part of adults in learning the skills that children possess, as well as assumptions about the direction of learning; thus, adults rarely find themselves in the position of novices to a child expert. A critical social science perspective suggests new ways of thinking about the relationship of children and adults in sociocultural learning theory.[18]

Language brokering work is another domain in which the assumption that adults are experts and children novices should be challenged. Language brokering involves activities in which children, often taking the lead with adults, facilitate their parents' abilities to accomplish tasks that these adults would not be able to accomplish on their own. In the process, children also support their parents' acquisition of English language and literacy skills. Thus, in many ways, translation episodes represent zones of proximal development *for parents*, where children serve as the experts.[19]

At the same time, parents also support their children's work as translators in various ways. They ask questions, call for clarification, prompt their movement through text, offer procedural guidance, provide background information, correct children's Spanish pronunciation, grammar and vocabulary, and otherwise work with the children to make sense of texts. They do this in varying degrees, across contexts, relationships, situations and tasks, and the nature and degree of their support certainly matters for children's experiences of translation and for what they learn from their experiences. Thus, zones of proximal development of language brokering are dynamic and shifting. Children and parents mutually scaffold each other's learning in these events, and they advance their skills together. This can include their acquisition of the two languages, literacy skills, procedural knowledge, and knowledge about the social world. Both parent and child may provide different kinds of expertise, and zones of proximal development may modulate dynamically in interactions over the tasks.

The following transcription documents a day when Junior was seated with his mother at their kitchen table, reading a letter that they had received in the mail from the program on Women, Infants and Children (WIC), regarding healthy food habits. Sra. Fernández began by telling Junior that she wanted him to read this paper that had come in the mail from WIC. Junior had gone with his mother to the WIC program, and so he had some context for understanding. He hesitated as he began to decipher the note and attempted to explain it in more general terms, when he switched to "es como" [it's like]. His mother seemed to respond to his hesitation and provided additional background information for him, by saying, "it's about the foods," a colloquial reference to the food program that WIC runs:

> JUNIOR: Dice? De::, es como= [It says? About::, it's like=]
> SR. FLORES: =es de las comidas [=it's about the foods]

Thus, in the very first half-sentence of their exchange, Junior and his mother were involved in a process of coconstructing meaning, as they set the context of what this paper is about. Struggling with the word "iron," Junior managed to identify the Spanish equivalent of this term and explained what iron was needed for. Sra. Fernández then stepped in to offer the scientific word for "little red balls of blood" (blood cells):

> JUNIOR: Sí, es de las comi-, dice lo que, es de la: sangre? Dice cuando [tomas] iron? Eh? Este, este, hierro. Que hierro es necesitado? Para buena salud. Eh, es para que haga? Um? Cells? Este, las bolitas rojas de:: sangre? [Yes, it's from the foo-, it says, it's about blood? And it says when you take iron, that is, that is, iron. That iron is needed? For good health. Eh, it's to make, um, cells? That is, little red balls of:: blood?]
> SRA. FLORES: Uhuh, las células. Rojas. [Uhuh cells. Red ones.]
> JUNIOR: Mhm, las células. Cada día? Tienes que comer, este, hierro? Y si no comes? Este, tu dieta regulario, las células rojas? ( ) se llama anemia? [Mhm, cells. Every day? You have to eat, this, iron? And if you don't eat it, in your regular diet, the red cells? ( ) it's called anemia.]
> SRA. FLORES: Mhm.
> JUNIOR: Eh, se describe, son importantes. [Eh, it describes, they're important.]

Arguably, even in this brief episode—one in which Junior's mother provided only a minimal level of explicit scaffolding—a process of learning is evident. At a minimum Junior was exposed to health information that he was able to convey authoritatively to his mother. Similarly, in Adriana's translation of the jury summons mentioned in chapter 3, she learned something about how juries operate (her mother provided background information based on her own prior experiences in court), and she and her mother learned the words for jury in English and Spanish.

Teachers are probably the second most common recipients of young people's translation efforts, and some teachers leveraged their pedagogical expertise to make interpretation encounters into high-quality learning activities. In several parent-teacher conferences that I attended, teachers made considerable effort to chunk the information in short phrases, rephrase it when the children hesitated, and explain complicated terms. They were generally attentive to the children as they relayed the information to their parents. Ms. Salinger, for example, provided quite explicit supports by rephrasing information when María hesitated:[20]

> MS. SALINGER: This is for advanced students. Tell her it's for advanced students.
>
> MARÍA: Es para niños que (pause) [This is for]
>
> MS. SALINGER: It's because she's a very good reader.
>
> MARÍA: Que soy, soy muy, lo que dice que yo soy muy buena leer, de leer, leo bien, yo no sé qué más. [That I am, I am, what it says is that I am very good to read, to read, that I read well, and I don't know what else.]

Once clued in to the meaning that Ms. Salinger intended for "advanced students"—that she was a good reader—María had no problem explaining this to her mother. She initially seemed to search for a direct grammatical equivalent for being "a good reader" [Que soy muy buena leer] [literally, "that I am very good to read"] but then rephrased to a more grammatically correct and appropriate way of saying this: "que leo bien" [that I read well]. Thus Ms. Salinger's rephrasing was an effective way of pushing María past a stuck point in the translation process.

Estela's teacher, Mr. Vick, was similarly careful not to overwhelm Estela with too much information all at once. Here, he explained the meaning of the numbered system on the school report card. He also seemed to sense Estela's hesitation at the word "standard" and explained this concept step by step:

> MR. VICK: Uh, let me try to explain what these numbers mean.
>
> ESTELA: Dice no más lo, e::l va a tratar de explicar qué significa. [He says that he just, he's going to explain what it means.]
>
> MR. VICK: Everything on this report card has to do with, standards.
>
> ESTELA: Um, todo esto? El= [Um, all of this? He=]

MR. VICK: =You can just use the word standard.

ESTELA: But I don't know what it means.

MR. VICK: You can just say it in English.

ESTELA: Dice que um, esa? Ese con-, ese, todo eso en la de ésta? Significa, standard. [He says that, um, this? That, with, this, all of this in this thing? Means, standard.]

MR. VICK: A standard is where we expect our kids to be at the end of the year.

ESTELA: Una estandard es cuando um, los maestros expec-, expectan? Tener? A los niños? Al ultimo del año. [A standard is when, um, the teachers expect[21] to have? All? The kids? At the end of year.]

Estela participated in the coconstruction of this zone of proximal development when she admitted to Mr. Vick that she did not know the word for "standard" and thus solicited his support. Young people did not always seem to feel comfortable admitting to adults when they did not understand something, but Mr. Vick had created a comfort level that facilitated the construction of this learning zone for Estela. In this case, Mr. Vick seems to recognize Estela's dilemma over how to translate the word "standard," and his step-by-step approach to explaining the meaning of this term models an effective translation strategy for concepts that are inherently difficult to translate.

Adults varied in the degree to which they supported children's language brokering work. Certainly, few participated as explicitly as Ms. Salinger and Mr. Vick did. The popular belief that translation is a straightforward, transparent process of moving words from one language to the other, a process that any bilingual can perform "naturally," may delimit coparticipants' awareness of the supports they can and should provide. In one parent-teacher conference, Junior's teacher spoke more than five hundred words without pause to explain the school district's complex new numerical rating system before turning to Junior to say, "Explain that to your mom." But scaffolding can also include less explicit supports, including efforts to direct the translator's attention in particular ways, prompt them, ask questions, correct errors, and provide contextual information. Adults also expand children's knowledge bases by supplying vocabulary. This is revealed in a few brief interactions involving María, Estela, and Junior.[22]

In the next transcription excerpt, María attempted to skip translating the term "strong performance" as she explained her report card to her mother; instead, she repeated the English phrase (much as Mr. Vick encouraged Estela to do with the word "standards"). However, her mother stopped her to press for meaning. María did her best to explain the term, doing so in a way that revealed her understanding of the school's value system, one that rewarded "having a lot of good ideas":

> MARÍA: Dice que tengo, que practicar más en drama. En music? Dice que tengo strong performance, y también que::= [It says that I have, that I have to practice more in drama. In music? It says that I have strong performance, and also that::=]
>
> SRA. GUTIÉRREZ: =¿Pero qué es strong performance? [=But what is strong performance?]
>
> MARÍA: Es así cuando, um tienes muchas ideas. [It's like, when you have a lot of ideas.]
>
> SRA. GUTIÉRREZ: ¿Y en español y en inglés? ¿Qué más? ¿Qué dice más? [And in Spanish and in English? What else? What else does it say?]

In this case, Sra. Gutiérrez's meaning-focused questions served as scaffolds because they pushed María to draw further on her own cognitive and linguistic resources to explain a tricky concept rather than gloss over it. This reveals the social process of meaning-making that interpreting involves. Parents also provided much more direct supports, for example by supplying Spanish vocabulary words that children did not know. Here, Sra. Balderas provided the word for "cash":

> ESTELA: Do not mail cash. O que uh, Que no tenemos que mandar por um, así dinero suelto. [Do not mail cash. That, uh, That we don't have, that we send, um, loose money.]
>
> SRA. BALDERAS: En efectivo. [In cash.]
>
> ESTELA: Aha, en efectivo. [Aha, in cash.]

In another example, Junior was translating a school dress code letter.[23] The letter is a good example of the convoluted prose that children were often expected to render meaningful to their parents. Arguably, the English original was confusing even for English audiences.

Dear Parents/Guardians:
TWO IMPORTANT MATTERS FOR YOUR CONSIDERATION

We at XXX Middle School are asking you to cooperate with us concerning a rule for student dress. We would like our school to appear more business-like than beach-like. In this light we are requesting students to follow these simple rules of thumb regarding their school attire:

Boys will not wear shirts, basketball jerseys, or similar-to-basketball jerseys, such as sleeveless tee shirts without a sleeved tee shirt beneath.

> Girls will not wear tops that expose midriffs or "spaghetti strap" tops. Blouses and tops will cover the shoulders. Sleeveless tops or blouses are permitted. These would be those which begin to be sleeveless at the junction of the arm and the shoulder . . .

(The letter continues in this tone, warning that "students not in compliance will be asked to comply by using PE clothing or options possessed in their lockers.")

When Junior struggled with how to explain the term "spaghetti straps," his mother stepped in to supply a word that is reasonable within this context, easing the meaning-making process for Junior even if this was not the precise meaning of the letter:

> JUNIOR: Niñas no pueden traer, midriffs o spaghetti straps [English pronunciation], straps [Spanish pronunciation], asina blusas, como, asina, que va, este [gesturing] [Girls can't wear midriffs or spaghetti straps, straps, like blouses, like, like, that go like]
> SRA. FLORES: pegadas [Skin tight].

In discussing this incident, Sra. Flores made clear that she knew she might not get the precise meaning of the material but that Junior facilitated her general understanding of the gist of the letter: "O sea, que no exacto como está allí, pero él me da a entender" [Or rather, not exactly as it is there, but he helps me to understand].

A number of parents noted explicitly that they saw interpreting as a vehicle for the development of their children's native language abilities. Junior's mother felt that "it helps them a lot because later they know two languages well" [les sirve mucho para que después sepan los dos idiomas bien]. Nova's mother described translation work as "an opportunity for him too, so that he can get better . . ." [una oportunidad para él también, para que él sea mejor]; she sometimes asked her younger daughter to translate, just "to animate her" [para animarla]. She further noted that she learned a lot from Nova: "because there are times that I notice how he said something, and I'll say, that's how you say that, and I'll ask him" [porque hay veces que yo me fijo en como él dice algo y yo digo así se dice allí, y le pregunto]. Sra. Gutiérrez named the dynamic and mutually supportive nature of language brokering when she talked about how she and María worked together to interpret text: "Pero a veces ella no, no me puede decir bien, y como yo le digo, estoy yendo a mis clases, hay cosas que sí sé también lo que quieren. O sea, entre las dos nos ayudamos" [But sometimes, she doesn't, she can't explain it well to me, and since, as I tell you, I am going to my classes, there are things that I also know what they mean. In other words, between the two of us we help each other]. I presented other examples of this collaborative work chapter 3.

At the same time, children did not always perceive their parents as support-ive of their work; rather, parents appeared critical of children's performances. Parents often monitored the children's pronunciation and grammar in Spanish and interrupted to correct their errors. They also monitored their behavior—their willingness to offer their English skills and the attitudes they conveyed while doing so. Correction, however, was an action that could be taken by chil-dren as well as adults; Nova's mother noted that Nova often corrected her English, though he usually waited until they were in private to do so.

Social and Cognitive Processes

Even when translations were not explicitly guided, they still involved social interactions, and the mere fact of having to explain something to someone else, for real purposes, arguably enhances the learning potential of translation encounters. The youth I observed showed keen social skills when they noticed people who "needed" translation, as Sammy recounted during his excursion to Toys R' Us and as Briana displayed at the doctor's office. They also revealed their awareness of the audience for whom they were reading when they provided additional contextual information to the recipient, as when María explained to her mother what "specials" subjects were. Further, the situations they worked in often required that they be especially attentive to politeness norms and to choose words in order to present themselves and their families in a particular light. As Luz said, "I became a huge 'May I help you' kind of person."

These social processes were tightly intertwined with cognitive ones, and the maneuvers that some translators engaged in as they made sense of material and explained it to others suggest why these events seem likely to produce powerful learning effects. In the following transcript excerpt, Estela appeared to take a certain kind of pleasure in facing the challenges of translating the book, "The Night Before Christmas," to her sister. She self-corrected contin-uously in her search for the precise words:

> That was the night before Christmas,
> Esa era la navidad, la noche después, [That was Christmas, the night after,]
> De na-, de, [Of Chris-, of,]
> Después de navidad, [After Christmas,]
> Antes de navidad. [Before Christmas.]
> When all through the house
> Twas the night before Christmas
> When all the houses,
> Ok
> Twas the night before Christmas,

Es la [It is the]
La noche de, de, antes de navidad. [The night of, of, before Christmas.]
Digo, después de navidad. [I mean, after Christmas.]
when all through the ni—the house,
cuando todo, eh, adentro de la casa. [when all, uh, inside the house.]
Not a creature was s::tirring.
Ni siquiera un animal estaba, [Not even an animal was,]
Staring,
Em, mirando. [Um, watching.]
Not even a mouse.
Ni siquiera un ratón. [Not even a mouse.]
The stockings were hung by the chimney.
Las, las medias estaban colgadas en la chimenea, [The stockings were
    hung on the chimney,]
por la chimenea. [by the chimney]
with care.
con, con::, con::, [with, with::, with::]
con: con, con: cuidado. [with, with, with: care.]

A number of times Estela guessed about words she didn't recognize by using context cues, illustrations, and both the phonology and morphology of the words themselves, as she attempted to explain their meaning. For example, she told her sister: "No sé que son dimplings, pero algo de su cuerpo." [I don't know what dimplings are, but it's something on his body.] Similarly, she explained that a pipe was "una de estas como que fumas pero de los viejos tiempos" [one of those things that you smoke but in old times]. Occasionally, she mistranslated, as when she said that no creatures were "watching" rather than "stirring" in the above segment, but only rarely did this transform the meaning, as when she indicated that Santa's "broad" face was "aburrida" [bored], or, more humorously, when she read "In spite of myself" as "Escupí a mí misma" [I spit on myself]. Seemingly aware of her uncertainty about exact word choices, she signaled this through upward inflection as well as explicit wonderings aloud. All of this showed Estela to be engaged in a cognitively and linguistically demanding practice. Estela's reading was not scaffolded by anyone, but she was motivated by the social situation—reading to her sister as part of Estela's home responsibilities.

Accumulating Experiences Over the Adolescent Years

ONTOGENETIC DEVELOPMENT

Thus far I have focused on the learning opportunities embedded in specific language brokering encounters, what might be considered the microgenetic level. Ontogenetic development refers to changes over the lifespan, the more gradual kinds of learning and development that accumulate over time. The many kinds of translation encounters that children like Estela engage in over the course of their childhood and adolescence may have cumulative learning effects. Ontogenetic development involves a complex interplay of developmental processes, all of which unfold in relation to experiences, and translation work may both shape and be shaped by these various developmental trajectories. That is, children change in many ways as they grow older: their linguistic, literate, and cognitive capacities expand; and they gain greater social competencies as they acquire procedural knowledge about how things are done in the social and cultural world. Their confidence may grow. As seen in chapter 3, changes in youths' experiences are interrelated with changes at the level of the family, as parents and younger siblings acquire English, and other such dynamic processes are set in play. How families change is shaped by social and cultural values and beliefs, such as about what children of different ages should be allowed or expected to do.

As most children grow older, their spheres of movement expand. They may spend more time outside the home, in after-school activities, working at official jobs, and getting themselves to and from school. Estela, though confined to the home after school owing to her mother's work schedule and the expectation that she care for her younger sisters, still got out more on weekends than she did when she was younger; she went to her babysitting job and walked around the town or drove in a car with her older cousin. Junior began helping his father fixing cars in a shop, and he walked or took the bus around town. María and Nova became quite active in after-school activities; María sometimes rode her bike to attend these. The children chose to spend more time out of the house at these activities or with friends, and they were also sent out more by their families. All four youth spent some time on the Internet, another way of expanding their social worlds.

As youths' spheres of movement expanded, so too did their spheres of language brokering. They encountered more and more situations in which their skills could be of service to others—translating for extended family, neighbors, friends, and strangers in public spaces. Ashley and Marina spoke about translating for strangers at bus stops. Tony's mother asked him to accompany a neighbor (a recent immigrant) to the county hospital for an M.R.I. María's mother noticed an English speaker having trouble communicating with a clerk at a Mexican bakery, and asked María to help him, which she did. Sammy wrote about helping a "lost woman" at his school and other people such as the woman he assisted at Toys R Us. Nova used his bilingual/translation skills on his website development, with clients in both Mexico and the United States.

Not all of the people that youth encountered in these "outside excursions" recognized or validated their skills, however. As presented in previous chapters, these situations may mark children and their families as immigrants and expose them to treatment colored by racism and xenophobia, in both overt and covert ways. The emotional tenor of the particular situations likely influenced what they learned from this work, as well as their motivation to engage in it. As they grew older, they were more able to articulate their awareness of racism and to identify how this shaped their own work as translators. Nova, for example, realized that it was easier for him to just speak to people in English than it was for him either to translate for his mother (an act that marked the family as immigrants) or to request a Spanish speaker because, as he explained, "You know, if you ask them, you know, like 'I want to speak to someone in Spanish,' they're gonna be like 'oh, ok, Spanish-speaking people, alright, blah, blah, blah.'"

GROWING RELATIONALLY

Traditional developmental theories as well as popular beliefs in the United States treat adolescence as a time of breaking away from the family and developing an independent, autonomous self.[24] Children are expected to engage in processes of "individuation" in which they loosen ties with their parents and shed family dependencies. This dominant developmental script also assumes that children take on greater responsibilities as they grow older; autonomy is linked with responsibility and set in contrast to dependence. In other words, taking on more responsibility is associated with becoming more independent. But what about taking on responsibilities to others? What about relational development? "Interdependence"[25]—growing in one's ability to take care of others and to feel responsible *for* them—may be a more culturally resonant developmental script than independence in immigrant communities. Youth translators seem to grow in these relational abilities as they offered their skills in ever wider circles in their social worlds. Indeed, Jessica marked her ability to help as a sign of maturity: "I feel that I'm a big girl now and I could help the family more." Kathy also saw it as a sign of her maturity that she could "take over her mother's place."

The youth I spoke with seemed to value interdependence. Tony put it this way: "I think it's fair. I have to help out. I can't just be here, come home and do nothing and go to sleep. I have to help out." Nova said, "I'm the oldest. I'm supposed to do it. I don't say anything about it. I just do it, you know. If I'm gonna' help my mom with something I'm just gonna' do it because my mom does her job and I just do my job to help." This sense of interdependence was further revealed in the ways in which they positioned themselves in and through language. They took ownership of family activities and presented themselves as integral to family decision-making processes. Josh spoke of how he and his family purchased a truck: "We bought the truck in 2000, and we were only getting two thousand cash back for the trade-in, which is real bad." Tony similarly used the pronoun "we" when he spoke of the work he and his family did in a family restaurant: "We owned a restaurant last year. . . . Last year when we started, we had the whole thing and I worked there every day after school." His ownership in this project extended to its eventual failure, when the building that housed the restaurant was sold: "We're just trying to recover the losses we had from there."

DEVELOPMENT THROUGH TRANSLATION

In addition to the linguistic, cognitive, social, transcultural, and relational skills that may be developed through translation, some evidence suggests that language brokering leads to positive outcomes on more traditional measures of learning and achievement. When Lisa Dorner, Christine Li-Grining, and I categorized the Regan fifth- and sixth-graders into three groups on the basis of their responses to a survey of their language-brokering experiences—those who had extensive experience interpreting for their families, those who had some experience, but to a lesser degree, and those bilingual children who rarely translated for family members—we found that the most active translators had significantly higher scores on tests of reading and math achievement than did the children who had little experience as translators. This was true even when we controlled for test scores in first and second grade. That is, these students did not start out as stronger students, but they surpassed their peers in later years, which suggests that translation experiences could have propelled the higher achievement.[26] We have speculated on why this might be so. Translation experiences may build vocabulary and familiarity with a range of written genres, thereby advancing the literacy skills that are demanded on tests. Perhaps they enhance children's abilities to handle problems of all sorts because of the many "tests" that they experience in daily life. Like bilingual skills more generally,[27] language brokering may boost children's metalinguistic capacities, literally making them smarter, as Guadalupe Valdés suggests when she argues that translators should be viewed as gifted.[28] The fact that standardized test scores increased is noteworthy because of the high stakes nature of such scores in today's test-driven school era; however, if translation skills enhance test scores it seems at least as likely that they advance everyday linguistic and cognitive skills as well, perhaps in more far-reaching ways.

I was particularly intrigued by the metalinguistic competencies that some youth displayed, as they talked about the decisions they made in language-brokering events. Sammy spoke extensively about how he struggled to choose the right words to convey nuances of meaning when he mediated between speakers from different world views, as well as his reading of social cues. He wrote one journal entry about translating between a parent and an ROTC instructor teacher (MC) at his school:

> . . . I overheard MC trying to mumble out an answer (to a parent's question) in the little Spanish that he knew. So I went over and told him that I would help. I(t) was pretty funny because every time I told her about discipline or pain she would get a dark smile out. The only thing that kept me nervous was trying to act professional because MC was there, without seeming too serious to the mother and her son.

In a particularly powerful display of metacultural awareness, Sammy also recounted a time when he translated on a golf course between a "rich lady" and some fieldworkers:

> Today I was caddying for Ms. Johnson. She's pretty nice but a little cocky and uptight. Well anyway it was pretty hot and we were walking to the tenth hole. It's a pretty large walk so one of the field workers offered to give us a ride. We hopped on and began talking. I translated back and forth. I felt weird though because I felt that Ms. Johnson didn't really want to talk to him. It made me think that the guy was thinking of me as a stuck-up rich kid. Of course I'm not. It was like Ms. Johnson's attitude was being shown through my translating.

Here, Sammy showed his understanding that the translator is an active participant, not a passive conduit of words between parties and that translation involves a presentation of self as well as the transmission of information between speakers. This recognition parallels what the linguist Paul Ricoeur noted in an essay on written translation:[29] "The work of translation might thus be said to carry a double duty: to expropriate oneself as one appropriates the other. We are called to make our language put on the stranger's clothes at the same time as we invite the stranger to step into the fabric of our own speech." Sammy further displayed his metalinguistic capacities when he explained the word choices he made as he negotiated meaning between these two speakers. He said that he used the slang word "chido" with the fieldworkers, and the English word "nice" with the lady—words that are equivalent, but distinctly nuanced. Each was appropriate for the audience, but each served to represent himself in different ways.

Sammy also felt that translating helped him with overall language skills: "The kids that translate, I think they are better off because it really helps them to learn other languages. And it gives them good experience." This viewpoint was echoed by parents and other youth as well.

Conflict, Tensions, and Stressors

But of course, translation work *can* put children into situations of high anxiety and may cause stress that can adversely affect child development, as some researchers have suggested.[30] How stressful translation work is likely depends on the availability of supports, the attitudes that participants have toward child translators and their families, and the weightiness of the transactions. Do children feel that their translations will affect either their families' abilities to access resources or secure opportunities or the ways they are seen and treated by others? Do they feel uniquely responsible for these outcomes, or do they share the responsibility with others? Do they sense that they are valued and appreciated by those for whom they speak?

On several occasions when we visited with Estela and her mother, Estela ended up in tears—Estela presumably frustrated that her mother did not understand her. Her mother in turn seemed very worried about Estela's activities and peer networks. Lacking facility in the English language and having to depend on her daughter to understand this "outside" world that lurked with dangers of teen pregnancies and gangs may have triggered greater tension and worry than would otherwise be the case. Though intergenerational tensions might exist even without a language barrier, the language barrier may have exacerbated Sra. Balderas's concerns and complicated Estela's position as interpreter of her own social worlds.

At the same time, as I have argued throughout this book, parent-child "role reversal" did not necessarily cause tension in translation encounters. What constitutes role reversal and what causes tension in both translation work and in parent-child interactions bear reconsideration. Perhaps conflict emerges most as children experience the tensions of living between two cultural worlds—those of their homes and their new expanding public lives—where there are different expectations and beliefs regarding responsibility, independence, and interdependence. This is then complicated by the fact that, as adolescents, these children are in between two developmental worlds—childhood and adulthood, with expectations of responsibility and independence changing over time.[31]

The different worlds that immigrant children straddle are also not equal in terms of privilege and power, and the tensions that Estela's family experienced were at least in part created or aggravated by the position they were in as members of the working class who were struggling to survive alongside middle- and upper-income families in Engleville. "Bicultural" youth are the objects of racism and xenophobia and are often treated as second-class citizens. Researchers miss an important aspect of the immigrant experience in focusing on the presumed inversion of appropriate parent-child relations in language-brokering encounters while ignoring the huge other stressors that immigrants live with everyday.

Chapter 7   Translating Childhoods

THERE ARE MANY ways to understand children's work as translators and inter-preters for their families. We can focus on the burdens it sometimes places on youth and on how stress affects children's growth and development. Turning this perspective around, we can highlight the cognitive, social, emotional, and linguistic benefits these experiences may offer to youth. We can either reject children's involvement as a form of youth exploitation or applaud youths' con-tributions to homes, schools, communities and society. We can talk about character formation, skills acquisition, and the pathways that are opened or closed through engagement in these activities, or we can view the practice as just a "normal" part of everyday life.

But understanding language brokering in all its complexity involves see-ing it as all of these things. Sociologist Patricia Hill Collins argues that Western scientific thought emphasizes dichotomies—orienting us to see things as either good *or* bad, about the present *or* the future, focused on indi-viduals *or* social processes.[1] Non-Western epistemologies, such as the black feminist epistemology that Hill Collins advocates, better accommodate seeing that things like translation work as many things all at the same time.

Translation Shapes Children's Experiences of Childhood and Their Pathways to the Future

Throughout this book, I have probed language brokering as an everyday set of activities, exploring how children participate in the functioning of their households, schools and communities, and in helping and caring for people.

In doing these things, children and families didn't usually have an eye to the future; their attention was on accomplishing the tasks of daily life. But everyday practices certainly influence pathways of development, often in more profound ways than most people realize. This is true in immigrant households just as it is in middle-class homes. Anthropologists, sociolinguists, and sociocultural researchers have studied the discourse norms that children pick up through family dinner conversations in middle-class families, the literate skills that children acquire when parents read them bedtime stories, and cognitive and social outcomes of engagement in other everyday practices.[2] These fields of study could benefit from examining a much wider range of practices than has been studied to date, contemplating everyday practices in homes that are not middle class, English-speaking, and "American," and outcomes that include cognitive development but also social processes, intergenerational relations, and the values and beliefs that accompany them. This could include studying the development of empathy, compassion, kindness, and transcultural or intercultural skills. There may be diverse pathways to similar outcomes and valuable outcomes that are not typically identified when using a white, middle-class, achievement-focused lens.

Language brokering is ubiquitous in immigrant households and communities. As a language and literacy practice, it is different from typical middle-class home activities like bedtime storybook reading, but it may be no less significant for children's language and literacy development. Arguably, it may be more so, because brokering activities expose children to a much wider array of genres, domains, forms and ways of using language than do practices like reading stories or participating in dinnertime conversations. Children's work as translators matters for the functioning of households; it matters for their own developmental pathways as well.

Language Brokering Has Both Positive and Negative Implications for Youth Learning and Development

But social practices do not have simple, clear-cut, uniquely positive *or* negative implications for learning and development. Children whose parents read them regular bedtime stories may learn a great deal about narrative structures, storybook genres, vocabulary, and certain kinds of subject matter. They may simultaneously learn to be more passive consumers of literacy than do children who have no parent available to read to them, but who are, instead, expected to read to their siblings, as in the case of Estela and Junior. My own parents rarely read to their eight children, undoubtedly because they were too busy working and running the household, but my siblings and I were quite motivated to read on our own. As an adult, I read faithfully each night to my own daughter, and watched her become a reluctant independent reader, at least initially; I always wondered if this was because she learned to see reading as a social activity. Any practice can have various effects, and it is much easier to see outcomes that accord with normative ideas about such practices than it is to see other results. It is also easier to see things in retrospect than it is to imagine them into the future.

To say that an activity has either positive or negative implications is to assert a value judgment about what counts as positive or negative. Value judgments are particularly difficult to avoid when we talk about youth development, because all parents and cultural groups have opinions about what is good and bad for children. All evaluations are value-laden, and different people may view the same practices in very different ways, rendering distinct judgments about what children of particular ages and genders should be allowed or expected to do. At the same time, it's likely both impossible and irresponsible not to make any evaluation at all, and so I will stake a few claims about what counts as "good" or "bad" from my vantage point—a position that aims to take seriously the views of immigrant families and youth translators themselves.

Certain translation events and ways of engaging in them clearly did seem to cause stress and anxiety for some youth. This was likely true even if youth did not *say* this directly. Stress was increased when children felt judged by adults, when they sensed that they and their families are being critiqued for who they were or were assumed to be, and when they felt that their words could cause harm to family members. Excessive stress and anxiety is not good for children—or for anyone—especially without adequate supports to buffer these feelings. (When people feel supported by others, some of the most damaging aspects of burdensome situations may be mitigated.)

In other situations, relationships, and forms of translation activities, however, children felt very good: smart, capable, and grown up, as well as just happy to help others. Too often children (and others) are not given opportunities to feel needed, useful and appreciated. Indeed, the world might be a better place if all people had opportunities to be needed and valued by others. Given that the children of immigrants are going to translate for their families whether or not we condone it, we would do well to provide scaffolds for their work, and to value and validate their skills.

Knowing that the practice can be both stressful and exhilarating can guide our ways of responding to it. Sociologist Mihaly Csikszentmihalyi[3] writes about the sense of creative intellectual "flow" that people can achieve when they engage in tasks that are demanding but not overwhelming, and when the motivation to do them is high. Some translation situations fit a model of "flow," when adequate supports are in place, and youth are acknowledged and compli-mented for their efforts. Adults who are involved in translation encounters can try to reduce the most stressful dimensions of the experience by providing back-ground information to contextualize the information that will be translated; chunking the information in manageable ways; encouraging translators to ask for help and to request clarifying information; explaining the information in multiple ways; and valuing, honoring, and respecting the work that children do so that they can feel good about their hard work.

Translation Work Is Both Cognitive and Social

A linguist, I. A. Richards,[4] once wrote "translation is probably the most com-plex event in the evolution of the cosmos." He was speaking about the chal-lenges of finding equivalences of words and ideas across languages and cultures. When this is compounded with the social skills that are demanded of youth in everyday, informal translating, especially in cross-cultural encounters, the com-plexity of this practice is even greater. Translation demands cognitive and lin-guistic skills; it also involves social sensibilities, awareness of others, the take-up of appropriate roles and voices, and the management of others' emo-tions as well as the translator's own. The intertwining of the social and cogni-tive demands of the practice—and the emotional work that it involves—makes everyday language brokering even more complex than other translation acts.

Translating Has Effects for Individuals and Groups

In considering developmental implications, I have emphasized the effects that translating may have on individuals' processes of learning and development. But it has implications for groups as well. Children's efforts can open up pathways of development for others; the developmental possibilities of childhood spaces are altered, for example, when youth assist their siblings with homework, or foster interactions with computers and books. Children also advanced their parents' language skills as well as their understanding of how things are done in the United States. They facilitated their parents' abilities to access information and resources that in turn opened up further possibilities for family members.

Translation Work Involves Both Service and Surveillance

Cecilia Wadensjö[5] notes that translators in institutional settings always oper-ate in a paradoxical position of both service and surveillance. They open up access to institutional resources, even as they defend institutional norms. This is especially clear in interpretations during police interrogations and court proceedings, but it was evident as well when youth translated for school authorities in parent-teacher conferences, for representatives of social service agencies, and even in stores. Youth translators became unwitting gatekeepers, in that they were expected to relay institutional demands to their families, and to negotiate the assumptions about their own families that were embedded in the words they transmitted. At the same time, they helped their families to access the services these institutions provided. This placed them in contradictory spaces, as indeed, all mediational space likely are.[6]

There were added layers of surveillance in translation situations for immigrant youth. Because these were children speaking to and for adults, about topics that were considered the domain of adults, child language brokers were open to evaluation in ways that adult interpreters might never be judged. Youth were critiqued for their language skills, abilities to manage these social situations, and willingness to do the work, among other things. They were evaluated for how appropriately they assumed positions as children in relation to different adults in these encounters. Again, as seen in Chapter Five, adults brought divergent criteria to these evaluations as well, with children caught in the middle.

Immigrant youth were caught in an especially complex web in that their work took place within politically charged landscapes; their work involved the crossing of what Valerie Walkerdine[7] refers to as "anxious borders." Walkerdine, speaking more generally about working class people who move into the middle class, argues that in crossing social borders, people who grew up in working class families are forced to "inhabit a surveillant position in relation to their Othered family, the object of vilification experienced by pathologized family members as shame."[8] This involves considerable psychological pain. The children of immigrants may be pushed into an even more extreme position of surveillance, and greater psychological pain, when they are asked to be the direct bearers of messages that are laced with racist and xenophobic assumptions about their families. And the very act of relaying these messages further opens themselves and their families up to surveillance and critique by society, because interpreting serves to mark families' "alien" status.

Translation Work Can Both Sustain and Change Institutions

That language brokering can contribute to the functioning of diverse institutions should be obvious from the descriptions of the practice that I have sketched throughout this book. Children's labor helps to accomplish the daily work that institutions like families and schools do. If children did not do this work, someone else might do it. On the other hand, the work might not get done, at least not as effectively; or indeed, someone else would have to do it. Children's labor may change institutions by enhancing their functioning, either by freeing others for other tasks or by providing services that otherwise would not be available.

To treat this work as deviant is to suggest deviance in the roles that children have played throughout history and in many places around the world today. Indeed, even in middle-class homes, children contribute more to households than is generally acknowledged, because their contributions are obscured by the tendency to see children's activities as trivial.[9] It has only been in the twentieth century, in the Western world, that children have been seen as relatively helpless dependents in need of adult labor and care, domesticated and schooled, living within protected spaces, and engaged in activities defined as play or learning (not work).[10]

To see family interpreting as "role reversal" similarly reinforces a sense of deviance. Is some kind of intergenerational power shifting necessarily so dangerous? Gendered relationships have changed over time, and some people may find this troubling, but those who are concerned with equity celebrate a re-balancing of power. Is it always a bad thing for children to gain power vis-à-vis adults? What if families, schools, and communities were structured around reciprocity of power, and interdependent cultural scripts, with adults and children contributing, perhaps differently, but in balanced ways, according to their needs and capacities, to the common good?

Translators Are Both Powerful and Constrained

Youth like Junior, Estela, María, and Nova were active participants in their households and in immigrant settlement processes. They did not simply animate their parents' words; they did not merely operate, like apprentices, on the edges of adult activities; and they were not passive objects of adults' socialization efforts. They did not act only as conduits of information, but also as socializing agents who provided access to opportunities in their communities. Their expertise really mattered for families' health, survival, and social advancement. Their efforts had both immediate and long-term effects. In all of these ways, they were powerful social actors.

At the same time, the fact that these children were key players in their households should not be taken to mean that they had inordinate power either within their families or in the public sphere, or even that there has been any significant rebalancing of power towards the reciprocity of relations that I suggested above. Many translation activities took place within the framework of everyday activities, and were experienced by children as "just normal." Youth participated in family decisions but did not generally make these decisions themselves. The power to draw children into translation activities also generally remained in adults' hands, as evidenced by the many journal entries in which children wrote that they "had to" translate, as well as by the resistance they sometimes displayed. Indeed, parents talked about using translations as an important arena in which to ensure and monitor their children's bilingual and bicultural development. They sometimes used these activities to have more control over their children than they might otherwise have had.

The power that children had to help their families was also constrained by the fact that these actors are children operating in situations that were usually the domain of adults. Further, they were the children of immigrants, generally distanced from native-born, representatives of U.S. institutions by language, culture and social class. These things affected how they and their families were viewed and treated, as well as how entitled they felt to ask questions, make demands, or speak on behalf of their families. It's important to see children's actions within the power relations of their everyday lives, and in relation to what they saw as destabilizing or "just normal."

Translation Work Is Both Under-Recognized and Exploited

By calling children's translation activities work, I am suggesting that it has measurable economic value. And indeed, through their labor children contribute part of the cost of supporting, maintaining, or what sociologists refer to as reproducing[11] the working class. Child language brokers help make it possible for their parents to live, eat, shop and otherwise sustain themselves as workers, citizens and consumers in their host country. This is part of the labor cost equation that should be contemplated in this era of global economic restructuring, in which "First World" economies rely on immigrant labor. The entire society benefits from the invisible work that the children of immigrants do. This adds a new perspective to national policy debates about the costs and contributions of immigrants to U.S. society. Various costs and benefits have been measured, but the general assumption is that adults make contributions, while children are only a drain: they "take" from the educational and health systems without giving anything back. This is an assumption that bears reconsideration. The work immigrant children do is only as invisible as we allow it to be.

Translating Immigrant Childhoods

Immigrant childhoods are good cases to think with about transformations in the meanings of childhood at this point in the twenty-first century, as well as about the cultural and contextual construction of generational relations. Family interpreting both shapes and is shaped by beliefs about children and childhoods. Children serve as language brokers in part because their families believe that children should use their linguistic and cultural skills to benefit others. Like working class immigrants at the turn of the century, many immigrants today do not treat childhood as a protected space in the way that middle-class Americans tend to do, and families do not see children as "endangered" by language brokering. These assumptions influence how youth see their work, and what they learn from it.

But even as beliefs shape the practice, practices shape beliefs. The practices of the social world influence what people believe to be normal or appropriate, correct or good. Seeing different possibilities may shake those beliefs and open up other possibilities. Immigrant families' ideas about childhood may change through their experiences in this country; dominant culture notions may change as well, as indeed beliefs and practices change in all communities over time. In this time of rapid social change, with increased flows of people traversing national boundaries around the world, there are many visible variations in the structuring and meanings of childhoods. Images evoking different kinds of childhoods may challenge middle-class, Western conceptions of what it means to be a child. In less dramatic ways, children's work as translators—when we stop to notice it—challenges the meanings of childhood in the modern Western world and raises new questions about what the role of children in society should be.

Appendix A: Learning from Children

The young people represented in this book were some of the best teachers I have ever had. I learned more from watching and listening to them, and to the dozens of other young people that I talked with in the course of my investigations into immigrant childhoods, than in any course of study. In this appendix I detail *how* I learned from them and reflect on my own processes of translating their childhood experiences. I first consider parallels between translation work and ethnographic representations and then share specific strategies and methods that I used in this program of mixed-method, multilayered, longitudinal research. This included methods designed to tap into children's thoughts, perceptions and feelings, as is called for by the critical social science of childhoods.[1]

The first challenge that translators face is not that of speaking, writing or presenting words and ideas to others. It is that of listening, hearing, and understanding what they are asked to do or convey. Cecilia Wadensjö emphasizes that interpreters have to be good listeners, as they attend to the expectations of different interlocutors in exchanges that would normally be dyadic.[2] But in most research on translation, as in most popular thinking, attention goes to what is produced, rather than what is received or understood. The often-overlooked receptive aspect of translation offers a starting point for my exploration of ethnographic work as an activity of translation and interpretation because the greatest challenge an ethnographer faces is to hear and really understand the viewpoints of others.

As ethnographers have long noted, hearing and understanding is immensely complicated when working across lines of difference that matter for social interactions, such as those based on age, gender, race/ethnicity, institutional positions and social class. Adults, for example, may *listen* to kids without really hearing them.[3] There are at least two distinct, rarely disentangled, sets of problems with outsider-insider relations in fieldwork. First, how do people view researchers, based on visible and audible identity markers such as phenotype, dress, speech and mannerisms? Who researchers are seen to be delimits what people say to us and how they do so. There are ways to minimize social distances, but social addresses can never be escaped and must be taken into account.

Second, how do lived experiences shape understandings and interpretations? This, the more slippery of the two concerns, is difficult if not impossible to redress. Lived experiences profoundly shape how we perceive things, often in ways that we do not recognize or fully understand ourselves. Just as there are steps to take to emphasize commonalities and deemphasize differences with participants, there are ways to expand our viewpoints on the world, but we can never completely step outside of them.

Being Seen by Others

The first problem centers on how surface, visible, marked aspects of my identity were likely to have been received by children, their family members, teachers, and others with whom I worked. This includes physical markings of socially salient categories like gender, race/ethnicity, and age, as well as more subtle indicators of social positioning, which are displayed through dress, mannerisms, shoes, hairstyle, makeup, dialect, and accent. It is not likely that the families I worked with would read any of these markings in quite the same way as I would read them, and so my challenge was to take on the perspectives of these different people in looking at myself. Children like Sammy display this sort of perspective-taking when they make decisions about what words to use in their translations for different audiences, to represent the words of the speaker, but also to display themselves in particular ways.

To understand how the people I worked with may have viewed me and how that may have shaped what they said to me, I thought about the histories of experiences they were likely to have had with people who look and act something like me. This in itself was a multilayered endeavor because there was variation in such experiences within and across families as well as within and across communities. Immigrant children generally had different kinds of relationships with "Americans" than do immigrant adults. Younger and older girls and boys were likely to have had very different kinds of intercultural experiences. Older children were more likely to have encountered both direct and indirect forms of racism in their interactions with white people, both because their teenage bodies were more readily viewed in racialized ways than those of younger children and because their spheres of independent movement were larger. Families in the Madison community probably had fewer and different kinds of intercultural contact than did families in Engleville, and families in the Regan community were operating in a context in which many whites were immigrants from Poland. Thus, the meanings of my whiteness, as it intersected with other aspects of my identity, likely varied across contexts.

In my earliest investigations into immigrant childhoods, in the Madison community, I was a white, adult woman who was undoubtedly seen by the children and families as a teacher because most white, adult women who moved about here were teachers. Indeed, children and parents alike often addressed me as "Maestra," even when I was not in school. I imagine that most children and parents interacted with me more or less as they would with a teacher, at least initially, and that this meant that they presented their words and ideas to me in particular ways and gave me access to some aspects of their thoughts and experiences, but not others.

At the same time identities are always mediated by social contexts. The geographical and sociopolitical settings of my work, activities, and relationships I engaged in and mediational tools I deployed influenced how I was seen, and these could serve either to widen or narrow the social distance between me and families. The context shaped the meanings that my identity took on in each landscape, as I argued above, as did my actions in the field. Different activities, such as playing basketball with children in after-school programs, talking with their teachers, and speaking in Spanish or English either marked or muted different aspects of my gendered, generational and ethnic/linguistic identity. Knowing this, I tried to engage in many different activities and to interact with people in different contexts, situations and relationships over a long period of time.

Experiential Influences

Ethnographers often address the problem of how our experiences shape our understandings by adopting an apologetic, confessional, and defensive discourse about our racial/ethnic, gendered, and social class backgrounds. Indeed, it is difficult to avoid a confessional tone as we invite readers to scrutinize our experiences and consider how they may have shaped our interpretations of social processes. And certainly our social addresses, especially along lines of race/ethnicity, gender, age, and social class, are likely to have positioned us to see the world in ways that are at great variance with the vantage points of people who are differently located along these important social axes. But for this second aspect of the ethnographic challenge a more profound issue is not who we appear to be, or who we are in terms of categorical labels, but how we have come to see the world through our engagement in activities, experiences, and relationships. These experiences become foils for examining social phenomena in addition to and in dialogue with other foils such as social science and everyday theories, beliefs, and values. Our life experiences exert their influence in part because they work on us at a deep and often unconscious level. They shape how we understand what we see and hear, as well as what we choose to look at and listen to, and what we notice or dismiss.

My research interests have been fundamentally shaped by my life experiences, not just by who I am at the juxtaposition of various categorical labels (for example, white, female, middle class), but by who I am in relation to the contexts I have engaged in, the life experiences I have gathered, the relationships through which I have cultivated those experiences, and the things that I have struggled with or tried to reconcile in my own life. The issues I explore reverberate with core concerns of my life, and I have revealed these in various ways throughout this book so the reader can contemplate potential dynamic influences on my translations of children's lives. I name here a few aspects of my experiences about which I have thought a great deal, and these have likely influenced my interest in the issues that I now study. I attempt to reach not just to surface features of these experiences, but to a deeper, even psychodynamic level—to contemplate the forces that motivated my research interests and may have influenced it in ways that I do not fully understand. I take inspiration from Valerie Walkerdine,[4] who turns the psychoanalytic frame that she uses to explore the construction of femininity on herself by sharing elements of her working-class girlhood and her own relationship with her father. Walkerdine calls for researchers to be attuned to one's own emotions, projections, and fantasies. Allison James and Barrie Thorne argue that researchers of childhoods in particular must grapple with memories and our relationships with our own childhood experiences in order to see how these inform our current readings.[5] Engaging in psychoanalysis during the course of writing this book helped me raise to conscious awareness some of the subconscious forces that influenced my thinking about children and childhoods.

TRANSLOCATIONS

My own movements far from the geographical, psychological, and cultural locations of my childhood reverberate with my interest in the movement of families who have traveled much greater geopolitical, psychological, and cultural distances. I have experienced some of the sense of loss that people feel when they move far from home, unable to return, at least as the persons that they were when they left. The conditions of my own translocations were quite different from, and far less constrained, than those of most of the families with whom I worked. Many immigrants can never really return home because their homes no longer exist or because they could be killed, jailed, or unable to leave again. Others can only return, even to visit, at great sacrifice, because of the costs involved.

Despite profound differences in the ease of border-crossing, my translocations offered at least some basis of experience for resonating with the pain I heard in the voices of people talking about family they left behind and for empathizing with their efforts to create community in their new locale. In my own way, I attempted to "go back home" at least twice: first, I moved from urban Los Angeles to Engleville, a suburban community that is closer (both geographically and culturally) to the New England I knew growing up; then, when I left Engleville to return to Los Angeles, the place that in the end has felt more like home than anywhere else, due to the history of experiences that I have cultivated there. Through both moves I learned many things, including that one can never really go back to where one came from because spatial contexts are also temporal ones, and people are constituent parts of their contexts, such that when we change, we change the contexts of which we are part.

TRANSCULTURATIONS

I am not an immigrant or a child of immigrants, and I grew up quite squarely in mainstream, English-speaking, middle/working class culture. But during the last twenty years my life has revolved centrally around transculturations. My relationships with immigrants and the children of immigrants have included those of researcher, teacher, activist, friend, wife, aunt, sister-in-law, daughter-in-law, and mother. To quote Rubén Rumbaut, a sociologist who coined the term for the 1.5 generation: "I not only study the children of immigrants, I have produced them."[6] (My children's father migrated to the United States from Guatemala at the age of sixteen.) These relationships gave me glimpses into immigrant experiences even as they also motivated my personal interest in the topics I research. Exploring the issues of the 1.5 generation helped me to understand the struggles that my own children face in their experiences moving between different cultures, social classes, languages and social worlds. It has helped me to probe my own experiences of what Juan Guerra has called "transcultural repositioning"[7]—the take-up and redefinition of one's own position and identity in and through movement across cultural spaces.

In studying immigrant childhoods I have also pondered my own experiences with childhood, as both a child and a mother. My own parents believed, more or less, that children should "do as they are told" and "be seen and not heard," attitudes that seem closer to those held by some immigrant families than the child-centered indulgences that reign among parents from the Baby

Boom generation in white, middle-class America.[8] Parenting has for me been a tremendous source of pride and satisfaction, but also anguish, as I struggled to determine my own beliefs and practices and to reconcile them with others I saw modeled around me and those I read or heard about in different forms. I have witnessed a diversity of parenting approaches, both close up and at a distance, and have seen both limitations and benefits to most established practices.

TEACHING, RESEARCH, AND ACTIVISM

My movement from teacher and activist to "researcher" did not feel easy, and I struggle to this day with the relationship between scholarship and efforts to create a more just social world. From 1983 to 1993 I solidified my identity as a teacher and activist as I spent countless hours working at my school and with local teachers' groups as well as with solidarity groups that were working to raise awareness about human rights violations in Central America, the role of the U.S. government in supporting repressive regimes, and the conditions of economic and political refugees from Central America to the United States. These experiences provided a conceptual grounding for my work as a researcher that goes far beyond "informing" it, as I have sometimes claimed. Rather, they drive it, infuse it with passion and vigor, and give me reasons for doing what I now do. The teacher and activist subject positions that I bring to my work affect the quality of the research I produce, not necessarily in the direction that some might assume. That is, rather than a negative distortion induced by subjectivity, these experiences provided an important base of what Angela Valenzuela calls "authentic caring"[9]—an emotional connection that arguably enhanced my ability to see and understand the life worlds of the families I studied. Without such authentic caring it would have been easy to focus on the problems that abound in any poor community (problems that are more open for scrutiny than the kinds of problems that abound in privileged communities) and not to see resources, resilience, power, and strength.

At the same time, my work as an activist induced in me much angst. In what ways could I inadvertently become complicit in power structures that oppress poor, working-class, immigrant families? How will readers interpret and recontextualize my words in this book? I want my writing to be a form of activism, even as I want it to have a place in the world of scholarship, but I recognize a tension between these goals. One way I have reconciled this tension is to use what I have learned about translation to help teachers leverage children's bilingual skills and parents to support their children's work. In ongoing work, I am working with teachers to design and implement curriculum that builds on translation skills and connects them to academic literacies.[10] We are using what we've learned to improve education for immigrant youth.

THE CHILD WITHIN

Undoubtedly, my interest in hearing children's voices was shaped by my own childhood experiences, especially as a middle child in a family of eight children. The critical social science of childhoods—a theoretical perspective that underscores the value of listening to children—had particular resonance for me in part, I think, because I often didn't feel listened to, heard, or understood as a child. I suspect, too, that my position as the middle daughter in a family of eight children had more than a bit to do with the fascination that I now hold for people who stand "in the middle" and who mediate between different perspectives and worldviews.[11] Words I wrote in a journal when I was seventeen, after mediating relations between my mother and a then-rebellious brother, reverberate in my research: "I don't mind being in the middle; I'm glad I can see both sides, but sometimes it's rough."

Methods for Learning from Children

Given the limitations of our own vantage points, what can we do to maximize our capacities to hear and understand the perspectives of others? What can adults do to listen to children, hear them, and learn from them? I will suggest a few approaches here, as I detail some methods I used to gather data. I built the eclectic tool kit of methods from my experiences as a teacher, activist, and parent as well as from my training as a researcher.

SECURE MULTIPLE VANTAGE POINTS

To remedy the most egregious aspects of the epistemological problems I have described I gathered a research team that included people from different social class and racial/ethnic backgrounds, as well as a range of life experiences. In Los Angeles I conducted the bulk of the observations myself, as a postdoctoral researcher on the California Childhoods project, but three research assistants (Anna Chee, Lucila Ek and Arcelia Hérnandez) assisted with observations and interviews, and we carried on an extensive dialogue based on our shared experiences as teachers in this community as well. When I moved to Chicago, grant support allowed me to more fully do "team ethnography" in the Regan community, with at least two researchers working with each child whom we observed at home and at school. This ensured at least two viewpoints on each child's experiences even as it made it possible to observe a wider range of experiences than I could alone. I participated in these observations, taking prime responsibility for logging observations of the children most featured in this book, but two research assistants (María Meza and Lisa Dorner) also contributed with many observations that again facilitated multiple perspectives on each child. Lisa stayed in touch with the families after I moved to Los Angeles, as she developed her own dissertation project with them, and I visited and interviewed the children on several return visits throughout a period of five years. Lisa and María visited the youth to talk with them about the final manuscript and secure their approval for the ways they are represented in this book, as detailed below.[12]

Given my interest in children's work as translators/interpreters, it was critical to have team members with different sets of language capacities, including monolingual, quite fully bilingual and bicultural, and others whose bilingual capacities lay somewhere in between these two extremes. Monolingual fieldworkers were better able to understand the perspectives of teachers and parents who relied on children for translation, and when they were observing it was more natural for children to step into roles as translators because when bilingual adults were available, children would not as naturally take up this work, deferring instead to adults. All the children we studied were comfortable in English; most preferred English over Spanish for talk with peers, but it was important for us to be able to communicate with parents as well, and most parents preferred to speak in Spanish. To analyze the children's translations—what was said, and how—bilingual skills were critical.

Uniting people from different subject positions in a common research endeavor addresses the two core issues I have laid out here. We capitalized on the fact that different young people, parents, and teachers were likely to open themselves up in different ways to differently aged, gendered, and racialized researchers with distinct language skills and deployed ourselves strategically in the data-gathering process to gain access to the perspectives of parents, children, and teachers. Older members of the research team conducted most of the teacher and parent interviews, and the younger members of the team did more of the "hanging out" time with the children.

Second, we took advantage of the insights that relative "insiders" and "outsiders" (on various dimensions, especially those of ethnicity and language) bring to a phenomenon by deliberately overlapping in fieldwork; sometimes we went in pairs to visit families or observe students in their classrooms. On other occasions we observed the same kids on different days and compared our observations. Partners recorded separate impressions before sharing them.

Of course, deploying the team in these ways was not enough; our conversations were critical. These dialogues presented us with some of the same challenges of translating across worldviews that child translators face: working to understand each other and to challenge each other gently when we disagreed in our interpretations. This process was not simple, for many reasons, including the fact that members of the research team had different degrees of investment in and long-term commitment to the project. I was the only person involved at all stages of the work; all others participated in it as a training experience, but moved on to other things and followed their own trajectories of professional development. And, of course, we could never escape all power relations; I was the professor, researcher, Principal Investigator, and the only team member who was involved in all stages, aspects, and sites of the research. The unequal distribution of ownership over this project shows up in the fact that I am the author of this book. (Students shared authorship in many other publications, but here I speak with a solo voice, albeit one that is refracted through with the voices of the many people who have participated in this work over the last ten years.) For my own part, I experienced considerable tension between the different identities I assumed— as teacher, advisor, mentor, researcher, friend, and "boss."

UTILIZE MULTIPLE METHODS

Just as it is valuable to have multiple vantage points on a researcher project, there is value to using multiple methods when studying things as complex as translation and the changing nature of childhoods. In social science research there have been increasing calls for "mixed methods" research—methods that allow one to understand processes as well as outcomes and to study phenomena close up as well as to connect them to larger social processes. I was interested in approaches that allowed me to focus in at different levels of inquiry (individual, family/household, classroom, and community), and to examine kids' experiences as they unfolded over time.

The specific methods that I used are perhaps less important than what drove them: a continual pursuit of children's own understandings of their lives and experiences. Such pursuit involves both listening and observing, while trying to suspend one's own judgments in order to really listen and see. Ethnographers, like translators, of course listen while they observe and observe while they listen, but for the sake of clarity I separate for discussion here those methods focused on soliciting children's ideas through their talk (processes that centrally involve listening) and those focused on observing kids' actions and interactions and examining their expressed viewpoints in drawings and other forms.

LISTENING. As a teacher and a parent, I learned early on that one can't ask children straight questions and expect to get straight answers, given relationships of power between children and adults. How questions are phrased, and what is perceived to be behind them, really matter for what children say. Children know how to read what adults are looking for and give answers adults expect. They may open up most when they are not responding to direct questions. When I ask my own children, "How was your day?" or "What did you do in school?" I usually get a mere mumble in reply. But if I'm ready to listen when they initiate a conversation—often in the context of doing things together—I may learn a great deal about their experiences and feelings. My challenge as a researcher was to create spaces in which we could hear things that might not be said if we directly probed kids with questions. We did this by "hanging out" with kids on their own time and observing them in a variety of contexts, situations, activities, and relationships. We also established our own space—what we came to call "Junior Ethnographer" meetings—for kids to talk together and with us about their experiences as translators.

To explore a wider range of kids' experiences, in systematic ways, I relied on interviewing. Through prearranged, semistructured encounters, and with María Meza's assistance as an undergraduate research aide, I was able to talk with about seventy-five young people in Los Angeles and Chicago. The interviews probed the range and nature of children's translation experiences, their feelings about the encounters, and how they managed the tasks. Through these interviews I was able to learn from many more children than would be possible to observe in any depth. The interviews were also useful for learning about kids' metalinguistic awareness of their translation practices and their metacultural understandings of transcultural encounters. I have quoted from these interviews throughout this book.

In the interviews, I tried different formats to see what facilitated the freest expression. Group interviews were generally more productive than individual ones because the higher ratio of young people to adults helped to adjust the imbalance of power; and when kids talked with each other they allowed me some of the best insights into their perspectives. On one occasion, when four girls in a group interview seemed reluctant to talk, I left the tape recorder running (mentioning this to the girls, so that they were informed) and left the room. I suggested that they talk among themselves until I got back. They did so, commenting on how nervous they felt about the interview, which led to talk about how nervous they sometimes felt when translating.

In these group interviews, another approach I took involved asking kids to reenact translation situations that they had talked about or written about in journals. These enactments don't necessarily reveal what children actually do, or would do, in authentic translation situations. Nevertheless, they were useful for thinking about translation practices with the children, and for on-line processing of what they do in such encounters. We sometimes stopped the play to ask about the particulars of the experience, check on the "accuracy" of the enactment, and probe for strategies kids used when they encountered problems. The enactments also helped draw out details about actual translating episodes, more than simply talking about them did. Sometimes the plays triggered additional memories from the children and more explicit discussion of their emotions than emerged in the interviews. They revealed how children understood the various social situations in which they had translated—how different actors engaged in doctor appointments, restaurants, stores, and parent-teacher conferences, and how they and their parents were positioned in these. These activities also gave kids a chance to demonstrate strategies that they may not have been able to put into words in response to interview questions.

OBSERVING. As ethnographers know, listening is most effective when it is accompanied by observations. Through interviews we learn what people think or believe, or at least, what they think they should think or believe, and how they think they should present what they think or believe to the interviewer. This does not necessarily map on to what people actually do in practice. Further, people can only talk about things for which they have some level of conscious awareness. This point is especially important to consider when asking about translation encounters because kids may not be aware of the many ways in which they use their knowledge of English to help their families. They may only report on translation experiences that were marked and salient to them, that they remember, or that represent the kinds of things that they think count as translating.

One question when engaging in participant observation is where to set the frame. If we use the analogy of a camera, then how far should we zoom in? Should we focus on specific activity settings, particular children, or a given context? Do we pan out to see broader contexts—at the level of classrooms, households, schools, neighborhoods, or beyond? In my work on these projects I wanted the flexibility that a "zoom" lens offers on a camera. My aim was to observe individual children as they engaged with others in particular activity settings, especially in and around translating. I also wanted to watch those same children as they moved into other activity settings and changed over time. And I hoped to understand how their experiences fit within and were shaped by larger social and cultural contexts.

At the "zoom lens" level, in each community I worked closely with individual children, following them into the various activity settings of their daily lives. In the California Childhoods Study in Los Angeles, my focus was on general life experiences, not specifically on children's translation activities, and so

I concentrated on the domains in which kids spent most of their time—home and school. Translation became an aspect of children's daily lives that held special interest for me, but it was not particularly salient in my early observations, for a host of reasons, including the fact that children were not likely to act as translators when bilingual adults were around. In the work in Engleville and Regan I had to devise methods to work around these challenges to focus on this practice; this included attending carefully to the contexts in which children might be called upon to translate for others and asking families to alert us to times when they might need their children's translation services.

To understand these children's experiences within a larger social context, and to consider broader patterns of those experiences, I also worked with my research team to observe many kids interacting within the same neighborhood or school. I spent time physically moving around each community while keeping an eye out for places that children frequented and resources targeted for young people (for example, parks, public libraries, after school programs, clinics, and some kinds of stores). I traveled to Mexico and visited farming areas in the states of Guanajuato and Michoacán that most of the Chicago families came from in order to learn more about families' background experiences, visiting with family members of Balderas, Flores, and Aguilera families in their hometowns. These observations helped me consider how local and global contexts contributed to the structuring of children's daily life experiences and their pathways of development.

What really helped me to see a community from the vantage point of children and to question my own views, however, was walking with children in each locale, talking with them about what they saw. In Los Angeles, I also gave kids cameras to take pictures of their choosing; I then looked with them at their photographs, and we discussed their selections. Through this I could approximate seeing things through their eyes. I found that kids invariably noticed and took interest in very different things than I did; their angles of vision seemed shaped by their physical and social positioning as well as their relationships to their communities. Often, they looked at their locales in ways I had never considered—climbing to the top steps outside apartment buildings to see out over the rooftops, for example, or leaning down, looking up, or pushing the camera through a fence to see what was on the other side. Noticing what they noticed and listening to what the kids had to say about their pictures helped me to examine critically the implicit interpretive frameworks that shaped my own picture-making, my reading of the children's viewpoints, and ultimately my understanding of their lives.

For example, many photographs taken by kids in Los Angeles focused on greenery. This surprised me because to my eye this community had rather little plant life, at least in comparison with the other communities. But children helped me to see elements of nature I hadn't noticed: a patch of nopal cactus growing in front of a house, a small garden in front of another, two young trees on the side of a new apartment building. Some of these gardens were behind fences and locked gates, and I realized that my own attention was drawn to the fences. But some kids with whom I walked peered through the fences with their cameras to shoot the flowers (with no signs of bars in their pictures). In following their gaze, I learned to open up my own angle of vision and to appreciate children's aesthetics of place.[13]

AUDIOTAPES OF TRANSLATION SITUATIONS. As I have noted, an important aim of our observations in the Regan community and in Engleville was to document actual translation situations. Interviews and observations helped to direct our attention to the kinds of situations in which participants were likely to interpret for others, and I sought to record examples of the full range of experiences that the children we had talked with had engaged in, as well as representations of each individual's repertoire.

Securing naturally occurring, "live" translation data was an extremely difficult data-gathering task, however. It required building a high degree of rapport with each family so that families would feel comfortable alerting us to medical or dental appointments, shopping trips, parent-teacher conferences, and other situations in which their children might translate for them. And even with extensive groundwork, it was not always possible to be present for translation moments. As Sammy told us, translations "happen everywhere," and they often arise spontaneously; furthermore, we were reluctant to be too invasive with our observations and recorders. Finally, participants did not often recognize what they did as translating.

After numerous missed opportunities, we gave participants tape recorders and asked them to record themselves. We secured consent in advance from the people for whom they were likely to translate. We paid the youth for what we viewed as their work on this project, and this increased the number of recordings that we were able to gather. Again because participants did not always recognize what they do as translating and because they did not always have their recorders handy, it took a long time to gather a larger corpus of samples. Over time, we were, however, able to gather more than ninety examples of formal translation events (in addition to many informal, spontaneous, small translations in our observations): parent-teacher conferences, doctors' offices, stores, and at home. When we were able to be on the scene, our presence and our tape recorders undoubtedly changed the nature of the interactions. When participants recorded themselves, we were not a distracting audience; although this better captured the events as they might naturally unfold, we were not able to observe many details of the interactions. As with all approaches to fieldwork, there were trade-offs to each approach, and securing completely "natural" data was difficult if not impossible. The combination of these approaches helped to compensate for the limitations of any single approach.

OTHER METHODOLOGIES. My experiences as a teacher and a parent provided me with more than just sensitivity to power relations, vantage points, and epistemological insights. They have also helped me cultivate practical methods for eliciting the viewpoints of children. As a teacher, I most liked to use open-ended pedagogical methods that gave students freedom to express themselves and opened a window for me into their worlds: asking kids to write and/or draw about their own experiences and those of their families; giving them assignments that involved looking closely at their neighborhoods; interviewing family members, and reflecting on their everyday experiences. As a researcher, the approaches I employed were similarly designed to capture children's experiences from their vantage points. I asked children to draw pictures of themselves, their families, and their daily life activities, to envision their futures, and sketch their communities. Jessica's words, which opened this book, were actually taken from a map she drew of her daily life:

One final "wide angle" approach involved administering surveys. By surveying students in all fifth- and sixth-grade "mainstream" and "bilingual Spanish" classrooms at Regan, we could identify community-level patterns of language practices such as translating. We used this survey as a basis for selecting "case study" participants and then for locating each individual's experiences in relation to his or her peers. The questionnaire was offered in Spanish and English; it asked the children about the practices of their daily lives and especially about their translating, interpreting, reading, writing, and technology experiences. Of 313 students in these fifth- and sixth-grade classrooms, 280 filled out the survey. On the days we administered it 23 students were absent, and 10 parents did not give consent.

Respecting Children's Right to Silence

In my discussion thus far I have concentrated on how to elicit children's talk and understand their viewpoints. But sometimes kids may not want to talk—with parents, teachers, researchers, or anyone. As a parent, even when I am burning with curiosity about my children's lives, I try to read whether or not my children want to share their thoughts with me, and I respect their rights to silence when they do not. In research, I have similarly tried not to put children in a position where they may feel compelled to tell me things they really don't want to share. Despite all the assurances I might give, I am still an adult, a teacher, and an authority-like figure, and so kids may not feel free to *tell* me that they don't want to talk. Thus, I tried to be attentive to signs of discomfort and back off from questioning when I *sensed* that I was overstepping in the slightest degree. Reading such nonverbal communication is a skill that child translators also deployed when they mediated between different speakers; as we saw in the case of Sammy, some children were quite explicit in their reflections on how they "read" their audiences.

Sense-Making

As this brief exposé should make clear, data collection for this program of research was not a simple process. Each method revealed certain things and obscured others. Just as every translation should be understood in its context—with consideration of who was translating, for whom, and why, with what texts, tools and artifacts—I tried to interpret each data source in relation to the contexts in which they were gathered.[14] The combined use of multiple data sources offers the greatest possibilities for documenting a complex social phenomenon like language brokering in all its richness, as well as for capturing the varied nature of childhood experiences.

The multiple data sources gathered using these methods allowed me to focus on particular kids, families, classrooms, and communities from different angles and at different points of time. They offered varied and multiple points of comparison for contrasting the experiences of kids both within and across households, communities, and classrooms. Multiple lenses and perspectives were useful for building a rich understanding of each child, family, classroom, community, and constellation of experiences that shaped each form of childhood. I have drawn on the totality of that understanding in this book.

Last Words from Junior, María, Estela, and Nova

My research team and I shared the products of this research with the children and their families in different ways throughout the years. In early home visits, we did our best to explain the research enterprise, its purpose, audiences, and conventions (such as the reasons for using pseudonyms—not an easy concept to make transparent to children). When we brought the children to North-western University for "Junior Ethnographer Meetings," we toured our offices and labs and talked about life in the Academy. After creating a brochure that summarized early findings from the research and that included implications for teachers, parents, and coparticipants in translation encounters, we brought families to the university for a celebration and sharing of the brochure.[15] Later, on return visits after I moved to California, I brought data samples to share with Junior, Estela, Nova, and María. I showed them some of the presentations I had made, and explained how I was using what I learned from their experiences to reveal their skills to teachers and others.

I also gave a draft of this book to Junior, Estela, Nova, and María to read and comment on, to check for accuracy as well as to be sure they felt comfortable with my representations of them, asking Lisa Dorner and María Meza Peate to serve as intermediaries so the youth could feel more free to request any changes of the text. María and Junior said they didn't remember the episodes I recounted but that they seemed accurate; Junior graciously thanked us for "letting (him) be part of something meaningful." Estela cried when she read it and said she wanted to be the first to buy the book. Nova's email to Lisa seems a fitting way to end:

> I'm kind of excited and surprised that our "work" (as we thought it was just a way for us to get paid) would turn out to be part of a book. It is very exciting that Marjorie will tell part of what most Spanish-speaking individuals who have parents that can't speak English well, go through as part of their lives. I appreciate the effort and all the time she spent with us and I'm glad to be part of her journey as she was for us.

Appendix B: Transcription Conventions

For conversations that were in Spanish, I provide the original along with my translation. Extended quotations are followed by my translations. These involve my translations of the translations that youth themselves had rendered. These presented me with the same translation challenges that I address in this book. I tried to be faithful to the spirit, tone and meaning of the original text. Translations were checked by a professional translator and native speaker of Mexican Spanish.

I use a few basic transcription conventions in these transcripts:

= indicates "latching" speech—where one speaker is cut off or cuts off another speaker.

( ) indicates words that were inaudible or unclear.

: A colon or colons following a vowel indicates that the sound was drawn out by the speaker.

[ ] Square brackets are used to provide clarifying information, features of nonverbal communication (such as laughter), and comments to aid interpretation.

? Question marks are used to indicate rising intonation. In this sense, punctuation marks do not serve the same purpose as they do in written texts. I did, however, use inverted question marks in the Spanish text for comments that were clearly intended as questions, spoken with rising intonation, because Spanish readers would expect these.

Commas indicate a brief pause or in-breathe. Long pauses are marked by brackets.

" " Quotation marks are used for reported speech.

Capital letters are used to indicate increased stress, loudness, or marked emphasis by the speaker.

Appendix C: Domains of Language Brokering

All reported and observed instances, organized by domains.

Educational

Translate at parent-teacher conferences for themselves and siblings, cousins, friends

Visit and evaluate preschools for younger siblings

Locate, participate in, and help parents study for their ESL classes

Translate between staff members/teachers and other parents or community members (at random moments, in the hallway, in the classroom, and so on)

Call schools to report their own or siblings' absences

Interpret letters about dress codes/school programs, invitations to apply for programs or other schools, report cards and interim grade reports, consent and field trip forms, notes from teachers, and telephone calls from school staff

Help siblings with homework from school or Sunday school religious course

Translate at community service center that provides ESL, tutoring for kids, babysitting

Medical/Health

Fill out report/give insurance information in emergency room

Translate at doctor's and dentist's offices during family visits

Fill prescriptions at pharmacy

Answer or make phone calls to doctors regarding family treatment

Make appointments or cancel appointments with doctors, dentists

Interpret instructions for medicine, vitamins, other health-care products

Interpret letters asking permission to transfer medical records, appointment reminder cards, information from WIC regarding proper nutrition

Translate details during own and others' operations at hospital

Commercial

Shop for or with parents at pharmacies and drug, grocery, home improvement, pet, and computer stores (for example, BestBuy, Walgreens, Home Depot, Wal-mart, Mega Mall)

Complete refund transactions, settle disputes and check for mistakes in sales transactions

Interpret receipts, ads, product labels

Answer phone calls from solicitors and market researchers

Order such services as DirectTV, CallerID, voicemail

Sign for delivered packages

Fill out rental applications (for example, for musical instrument)

Shop for and buy new homes, cars, and so on

Cultural/Entertainment

Translate plot and dialogue at movies

Obtain discounts at movie theaters

Buy computer games

Interpret at "Six Flags" amusement park

Interpret TV shows, newspapers at home

Read and translate storybooks, self-help guides, song lyrics, instructional manuals (for games, videogames, computers and other electronic devices) and joke books for families

Interpret letters about community events (for example, at church and school)

Read and interpret letters or email from family

Obtain library card/take books out of library

Legal/State

Fill out police reports regarding disturbances in neighborhood or home, robberies, and so on

Translate a witness account about a fight at school to guard/police

Call insurance company regarding car damage, car accident

Interpret phone calls and door-to-door sales visits from insurance company representatives

Interpret letters from Social Security Office

Obtain welfare or social security by accompanying parents to office, answering questions, and so on

Fill out applications for WIC or welfare

Interpret letters from WIC

Help parents study for citizenship exams

Help to renew immigration papers at INS office

Interpret letters from Congress, representatives, voting materials

Decipher jury summons and other mail from the state

Translate public thank you note/speech for firefighters after 9/11

Financial/Employment

Cash or deposit checks at the bank or currency exchange

Open bank accounts

Interpret and pay bills

Obtain credit cards

Interpret informational letters from banks and insurance companies, bank statements, and mortgage payment year-end summaries

Translate financial interactions between parents and tenants

Translate for parents at parent's place of work

Call in sick for parents

Help parents fill out applications for work or for unemployment benefits

Coordinate rides to work for parents

Help with fax machine for contracting work at home

Call to inquire about jobs

Translate between people at their own (kids') work (for example, golfers and gardeners at a golf course)

Housing/Residential

Translate between parents and landlords; parents and tenants

Interpret flyers or notices regarding rental property

Talk to managers regarding things broken in apartment

Help settle rent disputes

Communicate with neighbors (regarding home, property concerns such as leaky gutters)

Notes

Introduction

1. I use the term immigrant because my focus is on children and families' actions in the country to which they have moved (in this case, the United States). This term presumes the vantage point of the receiving context; other labels, such as "migrant" emphasize movement across geopolitical borders more than entry into the host country. The term "emigrant" has had some recent take-up; see, for example, Coutin (2007), and Fitzgerald (2008). These serve as good reminders that transnational movements can be examined from the perspective of the home country as well as that of the host. "Emigration" has also been used in reference to the earlier major wave of movement from Europe to the United States. See Cordasco and Cordasco (1990) and Foerster (1924).

   Other terms, such as "transnational" or "transmigrant," emphasize people's movement between countries and their ongoing connections to each. For work establishing transnationalism as a focus of study, see Smith and Guarnizo (1998). Researchers have described active transnational social fields developed and to some degree sustained by different groups of migrants; see, for example, the detailed ethnographies of Levitt (2001) and Smith (2005). Barrie Thorne, Wan Shun Eva Lam, Anna Chee, and I examined children's participation in transnationalism, using data from the California Childhoods project (1995). Nevertheless, very real political borders generally prohibit living fully transnational lives, and other questions about the explanatory power of the concept have been raised. See Waldinger and Fitzgerald (2004). The families I worked with maintained varying degrees of ties to their home countries, but my focus in this book is on their activities in the United States.

2. All names are pseudonyms. Most were selected by participants. In earlier work, "Junior" was "Miguel." Junior requested the change when he read the manuscript of this book; he noted that it "felt weird" to read about himself as Miguel because his family had "had problems" with someone named Miguel. When they read the final manuscript before publication, Estela and María recognized their pseudonyms, but were perplexed to see a different last name attached to their parents and a different name for their city.

3. Portes and Rumbaut (2001). See also Suárez-Orozco and Suárez-Orozco (2001); they note that 12.4 percent of the U.S. population were immigrants in 2005, and 20 percent of children growing up in the United States have immigrant parents.

For additional statistics on changing demographics in the United States, see Suárez-Orozco, Suárez-Orozco, and Todorova's comprehensive summary (2008) of the current state of immigrant children in the United States, which is based on their longitudinal mixed-method study. Such statistics about immigrant children are used by many writers for dramatic effect, as children are used to symbolize adults' hopes and fears for the future.

4. For example, Berrol's classic (1995) offers many fascinating details about the work, school, and play experiences of the children of immigrants to the United States in the early 1900s. She considers intergenerational conflict and other aspects of parent-child relationships without mentioning children's activities as linguistic or cultural brokers. Similarly, Klapper's report (2007) on children's experiences as immigrants at the turn of the century makes only minimal mention of language issues; in reporting on one family's experiences she notes, "They relied on other Mexican immigrants with a better command of English to help them when they needed to see a doctor or go to court or fill out a money order" (p. 55); there is no specific discussion of children's role in such negotiations.

5. In his autobiography, Covello (1958) recounts his experiences growing up as the child of immigrants from Italy in New York in the early 1900s, and later working with immigrant youth in Harlem. (See also the abridged version of Covello's story in Perrone (1998), which includes Perrone's reflections drawing connections between historical and contemporary immigration issues.) Covello addresses the prestige value of Italian as a foreign language in schools and makes brief mention of communication challenges between home and school, but he does not describe language brokering.

   I surveyed other memoirs about growing up as the children of immigrants at the turn of the century, and in most I found only brief mention of language issues and no discussion of translation; see, for example, Antin (2001), Shyne (2202), and Yezierska (1925). Hoffman (1990) highlights her own experiences translating cultural experiences and her very self, but she does not consider the work that children do to speak for others. Fass's memoir (2008) is an exception. Fass dedicates a few pages to reflection on the burdens she experienced as a child translator and her sense that this act inverted household power relations.

   A contemporary memoir, Dumas (2003) is another exception. Much of this book's humor is predicated on language issues, and the roles that the author and her siblings played as language and culture brokers for their Iranian immigrant parents (including her father, who had attended graduate school in the United States and who had a considerable degree of proficiency in English) are central to the story.

6. In their edited volumes, Gillan and Gillan (1995a, 1995b) compile almost two hundred compositions about the experiences of nondominant groups in the United States (not all are immigrants), with nary a mention of translation experiences. Santa Ana (2004) compiles more than forty personal reports that are specifically about language issues by multilingual speakers; only one of these addresses language brokering directly ("¿Qué dice? ¿Qué dice? Child Translators and the Power of Language?").

   In contemporary fiction about immigrant experiences, there is also remarkably little attention to language issues in general and language brokering in particular. The minimal attention to language brokering in historical reports and literature suggests the invisibility of both the practice and children as actors and agents. Hall and Sham (2007) note that many people have anecdotes about child language brokering, a widely acknowledged phenomenon, but "it is a phenomenon that gets mentioned in passing, the paragraph here and there, rather than considered as an important subject of study in its own right" (p. 17).

7. The media, calling attention to children's interpretation work in medical, legal, and other institutions, has generally focused on high-stakes or emotionally burdensome situations, not more mundane translation work. See, for example, Associated Press (1991), Flores (1993), Gold (1999), Hedges (2000), and Wallace (2002).

8. See Zuñiga and Hernández-Leon (2005).

9. Thorne (1993) uses this term in her study of children's gendered social worlds in school in California (p. 3).

10. I take inspiration from Behar (1993), who reflects on her work as an anthropologist in reporting on the life of a Mexican woman.

11. Saler (2003, p. 209). The Latin term "pontifex" is overlaid with religious connotations that Saler explores in an analysis of the transmission of religious ideas, which serves as a good reminder that translations are always bound up with struggles over whose meanings or intentions will prevail. See also the other essays in Rubel and Rosman's edited volume (2003) for considerations of anthropologists as translators, and Tymocsko and Gentzler's edited volume (2002) for more discussions of power in translation.

Chapter 1   *Translating Frames*

1. I describe my transcription conventions and my approach to translating the original Spanish are described in Appendix B.

2. Thanks to Wan Shun Eva Lam for the data I used to develop this portrait. Eva worked with Cindy in the Oakland site of the California Childhoods project. Unlike the other children whose words and actions I detail in this book, I had no direct contact with Cindy. I include her in these initial portraits to establish the point that language brokering is not confined to Spanish-speaking communities in the United States.

3. Role reversal within the family system is presumed to take place when parents experience high levels of stress, owing to a major illness or disabling condition. See Bekir et al. (1993), Chase, Wells, and Deming (1998), and Stein, Riedel, and Rotherame-Borus (1999). Several studies document presumed short- and long-term negative effects of parentification on adolescents' development and on interpersonal relationships, including relationships with their own children; see Earley and Cushway (2002) for an overview. But the few studies that reference parentification among immigrant families posit mixed or even positive effects of language brokering, including boosts to children's confidence and academic achievement. See Acoach and Webb (2004), Buriel et al. (1998), and Walsh et al. (2006).

4. Minuchin (1974, p. 97). See also Boszormenyi-Nagy and Spark (1973), and Minuchin et al. (1967).

5. Pyke (2000) uses this term to describe the monolithic interpretive framework that the children of immigrants from Korea and Vietnam used as contrastive structures for understanding their own family life. Pyke argues that mainstream culture propagates ethnocentric images of family life that "can shape the desires, disappointments, and subjective realities of children of immigrant minorities" (p. 240).

6. My sister Virginia pointed out that when she was growing up as one of the eldest daughters in our family of eight children, she took on many responsibilities for the younger children—changing diapers, reading to us, and filling in as a surrogate mother on the emotional front as well. She said she enjoyed being a "mother's helper" or "little mother" and never considered it a burden. This is what Minuchin (1974) saw as a potentially positive version of the parentified child, as it takes form in large families. Yet as a psychotherapist today, she has reflected on how this shaped her own development, in both positive and negative ways.

7. I refer to an argument that has been made about other populations as well. Cohen (1994) critiques the "lament" that prefaces many studies of gerontology about the invisibility of the elderly in the literature. He argues that it is not the case that the elderly are invisible but rather that they are inscribed only in certain ways, and not generally treated as historical or social agents.

8. There are many wonderful ethnographies of immigrant family and community life that have made visible aspects of the immigration experience that are obscured in large-scale studies of the political economy. See, for example, Hondagneu-Sotelo (1994), Kibria (1993), Levitt (2001), Mahler (1995), Menjivar (2000), and Smith (2005).

9. Immigrant youth appear as central actors in school-based studies, and there is a growing number of qualitative studies of immigrant youth in schools. These center largely on processes of identity formation and academic engagement. See, for example, Carger (1996), Conchas (2006), Lee (2005), López (2003), Olsen (1997), Sarroub (2005), Stanton-Salazar (2001), and Valenzuela (1999b). Others ethnographies, such as Lewis's analysis of race relations (2003) and Flores-González's exploration of Latino identity construction (2002) are set in schools that service immigrant youth, but they do not directly address immigrant issues.

10. In much education literature, immigrant youth are addressed as "English Learners," a label that highlights a single dimension of their profiles, with the specifics of their immigration experiences unexamined. "English Learners" are generally assumed to be immigrants, but this is not necessarily the case.

11. Psychological studies of immigrant youth using mixed methodologies generally examine such issues as acculturation, ethnic identity formation, intergroup relations, and academic achievement. See, for example, Fuligni (2001a) and Marks et al. (2007). The work of the Súarez-Orozcos (2001) and Súarez-Orozco, Súarez-Orozco, and Todorva (2008), informed by psychological and anthropological perspectives, pursues these questions as well.

12. For studies of immigrant youth experiences based mostly in out-of-school contexts, see Hall (2002), Sun-Hee Park (2005), Song (1999), Vigil (1988, 2002), Waters (1999), and Zhou and Bankston (1998).

13. Rumbaut and Portes (2001), Portes and Rumbaut (2001, 2006), Súarez-Orozco and Súarez-Orozco (2001), and Súarez-Orozco, Súarez-Orozco, and Todorov (2008) are some of the most prolific researchers on immigrant youth experiences in the United States today, and they address the full range of issues pertaining to the new second generation in their longitudinal mixed-method studies. This includes attention to language acquisition and recognition of the work that children do as language and culture brokers.

14. Perusing the indices of immigrant ethnographies, I was struck by the fact that "language" and "childhood" often do not appear as key words; language brokering hardly ever does. Smith-Hefner (1999) devotes two chapters to child socialization in her portrait of Khmer-American families by addressing cultural issues centrally, but she gives only a nod to language insofar as it is tied to cultural identity. Guerra (1998) and Cintrón (1997) attend centrally to language and include attention to young people in their insightful explorations of Mexican transnational communities in Chicago, but neither directly examines youths' work as language brokers. My intent is not to critique these works for their lack of attention to the topics that are of prime interest to me; rather, I note that language practices (and especially child language brokering) are not transparent aspects of social life.

An important exception is the journalistic ethnography by Fadiman (1998), who captures the perspectives of both the medical establishment and a Hmong family as they interact around a child's epilepsy; without demonizing or romanticizing either stance, she probes the complexities of translation in these interactions. In this book, children and language are both central, as is the work of language and culture brokering.

15. Formulations of these perspectives across disciplines abound since 1995. For general discussions of the framework, see Corsaro (2005), James, Jenks and Prout (1998), James and Prout (1997), Jenks (1996), Mayall (2002), Pufall and Unsworth (2004), Qvortrup (2005), Skolnick (1976), and Stephens (1995).

16. The large and rich body of literature on language socialization views children as active participants in bidirectional processes of socialization; socialization is achieved through the interaction of children and adults. It also treats children's language practices as worthy of study in their own right; see, for example, Goodwin (1990) for studies of African-American children's talk in everyday contexts and Goodwin (2006) for finely detailed explorations of children's talk in playground games, which is based partly on research conducted on a schoolyard not far from the one I studied in Los Angeles.

   For a review of the field of language socialization, see Garrett and Baquedano-López (2002). For foundational work, see Ochs (2002), Ochs and Schiefflin (1984), Schiefflin (1990), Schiefflin and Ochs (1987). For a recent historical overview, see Ochs and Schiefflin (1986).

17. Mayall (2002, p. 27).

18. Ibid.

19. Aries (1962). Aries's work has engendered much scholarship exploring the social construction of family life.

20. Jenks (1996) helps readers to understand Aries's argument on the "birth of childhood" by drawing parallels with the construction of adolescence in Western society since World War II. As he notes, "Here we have a quite clearly distinguishable group of people within our society (albeit only within the Western world) who occupy a now firmly establish twilight zone of the quasi-child or crypto-adult" (p. 55).

21. Zelizer (1995). See also Stephens (1995).

22. For a taste of this fascinating literature, see DeMause (1974), Fass (2007), Fass and Mason (2000), Hannawalt (1993), Hecht (2002), Mintz (2004), and Stearns (2006). For a history of changing parenting practices in the United States over the course of the twentieth century, see Stearns (2003).

23. Fass (2007).

24. See, for example, Rogoff et al. (1975). See also more recent crosscultural analyses in Rogoff et al. (2003). For an older comparison of childhoods from a human development perspective, see work by the father of ecological psychology, Bronfenbrenner (1970). The diversity of ways of growing up and raising children was established in classic anthropological work on childhood in diverse cultures by Mead (1928) and Whiting and Whiting (1975).

   There is a vast body of contemporary research that bridges with the language socialization literature to illuminate variations in children's experiences across cultural contexts. For a few rich examples, see Báquedano-López (2004), Ek (2005), García Sanchez (2007), Gaskins (1999), and Reynolds (2002).

25. Thorne (2008). See also Field (1995), Postman (2003), and Stephens (1995).

26. Given the heavy emphasis on schoolwork in modern childhoods, some, like Qvortrup (1985) have argued that children's schoolwork should be measured as labor and treated as economically valuable.

27. Stephens (1995).

28. Palmer, Song, and Lu (2002).

29. For more on imaginaries of space, see Le Espiritu (2003) in which she discusses Filipino immigrants' relationships with the their home country, both material and symbolic.

30. Pratt (1999).
31. Research crossing various disciplines documents youths' participation in the domestic sphere, though how this work is approached varies across disciplines. Psychologists such as Fuligni (2001b) have analyzed the impact of home obligations on immigrant youth's school achievement. Sociologists and political economists operating from a critical childhoods standpoint have focused on the contributions children make to households. See, for example, Bryson (1996), Morrow (1996), Schildkraut (1995), Solberg (1997), Song (1999), and Zelizer (2005). Valenzuela (1999) looks specifically at language brokering as one aspect of immigrant children's contributions to their households, along with tutoring and serving as surrogate parents. See also Orellana (2003) for a description of the home responsibilities of youth in the Regan community.
32. Different dimensions of "generations" to consider include those of kinship order and age cohort. A ten-year-old child, for example, may have a parent who is twenty-five, while his peer may have one who is fifty-five. These parents would share kinship order status (they are both parents), but they may be members of rather different sociohistorical age cohorts. Whether separated by fifteen or thirty years, a child and a parent must negotiate the individual relationships with each other, despite experiences in different social worlds. See Alanen and Mayall (2001) for essays on "generationing."
33. As translators of children's experiences, researchers contribute to the construction and reconstruction of childhoods. As James and Prout (1997) note in their summary of the key features of the new childhoods paradigm, "Childhood is a phenomenon in relation to which the double hermeneutic of the social sciences is acutely present. That is to say, to proclaim a new paradigm of childhood sociology is also to engage in and respond to the process of reconstructing childhood"(p. 9).
34. California's AB 292, authored by Senator Leland Yee, would prohibit the use of children under fifteen years as interpreters by government agencies or any entity or program receiving state funds. The bill was passed on the Assembly floor on June 3, 2003, and was passed by the Senate Judiciary Committee on July 1, 2003, but has since been held on the Senate Appropriations Committee suspense file.
35. Bucholtz (2002).
36. Ibid.
37. Vásquez, Pease-Alvarez, and Shannon (1994). See also McQuillan and Tse (1995), Shannon (1990), and Tse (1995, 1996a).
38. From the Oxford English Dictionary Online: http://dictionary.oed.com/cgi/entry /50256320?query_type=word&queryword=translate&first=1&max_to_show= 10&sort_type=alpha&result_place=2&search_id=C34m-p2pw29-9685& hilite=50256320.
39. Chu (1999).
40. Jones and Trickett (2005).
41. Valdés (2002).
42. Ellis, and Smaje (1999).
43. Harris first used the term in French ("la traduction naturelle") in "La traductologie, la traduction naturelle, la traduction automatique et la sémantique" [Translatology, natural translation, machine translation and semantics] (1973). The term and concept was picked up more widely after Harris and Sherwood used it in "Translating as an Innate Skill" (1978). Thanks to Harris for compiling an annotated bibliography of research on this topic, organized chronologically. The bibliography, which reveals the development of the topic, and related foci of study, over time and across continents, is available for downloading at http://www3.uva.es/ uvalal/Enlaces/B_Harris-Natural_Translation.pdf.

44. Sociocultural approaches to language and literacy treat language in its diverse forms as text, and examine different ways of engaging with both spoken and written texts. See Heath's classic *Ways with Words* (1983). For recent formulations of sociocultural perspectives on language and literacy within the "New Literacy Studies" paradigm, see Barton (1994), Barton and Hamilton (1998), Gee (1996), Lewis, Enisco, and Moje (2007), New London Group (1996), and Street (1984).
45. Toury (1995).
46. See Orellana et al. (2007). We introduced the term *para*-phrasing in a discussion of language brokering as a family literacy practice in part because it is useful for signaling the parallel between translating and school literacy practices. It also indexes the "unofficial" nature of the practice, as in the term paraprofessional.
47. Hill (1998).
48. I follow Johnson-Powell et al. (91997), García Coll and Magnuson (1998), and Juan Guerra (2004) in using the term "transcultural" rather than intercultural or crosscultural, as it better captures a sense of movement across borders.
49. Urciuoli (1998) makes an important distinction between "racializing" vs. "ethnicizing" discourses. Ethnicizing discourses construe immigrants as positively contributing to the ethnic diversity, albeit in essentialized and ahistorical ways. Racializing discourses construct immigrants as "Others" and strip the referent (a person or social group) of dignity. Omi and Winant (1986) introduced the terms racial formation" or "racialization" to capture the socially constructed nature of categories that are treated as fixed and real in the social world.
50. Davidson (2001). See also Cambridge(1999).
51. Farr (2006) details the speech styles of rancheros from Michoacán–a state close to Guanajuato, where most of the youth I worked with originated.
52. Junior first used an English grammatical construction but then corrected it to the proper Spanish grammatical form.
53. I traveled to this town as the locals do, taking a progression of buses from the capital of Guanajuato to another urban center to a small town, and finally to this farming community. On each leg of the trip the bus conditions deteriorated–the first had plush cushioned seats with individual television screens and air conditioning and the last was a rickety blue schoolbus with wooden seats, many with only open frames for seat bottoms. My aim in traveling here was to see with my own eyes from where these families had moved; I also hoped to visit María, who was there at the time. Unfortunately, María was on a trip to the nearby town the day I showed up, but I enjoyed a visit with her aunt and grandmother, then with Junior's family, who are from this same rancho, before moving on to the next farming community a mile or so away, where I met with Nova's family: his grandparents, an unmarried aunt, another aunt, and her eight-year-old son. (The child's father lived in Engleville with Nova's family.) These family members were typical of those who are "left behind" when families migrate, as Mexico serves as both nursery and the infirmary for the working class in the United States.

    See Smith (2005) for a discussion of transnational retirement and childcare arrangements in Ticuani, Mexico, in his in-depth, longitudinal ethnography of transnational life. The families I met with had children scattered in Atlanta, Chicago, Los Angeles, and Texas; they spoke proudly of the support their children provided for them in remittances even as María's grandmother noted how it felt to be left behind, in ghost towns: "Aquí vivimos como ratones en un agujero" [Here we live like rodents in a burrow], seemingly in contrast with the adventurous lives of their children and grandchildren.
54. Gutiérrez and Rogoff (2003) suggest this in their discussion of how to avoid "essentializing" cultural groups. All cultural practices are dynamic and changing;

ethnographic descriptions that are fixed in a single time point can obscure this. I have enjoyed extended dialogues with colleagues about other practices that avoid essentializing, homogenizing, and flattening the experiences of nondominant groups; see Cooper et al. (2005), Orellana and Gutiérrez (2006), Gutiérrez and Orellana (2006), Orellana and Bowman (2003).

Chapter 2   Landscapes of Childhood

1. Thorne (1993) notes the greater fluidity of age and gender groupings in out-of-school contexts than in schools, which utilize these social categories to organize routines.
2. For explorations of Los Angeles as a new global metropolis, see Davis (1992, 1999) and Gottlieb (2007). For an examination of the experiences of diverse immigrants within this global metropolis, see Chang and Leong (1993) and Waldinger and Bozorgmehr (1996).
3. For an entertaining expose on Latino immigrants in new receiving communities all over the United States, see Tobar (2005) for a collection of essays. For studies of Latinos in the "new diaspora," see Villenas (2005), Wortham, Hamann, and Murillo (2001), and Zuñiga and Hernández-Leon (2005).
4. The "California Childhoods" project was funded by the MacArthur Foundation Research Network on Successful Pathways through Middle Childhood, in a grant to Catherine Cooper and Barrie Thorne. I worked as a postdoctoral researcher on this project for three years. There were three sites to the research: Barrie Thorne led one based in Oakland, California; Catherine Cooper led one based in Santa Cruz; and I had prime data-gathering responsibility for the Los Angeles site. See Cooper et al. (2005) for a compendium of research from the network. For reports on work in the Oakland site, framed by the new social science of childhoods, see Thorne (2001, 2008).
5. In 1997 the school district reduced this number to twenty-four hundred when the legislature implemented a policy of "class size reduction." Under this policy primary-grade classrooms could have a maximum of twenty students (while grades three to five retained at least thirty students).
6. Chinchilla and Hamilton (1993).
7. Lavadenz (2005) and Loucky and Moors (2000).
8. At the time, the label used for such students was "LEP" ("Limited English Proficient.") These students were distinguished from "FEP" ("Functional English Proficient") students, and from "EOs" ("English Only" students). Today, the label that is used for students who speak another primary language is "English Learner."
9. This is precisely how a neighborhood not far from Madison is portrayed in a poignant film that was made by a local teacher around the time of Proposition 187 ("Fear and Learning at Hoover Elementary").
10. See Orellana and Thorne (2008) for more discussion of the logic of this way of carving up educational time, the implications of this schedule for family and community life, and how this tracking system played into and reinforced processes of racialization among youth. For additional research on the experiences of migrant populations in year-round schools in California, see Donato (1996).
11. For a more elaborated discussion of this volunteer labor and the ways in which it can be understood, see Orellana (2001).
12. Little research distinguishes between immigrants and refugees or considers the particular psychosocial stressors involved in fleeing war situations. Suárez-Orozco,

Suárez-Orozco, and Todorov (2008) offer some perspectives from some of the few researchers of immigrant youth who are attuned to these issues. See also Mosselson (2006).

13. Ek and Hernández and I explored parents' and children's views of bilingual education in Los Angeles during this time period; we reported our findings in Orellana, Ek, and Hernández (1999).

14. Kozol (1992) documents many disparities in public education that were also evident when I compared Regan and Madison with the schools in Engleville. The fact that funding for public schools is tied to the local tax base creates dramatic inequities across communities. Kozol makes no attempt to report in a detached or unemotional way about the savageness of the inequalities he documented, and, although his work has been critiqued by some for its heavy emotional investment, it is hard to imagine that any caring person would *not* to be outraged by the vast inequities in resources for children across communities and schools that he documents. For additional documentation of urban school inequities, see Oakes (1985). For analyses of the resegregation that is accompanying urban school deterioration in the current era, see Orfield and Lee (2007) and Orfield and Yun (1999).

15. I had strong reactions to the food and found it difficult to observe at lunch. The food looked unappealing (an opinion shared by most students), and it was hard to believe that it was considered nutritional. One relatively popular meal was nachos—fried tortilla strips covered in artificial cheese sauce, served with a small bit of iceberg lettuce (which always looked old and rusty to me), an optional apple and milk. Several of the girls we worked with said they ate nothing most days except a bag of Cheetos.

16. Pratt (1999).

17. The changes in Engleville somewhat mirror those in many cities across the nation, including my own hometown of Waltham, Massachusetts, a process I have observed on each of my home visits during the last three decades. In 1970, Waltham's population of sixty-two thousand was 80 percent "native-born." The Chamber of Commerce pronounced the "predominant nationalities" of the time to be "American, Canadian, Italian" (indeed, most of those who were not "native-born" were French-Canadian). By 1980 the ethnic make-up of Waltham had shifted considerably. The still-white majority (87.9 percent) was followed by 5.6 percent of the population who identified as Hispanic. In the 2000 census the percentage of whites had dropped to 82 percent, while the Hispanic population reached 8 percent, followed closely by 7 percent Asian. In the school-age population these figures shift even more, to 20 percent Hispanic, 7 percent Asian, and only 63 percent white. Of school age children 33 percent speak English as a second language. In this way, Waltham and Engleville are microcosms of much of the nation; new immigration is rapidly changing its face.

18. Farr (2005) sketches the history of Mexican and Puerto Rican migration to Chicago. See also Massey and Denton (1993).

19. Farr (2006, 2005).

20. Dorner (2006) discusses the various meanings that "community" took on in Engleville discussions and Latino families' perspectives on and positions within these debates.

21. See Lindholm-Leary (2001) for a detailed discussion of dual-language schools, also called Two-Way Immersion. See also Potowski (2007) for a mixed-method study of one school. For an incisive critique of the racialized politics of dual-language programs, see Valdés (1997). See also Hadi-Tabassum (2006).

22. See Thomas and Collier (2002).

Chapter 3   Home Work

1. Kralovec and Buell (2000) popularized these debates. See also Mayall (2002), which includes discussion of the competing demands of housework and homework in immigrant families in England.

2. Goodnow and Lawrence (2001), speaking generally about children's household contributions, suggest that we should think about children's work in homes as we would any other form of contribution (for example, love, money, respect, obedience, or honor). They call for enriched descriptions of what children do in homes, rather than mere quantifications of children's efforts, as researchers have sometimes done with domestic labor. They suggest that we look at the *person-specificity* of tasks: how are tasks distributed (for example, by gender, age or ability); whether tasks are shared, substitutable, or fixed; the degree of *consensus* that family members hold about children's efforts; and the *style* of these contributions (for example, mandatory or optional, volunteered or enlisted, taken-for-granted or reflected-upon). They suggest we need to look at how age, gender, competencies, preferences, family positioning, ethnic background, custom, needs, and availability as circumstances that influence who contributes what, and how those contributions are viewed and treated. They also call for a close examination of the *feelings people express* about housework in order to understand the role and significance of particular contributions. This framing is useful for understanding broad patterns of the *practice* of family translating across households: who tends to take up what kind of work, under what circumstances, and informed by what belief systems. It avoids ethnocentric norms and allows for variation in beliefs about children and childhoods. It helps us to think about how the beliefs and practices of immigrant families may change as they come into contact with other cultures and adapt to new circumstances.

3. See Orellana et al. (2003) for a summary of all of the text-based translation work children reported and for analyses of a few of these text-based translation episodes. See also Weinstein-Shr (1994). Classroom teachers might recognize and validate immigrant children's home-based translation work and support it, perhaps by giving students extra credit for this additional homework.

4. Dorner, Orellana, Li-Grining (2007).

5. Wong Fillmore (1991).

6. Waterman and Harry (2008) discuss the barriers to English Language Learner (ELL) parent-school collaboration and note that, while many parents of ELLs are interested in learning English, the demand for ESL classes exceeds the services available. Also see the Suárez-Orozcos's description (2001) of this imbalance.

7. Hall and Sham (2007) report on similar collaborative family interpreting.

8. Little attention has been given to the support that children offer to their siblings. For an important exception, see Gregory, Long, and Volk (2004).

9. On another return visit, a year or so later, María Meza similarly encountered María on the phone for her mother.

10. Jennifer Reynolds and I analyzed this incident together and discussed it at great length. We develop a more extended analysis of the paradoxes of María's positionality in this encounter in Orellana and Reynolds (2008).

11. Research in the field of literacy underscores the depth and breadth of everyday literacy practices in modern Western society in comparison with the relatively narrow range of literacy tasks at school. See Barton and Hamilton (1998), Barton, Hamilton, Ivanic (2000), Knobel (1999), Kress (2003), Lankshear and Knobel (2003), Purcell-Gates (1997), and Street (1984). See Orellana and Reynolds (2008) for a comparison of school literacy tasks at Regan and the demands in home literacy brokering.

12. See Orellana et al. (2003) for an analysis of how Adriana approached this task with support from her mother.
13. Thanks to Viviana Zelizer for calling my attention to the question of remuneration and for other helpful comments when I presented an earlier version of this chapter at the Princeton Economic Sociology program.

Chapter 4 Public Para-Phrasing

1. Luís Moll et al. (1992).
2. Gloria Anzaldúa's concept of "borderlands" (1999) is important here, as metaphorical sites of marked social difference.
3. Bourdieu (1984) describes how making classifications and establishing preferences—largely based on an individual's upbringing and social class status—are *strategies* of class distinction. In his words, "[A]rt and cultural consumption are predisposed, consciously and deliberately or not, to fulfil a social function of legitimating social differences" (p. 7). Preferred tastes, or "good" qualities, are defined by the dominant class and legitimized, while the preferences of the subordinate classes are viewed as inferior.
4. Jennifer F. Reynolds and I analyzed this incident together. We elaborate on it in Reynolds and Orellana (under review).
5. Hochschild (2003).
6. Solórzano, Ceja, and Yosso (2000) define microaggressions as "subtle insults (verbal, nonverbal, and/or visual) directed toward people of color, often automatically or unconsciously" (p. 60).
7. Wadensjö (1998).
8. García Sánchez (2007) shows evidence of this sort of "face-saving" translation work by Moroccan children in Spanish clinics.

Chapter 5 Transculturations

1. Ethnomethodological research on parent-teacher conferences in monolingual contexts shows that adult participants generally use these events to identify problems in children's academic and social developmental trajectories and to propose remediation. See Pillet-Shore (2003) and Baker and Keough (1997).
2. Wadensjö (1998).
3. Goffman (1981).
4. García Sánchez analyzed patterns in the data from across all of the parent-teacher conferences. We report on these patterns in García Sánchez and Orellana (2006).
5. Traditional theories of translation emphasized the importance of creating adequate linguistic equivalents across languages. Finding equivalent words was privileged over identifying equivalent pragmatic of ideological functions across the two languages. Haviland (2003) refers to this as the "verbatim theory" of language; it is one that relies on what Reddy (1993) calls the "conduit" metaphor of communication, whereby words serve as a pipeline through which meanings are passively transmitted between interlocutors. The translator/interpreter is assumed to be a mere message bearer who does not shape the form or function of the message.
   Other schools of thought on interpretation and translation hold quite different assumptions. Ricoeur (2006) summarizes the issue of written translation in one line: "Give up the ideal of the perfect translation" (p. 8). He argues that "it is this mourning for the absolute translation that produces the happiness associated with

translating. The happiness associated with translating is a gain when, tied to the loss of the linguistic absolute, it acknowledges the difference between adequacy and equivalence, equivalence without adequacy" (p. 10).

6. I use the word "transculturation" as a parallel to translation, to emphasize the cultural translations that are demanded in all translation work. In ongoing work, my colleague Rashmita Mistry and I are working to specify the skills involved in bridging cultural perspectives and identify ways teachers can cultivate such skills in school.

7. Educational deficit thinking views the historical underachievement of students from poor and nondominant groups as a result of the purported deficiencies (genetic, cultural, environmental, or otherwise) of children and their families, thus overlooking structural inequalities. Valencia (1997) offers a collection of essays on educational deficit thinking and its effects on educational policies and practices. Also see Valdés (1996), which questions the perceived disinterest in education shown by Mexican immigrant families, and Valenzuela (1999) for a description of how deficit thinking affects the educational experiences of Mexican immigrant youth in a Texas high school.

8. Davidson (2001). Jacquemet (1996). See also Berk-Seligson (2002) for sociolinguistic analyses of what actually transpires in courtroom interpretation.

9. Hill (1998) provides an anthropological perspective on the construction of "white public space" through the monitoring of the speech of racialized populations. She notes how "mock Spanish" is used by whites without impunity.

10. Many adults focus on spelling and punctuation errors in children's writing. It's important to note that Estela chose to write this in Spanish, after starting the first sentence in English, and she expressed herself clearly, though she had never had instruction in Spanish literacy; she had been in all-English classes since preschool.

Chapter 6   *Transformations*

1. In March 2008, I received an email from Junior. I had lost touch with him and the others during the previous year, when immersed in medical treatment. It read: "Hello, how is everything going with your family out there in California? You guys are still out there right? Haven't heard much in a while just thought I would check on how everything is going. I graduated a semester early from high school and I am getting my diploma soon if they are able to find it in the stacks they have. I was looking for your e-mail everywhere at home until i remembered that I could google your name like last time and find it again." This put us back in contact, and as we exchanged further emails Junior expressed his condolences ("I know that it's hard to talk about bad times so I won't extend conversation about it") and told me about his immediate plans: to work in order to save money to buy a car and take classes.

2. I was struck by the fact that Estela and I shared an understanding of the frustration involved in trying to get young children to go to sleep when they were not tired (but caregivers were)—she as a young teenager, and I as a middle-aged parent.

3. Though families experienced many forms of racist and xenophobic treatment, they also encountered many people who assisted them in their adjustment to life in the United States, valued their labor contributions, and found ways like this to support them. Parents told of "Americans" who helped them get jobs, paid them generously, gave them gifts, helped them purchase computers, cars, and other items, and gave them advice on how to help their children into college.

4. For rich, detailed portraits of sixteen children of immigrants from diverse backgrounds, covering their life changes over a period of five years, see Suárez-Orozco,

Suárez-Orozco, Todorov (2008). Such detailed glimpses into the lives of children over an extended period of time are quite rare in research.

5. Jenks (2007) counters the psychological approach to development with a sociological one. Discussing how parents compare their children's achievement of developmental milestones, he argues: "What I am suggesting is that the concept of development does not signify a "natural" process—it does, however, make reference to a socially constructed sense of change pertaining to the young individual which is encoded within a series of benchmarks." He further notes that those benchmarks may "move in and out of focus according to which aspect of the person we are attending to" (p. 37).

6. The recent emergence of this category suggests how the stages in stage theories are constructed and malleable.

7. Lisa Dorner, who read the manuscript with the eyes of a parent as well as a researcher, pointed this out.

8. See Lave and Wenger (1991) and Wenger (1999).

9. Rogoff (1990, 2003).

10. Vygotsky (1978).

11. Lee, Spencer, and Harpalani (2003) argue for understanding all learning through a profoundly cultural lens. Focusing on the experiences of nondominant students, she notes that to understand how and why youth engage in certain kinds of learning and development and not others requires an understanding of the relationships of individuals and groups within those cultural contexts.

12. Gutiérrez and Rogoff (2003). Sociologist Ann Swidler (2003) similarly treats culture as repertoire or tool kit by showing how a "common pool of cultural resources" can be used in many ways to make sense of experiences.

13. Ibid., p. 19.

14. See Scribner and Cole (1981) for elaboration of this idea.

15. See, for example, Lave (1977), Rogoff and Lave (1984), Scribner and Cole (1981), Nasir (2002), Saxe (1999). See also Rose (2005) for thoughtful consideration of the intellectual processes involved in and cultivated through blue-collar labor.

16. González (2006) illuminates the emotional as well as sociocultural dimensions of language learning in her beautifully crafted exploration of language learning in the borderlands.

17. Vygotsky (1978) defines the zone of proximal development as "the distance between the actual developmental level as determined by independent problem solving and the level of potential development as determined through problem solving under adult guidance or in collaboration with more capable peers" (p. 86). Vygotsky viewed the zone as human cognition-in-activity: "An essential feature of learning is that it creates the zone of proximal development; that is, learning awakens a variety of internal developmental processes that are able to operate only when the child is interacting with people in his [sic] environment and in cooperation with his [sic] peers" (p. 90).

18. What I am suggesting does not challenge the basic tenets of sociocultural theory in any way. I am only questioning the tendency—as in all of the social sciences—to assume adult-centric perspectives.

19. H. Julia Eksner and I (under review) hone in on the dynamic nature of zones of proximal development in "Translating in the Zone of Proximal Development."

20. See Orellana et al. (2003) and Eksner and Orellana (under review) for additional examples of how parents support children's translation work.

21. Estela used a false cognate for the word "expect," based on the English. "Expectan" has no meaning in Spanish. The correct translation might be "esperan." It seems reasonable to assume, however, that Estela's mother understood this meaning.

22. For additional and more elaborated examples, see Orellana et al. (2003), Eksner and Orellana (under review), and Reynolds and Orellana (under review).
23. Orellana and Reynolds (2008).
24. Blos (1979); Collins and Laursen (2004).
25. Greenfield (1994) introduces the notion of independent and interdependent cultural scripts to the field of psychology. Dorner, Orellana, and Jiménez (forthcoming)consider this further.
26. I am indebted to Lisa M. Dorner and Christine Li-Grining for developing and implementing this line of analysis and to Greg Duncan for encouraging this direction as well as for conceptual guidance. I had been skeptical that a measurable effect of language brokering on discrete measures of school achievement could be found. The details of these quantitative analyses are reported in Dorner, Orellana, and Li-Grining (2007). See also Buriel et al. (1998), who found a positive correlation between language brokering and biculturalism (for junior high students) and academic self-efficacy (for senior high school students). However, in a smaller cross-sectional analysis, Tse (1995) found that 50 percent of her sample of thirty-five Latino language brokers reported grade-point averages lower than 2.5 (average school performance).
27. Bialystock (2001) summarizes research showing the cognitive benefits of bilingualism.
28. Valdés (2002) studied the interpreting efforts of twenty-five mostly Spanish-speaking high school students who role-played conflictive situations in which they had to translate between a parent and a school principal. Valdés concluded that the metalinguistic competencies displayed by the bilingual adolescents constituted a form of giftedness. Malakoff and Hakuta (1991) have made a similar theoretical argument in claiming that bilingual interpreters, including children, develop greater metalinguistic awareness than do monolinguals.
29. Ricoeur (2006).
30. Weisskirch and Alva (2002) found that levels of brokering and measures of acculturative stress differed, along gender lines, among thirty-six fifth-grade Latinos from California. The bilingual girls in their sample tended to be more Spanish-dominant and have lower levels of stress associated with acculturation, while boys were more English-dominant and had higher levels of stress. In another study, Weisskirch (2006), twenty respondents to a questionnaire indicated that they felt helpful, proud, and useful; language brokering was associated with higher levels of self-esteem. The largest quantitative study to date on the consequences of brokering for parent-adolescent relationships found that youth's translating is negatively related to the psychological well-being of some groups; Korean and Chinese (but not Mexican) youth from immigrant families who reported more brokering had higher levels of "internalization" (that is, depression-anxiety, somatic complaints, and withdrawal); see Chao (2006). However, Mexican respondents in Chao's study did *not* report high levels of internalization. Likewise, Tse (1995) shows that a number of Latino children did not view the practice as stressful. Only 9 percent of her sample of thirty-five sixteen-year-old Latino students reported that brokering was a "burden," and only 9 percent felt "embarrassed" by it. In fact, more than 50 percent liked it, and 46 percent were "proud to broker" (ibid., p. 188).
31. Ironically, Regan students were expected to log a certain number of "service learning hours" in their high school years. Such institutional practices were ostensibly aimed at engendering a "helping orientation." When immigrant children help out at home, they do not do so to earn points, gain credit, or enhance their college applications. They are taking part in what feminist scholars call "care work." See Cockburn (2005) for an explication of how feminist notions of care work can be extended to children's home-based work.

Chapter 7 **Translating Childhoods**

1. Collins (1990).
2. See probably the most-cited research on this topic, Heath (1983). Heath details language socialization practices in middle-class European American, working-class European American, and working-class African American communities. She describes how children's interactive styles (including modes of storytelling) and literary practices develop, based on exposure to different language patterns and experiences with literature. The styles and practices cultivated in middle-class homes parallel more directly those found in classrooms than do working-class styles; this makes it easier for these children to be seen as intelligent and achieve success in school.
3. Cziksentmihalyi (1990).
4. Richards (1953), as cited in Brislin (1976).
5. Wadensjö (1995).
6. The story of the much-maligned Malinche is a case in point. See Esquivel (2006); this novel depicts the complexities of Malinche's position as mediator between Spanish and Náhuatl speakers.
7. Walkerdine (2006).
8. Ibid., p. 20.
9. Blair (1992), Gill (1998), and Morrow (1996).
10. Zelizer (1985).
11. Bourdieu (1973); Bourdieu and Passeron (1977).

Appendix A

1. James and Prout (1997) summarize the key components of the critical sociology childhoods; they argue that "ethnography is a particularly useful methodology for the study of childhood. It allows children a more direct voice and participation in the production of sociological data than is usually possible through experimental or survey styles of research." Speier (1976) calls for conscious work to escape the "adult ideological viewpoint" in studies of childhood. Thorne(1993) calls for approaches that deemphasize our adult status and align us better with youths' perspectives because adults are invariably "tethered to adults by lines of structure and consciousness" (p. 19). Critical childhood scholars have found thoughtful ways of exploring children's views of their social worlds even under very sensitive circumstances. See, for example, Bluebond-Langer (2000) and Clark (2003).
2. Wadensjö (1998).
3. Roberts (2003).
4. Walkerdine (1998). I take inspiration as well from postobjectivist essays by Behar (1996) and Rosaldo (1993), which highlight the emotional dimensions of ethnographic research and the role of memory in shaping our understandings.
5. James (1993). Thorne (1993) argues that "tugs of memory" and the "child within" should be attended to by adults who study children and that memories can be rich resources for understanding when raised to conscious awareness. Throughout my work, I noticed the memories and emotions that were evoked for me and took these into account in my efforts to understand and report on the perspectives of children and families.
6. Rumbaut (2004).
7. Guerra (2004). See also Guerra (2007).

8. See Schieffelin and Ochs (1986) for a discussion of child-centered and situation-centered socialization practices. See Lareau (2003) for explorations of social class differences in parenting practices.
9. Valenzuela (1999).
10. For reports on this work, see Orellana and Reynolds (2008), Orellana and Eksner (2006), and Martínez et al. (2008). See Lee (2007, 1995). Based in the cultural modeling tradition, we suggest ways of leveraging everyday translation skills for the development of academic literacy.
11. I draw parallels between children's movement between cultural worlds and my own work moving across disciplines; see Orellana (2007).
12. Smith (2005) describes a similar approach to what he calls "collective ethnography" and a similar approach to combining life course analyses and ethnography.
13. In Orellana (2003) I elaborate on this methodology and share photographs kids took as well as what I learned from listening to children and looking at their social worlds through their eyes. In Orellana and Hernández (1998) I describe what I learned about how children read their social worlds, as well as the print in their environment, again through the method of walking and taking photographs with urban youth in their neighborhoods. For other research involving young people with cameras, see Buss (1995) and Cavin (1994). See also Davies (1998), which includes a chapter on using visual methods (though not in relation to working with children).
14. My general approaches to fieldwork and to data analyses were shaped by Emerson, Fretz, and Shaw (1995), which offered guidelines for writing fieldnotes. I've been inspired as well by Becker (1998), who proffered excellent suggestions in the clearest of prose. Ethnography is perhaps best learned by reading good models, and the many ethnographic texts that I have cited here have been my best teachers.
15. The brochure is available for downloading at http://www.gseis.ucla.edu/faculty/orellana/Translations.html.

Bibliography

Acoach, C. Leah, and Lynne M. Webb. 2004. "The Influence of Language Brokering on Hispanic Teenagers' Acculturation, Academic Performance, and Nonverbal Decoding Skills: A Preliminary Study." *Howard Journal of Communication* 15: 1–19.

Alanen, Leena, and Barry Mayall, eds. 2001. *Conceptualizing Child-Adult Relationships.* New York: Routledge/Falmer.

Antin, Marie. 2001. *The Promised Land.* New York: Random House.

Anzaldúa, Gloria. 1999. *Borderlands/La Frontera: The New Mestiza.* San Francisco: Aunt Lute Books.

Aries, Phillipe. 1962. *Centuries of Childhood: A Social History of Family Life.* London: Cape.

Associated Press. 1991. "For Immigrants' Children, An Adult Role." *New York Times,* August 15.

Baker, Carolyn, and Jayne Keogh. 1997. "Mapping Moral Orders in Parent-Teacher Interviews." In *Analisis della conversazione e prospettive di ricerca in etnometodologia,* ed. Aurelia Marcarino, 25–42. Urbino, Italy: Quattro Venti.

Baquedano-López, Patricia. 2004. "Traversing the Center: The Politics of Language Use in a Catholic Religious Education Program for Immigrant Mexican Children." *Anthropology and Education Quarterly* 35 (2): 212–232.

Barton, David. 1994. *Literacy: An Introduction to the Ecology of Written Language.* Cambridge: Wiley-Blackwell.

Barton, David, and Mary Hamilton. 1998. *Local Literacies: Reading and Writing in One Community.* London: Routledge.

Barton, David, Mary Hamilton, and Roz Ivanic, eds. 2000. *Situated Literacies: Reading and Writing in Context.* London: Routledge.

Becker, Howard S. 1998. *Tricks of the Trade: How to Think About Your Research While You're Doing It.* Chicago: University of Chicago Press.

Behar, Ruth. 1993. *Translated Woman: Crossing the Border with Esperanza's Story.* Boston: Beacon Press.

———. 1996. *The Vulnerable Observer: Anthropology That Breaks Your Heart.* Boston: Beacon Press.

Bekir, Pamela, Thomas McLellan, Anna Rose Childress, and Peter Gariti. 1993. "Role Reversals in Families of Substance Abusers: A Transgenerational Phenomenon." *International Journal of the Addictions* 28: 613–630.

Berk-Seligson, Susan. 2002. *The Bilingual Courtroom: Court Interpreters in the Judicial Process.* Chicago: University of Chicago Press.

Berrol, Selma Cantor. 1995. *Growing Up American: Immigrant Children in America Then and Now*. New York: Twayne.

Bialystok, Ellen. 2001. *Bilingualism in Development: Language, Literacy, and Cognition*. New York: Cambridge University Press.

Blair, Sampson. 1992. "Children's Participation in Household Labor: Child Socialization Versus the Need for Household Labor." *Journal of Youth and Adolescence* 21: 241–258.

Blos, Peter. 1979. *The Adolescent Passage*. Madison, Conn.: International Universities Press.

Bluebond-Langer, Myra. 2000. *In the Shadow of Illness: Parents and Siblings of the Chronically Ill Child*. Princeton, N.J.: Princeton University Press.

Boszormenyi-Nagy, Ivan, and Geraldine M. Spark. 1973. *Invisible Loyalties: Reciprocity in Intergenerational Family Therapy*. Hagerstown, Md.: Harper & Row.

Bourdieu, Pierre. 1973. "Cultural Reproduction and Social Reproduction." In *Knowledge, Education, and Social Change*, ed. Richard Brown. London: Tavistock.

———. 1984. *Distinction: A Social Critique of the Judgment of Taste*. Cambridge, Mass.: Harvard University Press.

Bourdieu, Pierre, and Jean-Claude Passeron. 1977. *Reproduction in Education, Society, and Culture*. London: Sage.

Brislin, Richard W. 1976. *Translation: Applications and Research*. New York: Halsted.

Bronfenbrenner, Uri. 1970. *Two Worlds of Childhood: U.S. and U.S.S.R.* New York: Simon & Schuster.

Bryson, Lois. 1996. "Revaluing the Household Economy." *Women's Studies International Forum* 19: 207–219.

Bucholtz, Mary. 2002. "Youth and Cultural Practice." *Annual Review of Anthropology* 31: 525–552.

Buriel, Raymond, William Perez, Terri L. De-Ment, David V. Chavez, and Virginia R. Moran. 1998. "The Relationship of Language Brokering to Academic Performance, Biculturalism and Self-Efficacy Among Latino Adolescents." *Hispanic Journal of Behavioral Sciences* 20: 283–297.

Buss, Shirl. 1995. "Urban Los Angeles from Young People's Angle of Vision." *Children's Environments* 12 (3): 340–351.

Cambridge, Ian. 1999. "Information Loss in Bilingual Medical Interviews Through an Untrained Interpreter." *The Translator* 5 (2): 201–219.

Carger, Chris L. 1996. *Of Borders and Dreams: A Mexican-American Experience of Urban Education*. New York: Teachers College Press.

Castañeda, Antonia. 2004. "¿Qué dice? ¿Qué dice? Child Translators and the Power of Language?" In *Tongue-Tied: The Lives of Multilingual Children in Public Education*, ed. Otto Santa Ana, 66–69. Lanham, Md.: Rowan & Little.

Cavin, Erica. 1994. "In Search of the Viewfinder: A Study of a Child's Perspective." *Visual Sociology* 9 (1): 27–41.

Chang, Edward T., and Russell C. Leong. 1993. *Los Angeles: Struggles toward Multiethnic Community: Asian, American, African American, and Latino Perspectives*. Seattle: University of Washington Press.

Chao, Ruth K. 2006. "The Prevalence and Consequences of Adolescents' Language Brokering for Their Immigrant Parents." In *Acculturation and Parent-Child Relationships: Measurement and Development*, ed. Marc H. Bornstein and Linda R. Cote. Mahwah, N.J.: Erlbaum.

Chase, Nancy D., Marolyn C. Wells, and Mary P. Deming. 1998. "Parentification, Parental Alcoholism, and Academic Status Among Young Adults." *American Journal of Family Therapy* 26 (2): 105–114.

Chinchilla, Norma S., and Hamilton, Nora. 1993. "Central Americans in Los Angeles: An Immigrant Community in Transition." In *In the Barrios: Latinos and the Underclass Debate*, ed. Joan Moore and Raquel Pinderhughes, 51–78. New York: Russell Sage Foundation.

Chu, Clara. 1999. "Immigrant Children Mediators (ICM): Bridging the Literacy Gap in Immigrant Communities." *The New Review of Children's Literature and Librarianship* 5: 85–94.

Cintrón, Ralph. 1997. *Angel's Town: Chero Ways, Gang Life and Rhetorics of the Everyday*. Boston: Beacon Press.

Clark, Cindy Dell. 2003. *In Sickness and Play: Children Coping with Chronic Illness*. New Brunswick, N.J.: Rutgers University Press.

Cockburn, Tom. 2005. Children and the Feminist Ethic of Care. *Childhood* 12 (1): 71–89.

Cohen, Lawrence. 1994. "Old Age: Cultural and Critical Perspectives." *Annual Review of Psychology* 23: 137–158.

Cohen, Suzanne, Jo Moran-Ellis, and Chris Smaje. 1999. Children as Informal Interpreters in GP Consultations: Pragmatics and Ideology. *Sociology of Heath and Illness* 21: 163–186.

Collins, Patricia Hill. 1990. *Black Feminist Thought: Knowledge, Consciousness, and the Politics of Empowerment*. New York: Routledge.

Collins, W. Andrew, and Brett Laursen. 2004. "Family Relationships and Parenting Influences." In *Handbook of Adolescent Psychology*, ed. Richard M. Lerner and Laurence Steinberg, 331–362. New York: J. Wiley.

Conchas, Gilberto Q. 2006. *The Color of Success: Race and High-Achieving Urban Youth*. New York: Teachers College Press.

Cooper, Catherine R., Cynthia T. García Coll, W. Todd Bartko, Helen Davis, and Celina Chatman, eds. 2005. *Developmental Pathways Through Middle Childhood: Rethinking Contexts and Diversity as Resources*. Mahwah, N.J.: Lawrence Erlbaum Associates.

Cordasco, Francesco, and Michael Vaughn Cordasco. 1990. *The Italian Emigration to the United States, 1880–1930*. London: Junius-Vaughn Press.

Corsaro, William A. 2005. *The Sociology of Childhood*. Thousand Oaks, Calif.: Pine Forge Press.

Coutin, Susan Bibler. 2007. *Nations of Emigrants: Shifting Boundaries of Citizenship in El Salvador and the United States*. Ithaca, N.Y.: Cornell University Press.

Covello, Leonard. 1958. *The Heart Is the Teacher*. New York: McGraw Hill.

Cziksentmihalyi, Mihaly. 1990. *Flow: The Psychology of Optimal Experience*. New York: Harper &and Row.

Davidson, Brad. 2001. "Questions in Cross-Linguistic Medical Encounters: The Role of the Hospital Interpreter." *Anthropological Quarterly* 74 (4): 170–178.

Davies, Charlotte Aull. 1998. *Reflexive Ethnography: A Guide to Researching Selves and Others*. New York: Routledge.

Davis, Mike. 1992. *City of Quartz: Excavating the Future in Los Angeles*. New York: Verso.

———. 1999. *Ecology of Fear: Los Angeles and the Imagination of Disaster*. New York: Vintage.

DeMause, Lloyd, ed. 1974. *The History of Childhood*. London: Souvenir Press.

Delgado-Gaitan, Concha. 1992. "School Matters in the Mexican American Home: Socializing Children to Education." *American Educational Research Journal* 29: 495–513.

Donato, Ruben. 1996. "The Irony of Year-Round Schools: Mexican Migrant Resistance in a California Community during the Civil Rights Era." *Educational Administration Quarterly* 32: 181–208.

Dorner, Lisa M. 2006. "Constructing a Dual Language Policy in a New Immigrant Community: Conflicts, Contexts, and Kids." Ph.D. diss., Northwestern University.

Dorner, Lisa M., Marjorie Faulstich Orellana, and Rosa Jiménez. 2008. " 'It's Just Something You Do to Help Your Family': The Development of Immigrant Youth Through Relationships and Responsibilities." *Journal of Adolescent Development* 23 (5): 515–543.

Dorner, Lisa M., Marjorie Faulstich Orellana, and Christine P. Li-Grining. 2007. " 'I Helped My Mom,' and It Helped Me: Translating the Skills of Language Brokers into Improved Standardized Test Scores." *American Journal of Education* 113 (2): 451–478.

Dumas, Firoozeh. 2003. *Funny in Farsi: A Memoir of Growing Up Iranian in America.* New York: Random House.

Earley, Louise, and Delia Cushway. 2002. "The Parentified Child." *Clinical Child Psychology and Psychiatry* 7 (2): 163–178.

Ek, Lucila. 2005. "Staying on God's Path: Socializing Latino/a Immigrant Youth to a Christian Pentecostal Identity in Los Angeles." In *Building on Strength: Language and Literacy in Latino Families and Communities*, ed. Ana Celia Zentella, 77–92. New York: Teachers College Press.

Eksner, H. Julia, and Marjorie Faulstich Orellana. Under review. "Shifting in the Zone: Latino Child Language Brokers and the Co-Construction of Knowledge."

Emerson, Robert M., Rachel I. Fretz, and Linda L. Shaw. 1995. *Writing Ethnographic Fieldnotes.* Chicago: University of Chicago Press.

Esquivel, Laura. 2006. *Malinche.* New York: Atria Books.

Fadiman, Ann. 1998. *The Spirit Catches You and You Fall Down: A Hmong Child, Her American Doctors, and the Collision of Two Cultures.* New York: Farrar, Straus & Giroux.

Farr, Marcia, ed. 2005. *Latino Language and Literacy in Ethnolinguistic Chicago.* Mahwah, N.J.: Lawrence Erlbaum Associations, Inc.

———. 2006. *Rancheros in Chicagoacán: Language and Identity in a Transnational Community.* Austin: University of Texas Press.

Fass, Paula S. 2007. *Children of a New World. Society, Culture, and Globalization.* New York: New York University Press.

———. 2008. *Inheriting the Holocaust: A Second-Generation Memoir.* New Brunswick, N.J.: Rutgers University Press.

Fass, Paula S., and Mary Ann Mason, eds. 2000. *Childhood in America.* New York: New York University Press.

Fear and Learning at Hoover Elementary. 1997. VHS. Directed by Laura Angelica Simón. Los Angeles: Josepha Producciones.

Field, Norma. 1995. "The Child as Laborer and Consumer: The Disappearance of Childhood in Contemporary Japan." In *Children and the Politics of Culture*, ed. Sharon Stephens. Princeton, N.J.: Princeton University Press.

Fitzgerald, David. 2008. *A Nation of Emigrants: How Mexico Manages Its Migration.* Berkeley: University of California Press.

Flores, Veronica. 1993. "Language Skills Translate to Major Duties for Kids." *Chicago Sun-Times*, April 4.

Flores-González, Nilda. 2002. *School Kids/Street Kids: Identity Development in Latino Students.* New York: Teachers College Press.

Foerster, Robert Franz. 1924. *The Italian Emigration of Our Times*. Cambridge, Mass.: Harvard University Press.

Fuligni, Andrew. 2001a. "A Comparative Longitudinal Approach to Acculturation Among Children from Immigrant Families." *Harvard Educational Review* 71 (3): 566–578.

———. 2001b. "Family Obligation and the Academic Motivation of Adolescents from Asian, Latin American, and European Backgrounds." *New Directions for Child and Adolescent Development* 94: 61–75.

García Coll, Cynthia, and Kathryn Magnuson. 1998. "The Psychological Experience of Immigration: A Developmental Perspective." In *Immigration and the Family: Research and Policy on U.S. Immigration*, ed. Alan Booth, Ann C. Crouter, and Nancy Landale, 91–131. Mahwah, N.J.: Lawrence Erlbaum Associates.

García Sánchez, Inmaculada M. 2007. "Becoming Translators of Culture: Language Brokering Among Moroccan Immigrant Children in Spain." Paper presented at the 106th American Anthropological Association Annual Meeting, Nov. 28–Dec. 2, Washington, D.C.

García Sánchez, Inmaculada M., and Marjorie Faulstich Orellana. 2006. "The Construction of Moral and Social Identity in Immigrant Children's Narratives-in-Translation." *Linguistics and Education* 17 (3): 209–239.

Garrett, Paul B., and Patricia Baquedano-López. 2002. "Language Socialization: Reproduction and Continuity, Transformation and Change." *Annual Review of Anthropology* 31: 331–361.

Gaskins, Suzanne. 1999. "Children's Daily Lives in a Mayan Village: A Case Study of Culturally Constructed Roles and Activities." In *Children's Engagement in the World: Sociocultural Perspectives*, ed. Artin Göncü, 25–61. New York: Cambridge University Press.

Gee, James Paul. 1996. *Social Linguistics and Literacies: Ideology in Discourses*, 2d ed. London: Taylor & Francis.

Gill, Gurjeet. 1998. "The Strategic Involvement of Children in Housework: An Australian Case of Two-Income Families." *International Journal of Comparative Sociology* 39: 301–314.

Gillan, Maria Mazziotti, and Jennifer Gillan, eds. 1999a. *Growing Up Ethnic in America: Contemporary Fiction About Learning to Be American*. New York: Penguin Books.

———, eds. 1999b. *Identity Lessons: Contemporary Writing About Learning to Be American*. New York: Penguin Books.

Goffman, Erving. 1981. *Forms of Talk*. Philadelphia: University of Pennsylvania Press.

Gold, Matea. 1999. "Small Voice for Her Parents." *Los Angeles Times*, May 24.

González, Norma. 2006. *I Am My Language: Discourses of Women and Children in the Borderlands*. Tucson, Ariz.: University of Arizona Press.

González, Norma, Luis C. Moll, and Cathy Amanti, eds. 2005. *Funds of Knowledge: Theorizing Practices in Households, Communities, and Classrooms*. New York: Routledge.

Goodnow, Jacqueline, and Jeannette Lawrence. 2001. "Work Contributions to the Family: Developing A Conceptual And Research Framework." In *Family Obligation And Assistance During Adolescence: Contextual Variations And Developmental Implications*, ed. Andrew Fuligni. San Francisco: Jossey-Bass.

Goodwin, Marjorie Harness. 1990. *He-Said-She-Said: Talk as Social Organization Among Black Children*. Bloomington: Indiana University Press.

———. 2006. *The Hidden Life of Girls: Games of Stance, Status, and Exclusion*. Boston: Wiley-Blackwell.

Gottlieb, Robert. 2005. *The Next Los Angeles: The Struggle for a Livable City.* Berkeley: University of California Press.

———. 2007. *Reinventing Los Angeles: Nature and Community in the Global City.* Boston: MIT Press.

Graham, Hilary. 1983. "Caring: A Labour of Love." In *A Labour of Love: Women, Work and Caring,* ed. Janet Finch and Dulcie Groves, 13–30. London: Routledge and Kegan Paul.

Gregory, Eve, Susi Long, and Dinah Volk, eds. 2004. *Many Pathways to Literacy: Young Children Learning with Siblings.* New York: Routledge.

Greenfield, Patricia M. 1994. "Independence and Interdependence as Developmental Scripts: Implications for Theory, Research, and Practice." In *Cross-Cultural Roots of Minority Child Development,* ed. Patricia M. Greenfield and Rodney R. Cocking, 1–37. Hillsdale, N.J.: Erlbaum.

Guerra, Juan. 1998. *Close to Home: Oral and Literate Practices in a Transnational Mexicano Community.* New York: Teachers College Press.

———. 2004. "Putting Literacy in Its Place: Nomadic Consciousness and the Practice of Transcultural Repositioning." In *Rebellious Reading: The Dynamics of Chicana/o Cultural Literacy,* ed. Carl Gutierrez-Jones, 19–37. Center for Chicana/o Studies: University of California Santa Barbara.

———. 2007. "Out of the Valley: Transcultural Repositioning as a Rhetorical Practice in Ethnographic Research and Other Aspects of Everyday Life." In *Reframing Sociocultural Research: Identity, Agency, and Power,* ed. Cynthia Lewis, Patricia Enciso, and Elizabeth Birr Moje, 137–162. Mahwah, N.J.: Lawrence Erlbaum Associates.

Gutiérrez, Kris D., and Marjorie Faulstich Orellana. 2006. "The 'Problem' of English Learners: Constructing Genres of Difference." *Research in the Teaching of English* 40: 502–507.

Gutiérrez, Kris D., and Barbara Rogoff. 2003. "Cultural Ways of Learning: Individual Traits or Repertoires of Practice." *Educational Researcher* 32 (5): 19–25.

Hadi-Tabassum, Samina. 2006. *Language, Space, and Power: A Critical Look at Bilingual Education.* Clevedon, England: Multilingual Matters.

Hall, Kathleen D. 2002. *Lives in Translation: Sikh Youth as British Citizens*

Hall, Nigel, and Sylvia Sham. 2007. "Language Brokering as Young People's Work: Evidence from Chinese Adolescents in England." *Language and Education* 21(1): 16–30.

Hannawalt, Barbara A. 1993. *Growing Up in Medieval London: The Experience of Childhood in History.* New York: Oxford University Press.

Harris, Brian. 1973. "La traductologie, la traduction naturelle, la traduction automatique et la sémantique" ["Translatology, natural translation, machine translation and semantics"]. In French. In *Problèmes de sémantique* (Cahier de linguistique 3), ed. Judith McA'Nulty et al., 133–146. Montreal: University of Quebec Press.

Harris, Brian, and Bianca Sherwood. 1978. "Translating As an Innate Skill." In *Language Interpretation and Communication,* ed. David Gerver and H. Wallace Sinaiko, 155–170. New York: Plenum Press.

Haviland, John B. 2003. "Ideologies of Language: Some Reflections on Language and U.S. Law." *American Anthropologist* 105: 764–774.

Heath, Shirley Brice. 1983. *Ways with Words: Language, Life, and Work in Communities and Classrooms.* New York: Cambridge University Press.

Hecht, Tobias, ed. 2002. *Minor Omissions: Children in Latin American History and Society.* Madison: University of Wisconsin Press.

Hedges, Chris. 2000. "Translating America for Parents and Family." *New York Times,* June 19.

Heywood, Colin. 2001. *A History of Childhood: Children and Childhood in the West from Medieval to Modern Times*. Cambridge, England: Polity Press.

Hill, Jane H. 1998. "Language, Race, and White Public Space." *American Anthropologist* 100 (3): 680–689.

Hochschild, Arlie R. 2003. *The Managed Heart: Commercialization of Human Feeling*. Berkeley: University of California Press.

Hoffman, Eva. 1990. *Lost in Translation: A Life in a New Language*. New York: Penguin.

Hondagneu-Sotelo, Pierrette. 1994. *Gendered Transitions: Mexican Experiences of Immigration*. Berkeley: University of California Press.

Jacquemet, Marco. 1996. *Credibility in Court: Communicative Practices in the Camorra Trails*. New York: Cambridge University Press.

James, Allison. 1993. *Childhood Identities: Self and Social Relationships in the Experience of the Child*. Edinburgh, Scotland: Edinburgh University Press.

James, Allison, Chris Jenks, and Alan Prout. 1998. *Theorizing Childhood*. Cambridge, England: Polity Press.

James, Allison, and Alan Prout, eds. 1997. *Constructing and Reconstructing Childhoods: Contemporary Issues in the Sociological Study of Childhood*. London: Falmer Press.

Jenks, Chris. 2007. *Childhood*. 2d ed. New York: Routledge.

Johnson-Powell, Gloria, Joe Yamamoto, Gail E. Wyatt, and William Arroyo, eds. 1997. *Transcultural Child Development: Psychological Assessment and Treatment*. U.S.A.: John Wiley and Sons.

Jones, Curtis J., and Edison J. Trickett. 2005. "Immigrant Adolescents Behaving as Culture Brokers: A Study of Families From the Former Soviet Union." In *The Journal of Social Psychology* 145 (4): 405–427.

Kibria, Nazli. 1993. *Family Tightrope: The Changing Lives of Vietnamese Americans*. Princeton, N.J.: Princeton University Press.

Klapper, Melissa R. 2007. *Small Strangers: The Experiences of Immigrant Children in America, 1880–1925*. Chicago: Ivan R. Dee.

Knobel, Michele. 1999. *Everyday Literacies: Students, Discourse and Social Practices*. New York: Lang.

Kozol, Jonathan. 1992. *Savage Inequalities: Children in America's Schools*. New York: Harper Collins.

Kralovec, Etta, and John Buell. 2000. *The End of Homework: How Homework Disrupts Families, Overburdens Children, and Limits Learning*. Boston: Beacon Press.

Kress, Gunther. 2003. *Literacy in the New Media Age*. New York: Routledge.

Lankshear, Colin, and Michele Knobel. 2003. *New Literacies: Changing Knowledge and Classroom Learning*. Buckingham: Open University Press.

Lareau, Annette. 2003. *Unequal Childhoods: Class, Race and Family Life*. Berkeley: University of California Press.

Lassonde, Stephen. 2005. *Learning to Forget: Schooling and Family Life in New Haven's Working Class, 1870–1940*. New Haven: Yale University Press.

Lavadenz, Magaly. 2005. "Central Americans in Los Angeles: Issues of Language, Culture, and Identity." In *Building on Strength: Language and Literacy Practices in Latino Families*, ed. Ana Celia Zentella. New York: Teachers College Press.

Lave, Jean. 1977. Tailor-Made Experiments and Evaluating the Intellectual Consequences of Apprenticeship Training. *Quarterly Newsletter of Institute for Comparative Human Development* 1: 1–3.

Lave, Jean, and Etienne Wenger. 1991. *Situated Learning: Legitimate Peripheral Participation*. New York: Cambridge University Press.

Le Espiritu, Yen. 2003. *Home Bound: Filipino American Lives Across Cultures, Communities, and Countries*. Berkeley: University of California Press.

Lee, Carol D. 1995. "A Culturally Based Cognitive Apprenticeship: Teaching African American High School Students Skills in Literary Interpretation." *Reading Research Quarterly* 30: 608–630.

———. 2007. *Culture, Literacy, and Learning: Taking Bloom in the Midst of the Whirlwind*. New York: Teachers College Press.

Lee, Carol D., Margaret Beale Spencer, and Vinay Harpalani. 2003. "'Every Shut Eye Ain't Sleep': Studying How People Live Culturally." *Educational Researcher* 32 (5): 6–13.

Lee, Stacey J. 2005. *Up Against Whiteness: Race, School, and Immigrant Youth*. New York: Teachers College Press.

Levitt, Peggy. 2001. *The Transnational Villagers*. Berkeley: University of California Press.

Lewis, Amanda E. 2003. *Race in the Schoolyard: Negotiating the Color Line in Classrooms and Communities*. New Brunswick, N.J.: Rutgers University Press.

Lewis, Cynthia, Patricia E. Enciso, and Elizabeth Birr Moje, eds. 2007. *Reframing Sociocultural Research on Literacy: Identity, Agency, and Power*. Mahwah, N.J.: Lawrence Erlbaum Associates.

Lindholm-Leary, Kathryn J. 2001. *Dual Language Education*. Clevedon, England: Multilingual Matters.

López, Nancy. 2003. *Hopeful Girls, Troubled Boys: Race and Gender Disparity in Urban Education*. New York: Routledge.

Loucky, James, and Marilyn M. Moors. 2000. *The Maya Diaspora: Guatemalan Roots, New American Lives*. Philadelphia: Temple University Press.

Mahler, Sarah J. 1995. *American Dreaming: Immigrant Life on the Margins*. Princeton, N.J.: Princeton University Press.

Malakoff, Marguerite, and Kenji Hakuta. 1991. "Translation Skill and Metalinguistic Awareness in Bilinguals." In *Language Processing in Bilingual Children*, ed. Ellen Bialystok, 141–166. New York: Cambridge University Press.

Marks, Amy Kerivan, Laura A. Szalacha, Meaghan Lamarre, Michelle J. Boyd, and Cynthia García Coll. 2007. "Emerging Ethnic Identity and Interethnic Group Social Preferences in Middle Childhood: Findings from the Children of Immigrants Development in Context (CIDC) Study." *International Journal of Behavioral Development* 31 (5): 501–513.

Martínez, Ramón, Marjorie Faulstich Orellana, Mariana Pacheco and Paula Carbone. 2008. "Found in Translation: Connecting Translation Experiences to Academic Writing." *Language Arts* 85 (6): 421–431.

Massey, Douglas S., and Nancy A. Denton. 1993. *American Apartheid: Segregation and the Making of the Underclass*. Cambridge, Mass.: Harvard University Press.

Mayall, Barry. 2002. *Towards a Sociology for Childhood: Thinking from Children's Lives*. Buckingham, England: Open University Press.

McQuillan, Jeff, and Lucy Tse. 1995. "Child Language Brokering in Linguistic Minority Communities: Effects on Cultural Interaction, Cognition, and Literacy." *Language and Education* 9 (3): 195–215.

Mead, Margaret. 1928. *Coming of Age in Samoa*. New York: Harper Perennial.

Menjívar, Cecilia. 2000. *Fragmented Ties: Salvadoran Immigrant Networks in America*. Berkeley: University of California Press.

Minuchin, Salvador. 1974. *Families and Family Therapy*. Cambridge, Mass.: Harvard University Press.

Minuchin, Salvador, Braulio Montalvo, Bernard G. Guerney, Bernice L. Rosman, and Florence Schumer. 1967. *Families of the Slums*. New York: Basic Books.

Mintz, Steven. 2004. *Huck's Raft: A History of American Childhood*. Cambridge, Mass.: Harvard University Press.

Moll, Luis C., Cathy Amanti, Deborah Neff, and Norma González. 1992. "Funds of Knowledge for Teaching: Using a Qualitative Approach to Connect Homes and Classrooms." *Theory into Practice* 31 (2): 132–141.

Morrow, Virginia. 1996. "Rethinking Childhood Dependency: Children's Contributions to the Domestic Economy." *Sociological Review* 44: 58–77.

Mosselson, Jacqueline. 2006. *Roots and Routes: Bosnian Adolescent Refugees in New York City*. New York: Peter Lang.

Nasir, Na'ilah Suad. 2002. "Identity, Goals, and Learning: Mathematics in Cultural Practice." *Mathematical Thinking and Learning* 4 (2&3): 211–245.

New London Group. 1996. "A Pedagogy of Multiliteracies: Designing Social Futures." *Harvard Educational Review* 66 (1): 60–92.

Oakes, Jeannie. 1985. *Keeping Track: How Schools Structure Inequality*. New Haven, Conn.: Yale University Press.

Ochs, Elinor. 2002. "Becoming a Speaking of Culture." In *Language Socialization and Language Acquisition: Ecological Perspectives*, ed. Claire J. Kramsch, 99–120. New York: Continuum Press.

Ochs, Elinor, and Bambi B. Schieffelin. 1984. "Language Acquisition and Socialization: Three Developmental Stories and Their Implications." In *Culture Theory: Essays in Mind, Self and Emotion*, ed. Richard A. Shweder and Robert A. LeVine, 276–320. New York: Cambridge University Press.

———. 2008. "Language Socialization: An Historical Overview." In *Encyclopedia of Language and Education, Volume 8: Language Socialization*, ed. Patricia A. Duff and Nancy H. Hornberger, 3–15. New York: Springer.

Olsen, Laurie. 1997. *Made in America: Immigrant Students in Our Public Schools*. New York: The New Press.

Omi, Michael, and Michael Winant. 1986. *Racial Formation in the United States: From the 1960s to the 1980s*. New York: Routledge & Kegan Paul.

Orellana, Marjorie Faulstich. 2001. "The Work Kids Do: Mexican and Central American Immigrant Children's Contributions to Households and Schools in California." *Harvard Educational Review* 71 (3): 366–389.

———. 2003. "Responsibilities of Children in Latino Immigrant Homes." *New Directions for Youth Development: Understanding the Social Worlds of Immigrant Youth* 100 (Winter): 25–39.

———. 2007. "Moving Words and Worlds: Reflections from 'The Middle. '" In *Reframing Sociocultural Research: Identity, Agency, and Power*, ed. Cynthia Lewis, Patricia Enciso, and Elizabeth Birr Moje, 123–136. Mahwah, N.J.: Lawrence Erlbaum Associates.

Orellana, Marjorie Faulstich, and Phillip Bowman. 2003. "Cultural Diversity Research on Learning and Development: Conceptual, Methodological, and Strategic Considerations." *Educational Researcher* 32 (5): 26–32.

Orellana, Marjorie Faulstich, Lisa M. Dorner, and Lucila Pulido. 2003. "Accessing Assets: Immigrant Youth's Work as Family Interpreters." *Social Problems* 50 (5): 505–524.

Orellana, Marjorie Faulstich, Lucila Ek, and Arcelia Hernández. 1999. "Bilingual Education in an Immigrant Community: Proposition 227 in California." *International Journal of Bilingual Education and Bilingualism* 2 (2): 114–130.

Orellana, Marjorie Faulstich, and H. Julia Eksner. 2006. "Power in Cultural Modeling: Building on the Bilingual Language Practices of Immigrant Youth in Germany and the United States." *National Reading Conference Yearbook* 55: 224–234.

Orellana, Marjorie Faulstich, and Kris D. Gutiérrez. 2006. "What's the Problem? Constructing Different Genres for the Study of English Learners." *Research in the Teaching of English* 41 (1): 118–123.

Orellana, Marjorie Faulstich, and Arcelia Hernández. 1998. "Talking the Walk: Children Reading Urban Environmental Print." *The Reading Teacher* 52 (6): 612–619.

Orellana, Marjorie Faulstich, and Jennifer F. Reynolds. 2008. "Cultural Modeling: Leveraging Bilingual Skills for School Paraphrasing Tasks." *Reading Research Quarterly* 43 (1): 48–65.

Orellana, Marjorie Faulstich, Jennifer F. Reynolds, Lisa M. Dorner, and María Meza. 2003. "In Other Words: Translating or 'Para-phrasing' as Family Literacy Practice in Immigrant Households." *Reading Research Quarterly* 38 (1): 12–34.

Orellana, Marjorie Faulstich, and Barrie Thorne. 1998. "Year-Round Schools and the Politics of Time." *Anthropology and Education Quarterly* 29 (4): 1–27.

Orellana, Marjorie Faulstich, Barrie Thorne, Anna Chee, and Wan Shun Eva Lam. 2001. "Transnational Childhoods: The Participation of Children in Processes of Family Migration." *Social Problems* 48 (4): 572–591.

Orfield, Gary, and Chungmei Lee. 2007. *Historic Reversals, Accelerating Desegregation, and the Need for New Integration Strategies.* Los Angeles: UCLA Civil Rights Project/Proyeto Derechos Civiles.

Orfield, Gary, and John T. Yun. 1999. *Resegregation in American Schools.* Cambridge, Mass.: The Civil Rights Project, Harvard University.

Palmer, Julian, Younghwan Song, and Hsien Hen Lu. 2002. *The Changing Face of Child Poverty in California.* New York: National Center for Children in Poverty, Columbia University.

Park, Lisa Sun-Hee. 2005. *Consuming Citizenship: Children of Asian Immigrant Entrepreneurs.* Stanford, Calif.: Stanford University Press.

Perrone, Vito. 1998. *Teacher With a Heart: Reflections on Leonard Covello and Community.* New York: Teachers College Press.

Pillet-Shore, Danielle. 2003. "Doing 'Okey:' On the Multiple Metrics of an Assessment." *Research on Language and Social Interaction* 36 (3): 285–319.

Postman, Neil. 2003. *The Disappearance of Childhood.* London: W. H. Allen.

Portes, Alejandro, and Rubén G. Rumbaut, eds. 2001. *Legacies: The Story of the Immigrant Second Generation.* Berkeley: University of California Press.

———. 2006. *Immigrant America: A Portrait.* Berkeley: University of California Press.

Potowski, Kim. 2007. *Language and Identity in a Dual Immersion School.* Clevedon, England: Multilingual Matters.

Pratt, Mary Louise. 1999. "Arts of the Contact Zone." In *Ways of Reading,* ed. David Bartholomae and Anthony Petroksky. New York: Bedford/St.Martin's.

Pufall, Peter B., and Richard P. Unsworth, eds. 2004. *Rethinking Childhood.* New Brunswick, N.J.: Rutgers University Press.

Purcell-Gates, Victoria. 1997. *Other People's Words: The Cycle of Low Literacy.* Cambridge, Mass.: Harvard University Press.

Pyke, Karen. 2000. " 'The Normal American Family' as an Interpretive Structure of Family Life Among Grown Children of Korean and Vietnamese Immigrants." *Journal of Marriage and the Family* 62 (1): 240–255.

Qvortrup, Jens. 1985. "Placing Children in the Division of Labour." In *Family and Economy in Modern Society,* ed. Paul Close and Rosemary Collins. London: MacMillan.

———, ed. 2005. *Studies in Modern Childhood: Society, Agency and Culture.* New York: Palgrave Macmillan.

Reddy, Michael J. 1993. "The Conduit Metaphor: A Case of Frame Conflict in Our Language About Language." In *Metaphor and Thought,* ed. Andrew Ortony, 164–201. New York: Cambridge University Press.

Reynolds, Jennifer F. 2002. "Maya Children's Practices of the Imagination: (Dis)playing Childhood and Politics in Guatemala." Ph.D. diss., University of California Los Angeles.

Reynolds, Jennifer F., and Marjorie Faulstich Orellana. Forthcoming. "New Immigrant Youth Interpreting in White Public Space." *American Anthropologist.*

Ricoeur, Paul. 2006. *On Translation.* New York: Routledge.

Roberts, Helen. 2000. "Listening to Children and Hearing Them." In *Research with Children: Perspectives and Practices,* ed. Pia Monrad Christensen and Allison James, 225–240. London: Falmer Press.

Rogoff, Barbara. 1990. *Apprenticeship in Thinking: Cognitive Development in Social Context.* New York: Oxford University Press.

———. 2003. *The Cultural Nature of Human Development.* New York: Oxford University Press.

Rogoff, Barbara, and Jean Lave, eds. 1984. *Everyday Cognition: Its Development in Social Context.* Cambridge, Mass.: Harvard University Press.

Rogoff, Barbara, Ruth Paradise, Rebeca Mejia Arauz, Maricela Correa-Chavez, and Cathy Angelillo. 2003. "Firsthand Learning Through Intent Participation." *Annual Review of Psychology* 54: 175–203.

Rogoff, Barbara, Martha Julia Sellers, Sergio Pirrotta, Nathan Fox, and Sheldon H. White. 1975. "Age of Assignment of Roles and Responsibilities to Children: A Cross-Cultural Survey." *Human Development* 18 (5): 353–369.

Rosaldo, Renato. 1993. *Culture and Truth: The Remaking of Social Analysis.* Boston: Beacon Press.

Rose, Mike. 2005. *The Mind at Work: Valuing the Intelligence of the American Worker.* New York: Penguin Group.

Rubel, Paula G., and Abraham Rosman, eds. 2003. *Translating Cultures: Perspectives on Translation and Anthropology.* New York: Berg.

Rumbaut, Rubén G. 2004. "Ages, Life Stages, and Generational Cohorts: Decomposing the Immigrant First and Second Generations in the United States." *International Migration Review* 38: 1160–1205.

Rumbaut, Rubén G., and Alejandro Portes, eds. 2001. *Ethnicities: Children of Immigrants in America.* Berkeley: University of California Press.

Saler, Benson. 2003. "The Ethnographer as Pontifex." In *Translating Cultures: Perspectives on Translation and Anthropology,* ed. Paula G. Rubel and Abraham Rosman. New York: Berg.

Santa Ana, Otto, ed. 2004. *Tongue-Tied: The Lives of Multilingual Children in Public Education.* Lanham, Md.: Rowan & Little.

Sarroub, Loukia K. 2005. *All American Yemeni Girls: Being Muslim in a Public School.* Philadelphia: University of Pennsylvania Press.

Saxe, Geoffrey B. 1999. "Cognition, Development, and Cultural Practices." In *Culture and Development: New Direction in Child Psychology,* ed. Elliot Turiel, 19–35. San Francisco: Jossey-Bass.

Scheiffelin, Bambi B. 1990. *The Give and Take of Everyday Life: Language Socialization of Kaluli Children.* New York: Cambridge University Press.

Scheiffelin, Bambi B., and Elinor Ochs. 1986. "Language Socialization." *Annual Review of Anthropology* 15: 163–191.

———. 1987. *Language Socialization Across Cultures.* New York: Cambridge University Press.

Schildkraut, Enid. 1975. "Age and Gender in Hausa Society: Socio-economic Roles of Children in Urban Kano." In *Sex and Age As Principles of Social Differentiation,* ed. Jean S. LaFontaine, 109–137. New York: Academic Press.

Scribner, Sylvia, and Michael Cole. 1981. *The Psychology of Literacy*. Cambridge, Mass.: Harvard University Press.

Shannon, Sheila M. 1990. "English in the Barrio: The Quality of contact Among Immigrant Children." *Hispanic Journal of Behavioral Sciences* 12: 256–276.

Shyne, Millicent Petrov. 2002. *2943: An Immigrant Girl's Childhood in St. Louis*. Alamogordo, N.M.: Six Sisters Publishing.

Skolnick, Arlene, ed. 1976. *Rethinking Childhood: Perspectives on Development and Society*. Boston: Little, Brown & Co.

Smith, Michael P., and Luis E. Guarnizo, eds. 1998. *Transnationalism from Below*. New Brunswick, N.J.: Transaction Publishers.

Smith, Robert. 2005. *Mexican New York: Transnational Lives of New Immigrants*. Berkeley: University of California Press.

Smith-Hefner, Nancy J. 1999. *Khmer American: Identity and Moral Education in a Diasporic Community*. Berkeley: University of California Press.

Solberg, Anne. 1997. "Negotiating Childhood: Changing Constructions of Age for Norwegian Children." In *Constructing and Reconstructing Childhood*, ed. Allison James and Alan Prout, 126–144. London: Falmer Press.

Solórzano, Daniel, Miguel Ceja, and Tara Yosso. 2000. "Critical Race Theory, Racial Microaggressions, and Campus Racial Climate: The Experiences of African American College Students." *The Journal of Negro Education* 69 (1/2): 60–73.

Song, Miri. 1999. *Helping Out: Children's Labor in Ethnic Businesses*. Philadelphia: Temple University Press.

Speier, Michael. 1976. "The Adult Ideological Viewpoint in Studies of Childhood." In *Rethinking Childhood*, ed. Arlene Skolnick, 168–186. Boston: Little, Brown.

Stanton-Salazar, Ricardo D. 2001. *Manufacturing Hope and Despair: The School and Kin Support Networks of U.S.-Mexican Youth*. New York: Teachers College Press.

Stearns, Peter N. 2003. *Anxious Parents: A History of Modern Childrearing in America*. NewYork: New York University Press.

———. 2006. *Childhood in World History*. New York: Routledge.

Stein, Judith A., Marion Riedel, and Mary Jane Rotheram-Borus. 1999. "Parentification and Its Impact on Adolescent Children of Parents with AIDS." *Family Process* 38 (2): 193–208.

Stephens, Sharon. 1995. "Children and the Politics of Culture in 'Late Capitalism.'" In *Children and the Politics of Culture*, ed. Sharon Stephens. Princeton, N.J.: Princeton University Press.

———, ed. 1995. *Children and the Politics of Culture*. Princeton, N.J.: Princeton University Press.

Street, Brian. 1984. *Literacy in Theory and Practice*. New York: Cambridge University Press.

Suárez-Orozco, Carola, and Marcelo M. Suárez-Orozco. 2001. *Children of Immigration*. Cambridge, Mass.: Harvard University Press.

Suárez-Orozco, Carola, Marcelo M. Suárez-Orozco, and Irina Todorva. 2008. *Learning a New Land*. Cambridge, Mass.: Harvard University Press.

Swidler, Ann. 2003. *Talk of Love: How Culture Matters*. Chicago: University of Chicago Press.

Thomas, Wayne P., and Virginia P. Collier. 2002. *A National Study of School Effectiveness for Language Minority Student's Long-Term Academic Achievement*. Washington, D.C.: Center for Research on Education, Diversity and Excellence.

Thorne, Barrie. 1993. *Gender Play: Boys and Girls in School*. New Brunswick, N.J.: Rutgers University Press.

———. 2001. "Pick-Up Time at Oakdale Elementary School: Work and Family From the Vantage Points of Children." In *Working Families*, ed. Rosanna Hertz and Nancy L. Marshall, 354–376. Berkeley: University of California Press.

————. 2008. "The Chinese Girls and the 'Pokémon Kids': Children Constructing Difference in Urban California." In *Figuring the Future: Children, Youth, and Globalization*, ed. Jennifer Cole and Deborah Durham. Santa Fe, N.M.: School for American Research Press.

Thorne, Barrie, Marjorie Faulstich Orellana, Wan Sun Eva Lam, and Anna Chee. 1999. "Raising Children, and Growing Up, across National Borders: Comparative Perspectives on Age, Gender, and Migration." In *Gender and U.S. Immigration: Contemporary Trends*, ed. Pierrette Hondagneu-Sotelo, 241–262. Berkeley: University of California Press.

Tobar, Hector. 2005. *Translation Nation: Defining a New American Identity in the Spanish-Speaking United States*. New York: Riverhead Books.

Toury, Gideon. 1995. *Descriptive Translation Studies and Beyond*. Philadelphia: John Benjamins.

Tse, Lucy. 1995. "Language Brokering Among Latino Adolescents: Prevalence, Attitudes, and School Performance." *Hispanic Journal of Behavioral Sciences* 17 (2): 180–193.

————. 1996a. "Language Brokering in Linguistic Minority Communities: The Case of Chinese- and Vietnamese-American Students." *Bilingual Research Journal* 20 (3/4): 485–498.

————. 1996b. "Who Decides?: The Effects of Language Brokering on Home-School Communication." *Journal of Educational Issues of Language Minority Students* 16: 225–234.

Tymocsko, Maria, and Edwin Gentzler, eds. 2002. *Translation and Power*. Amherst, Mass.: University of Massachusetts Press.

Urciuoli, Bonnie. 1998. *Exposing Prejudice: Puerto Rican Experiences of Language, Race, and Class*. Boulder, Colo.: Westview Press.

Valdés, Guadalupe. 1996. *Con Respeto: Bridging the Distance Between Culturally Diverse Families and Schools (An Ethnographic Portrait)*. New York: Teachers College Press.

————. 1997. "Dual-language Immersion Programs: A Cautionary Note Concerning the Education of Language-Minority Students." *Harvard Educational Review* 67 (3): 391–429.

————. 2002. *Expanding Definitions of Giftedness: The Case of Young Interpreters from Immigrant Families*. Mahwah, N.J.: Lawrence Erlbaum Associates.

Valencia, Richard, ed. 1997. *The Evolution of Deficit Thinking: Educational Thought and Practice*. London: Falmer.

Valenzuela, Abel. 1999. "Gender Roles and Settlement Activities Among Children and Their Immigrant Families." *American Behavioral Scientist* 42 (4): 740–742.

Valenzuela, Angela. 1999. *Subtractive Schooling: U.S.-Mexican Youth and the Politics of Caring*. Albany: State University of New York Press.

Vásquez, Olga A., Lucinda Pease-Alvarez, and Sheila M. Shannon. 1994. *Pushing Boundaries: Language in a Mexicano Community*. New York: Cambridge University Press.

Vigil, James Diego. 1988. *Barrio Gangs: Street Life and Identity in Southern California*. Austin: University of Texas Press.

————. 2002. *A Rainbow of Gangs: Street Cultures in the Mega-City*. Austin: University of Texas Press.

Villenas, Sofia A. 2005. "Between the Telling and the Told: Latino Mothers Negotiate Education in New Borderlands." In *Narrative and Experience in Multicultural Education*, ed. JoAnn Phillion, Ming Fang He, and F. Michael Connelly, 71–91. Thousand Oaks, Calif.: Sage Publications.

Vygotsky, Lev S. 1978. *Mind in Society: The Development of Higher Psychological Processes*. Cambridge, Mass.: Harvard University Press.

Wadensjö, Cecilia. 1995. "Recycled Information as a Questioning Strategy: Pitfalls in Interpreter-Mediated Talk." In *The Critical Link: Interpreters in the Community*, ed. Silvana E. Carr, Roda P. Roberts, Aideen Dufour, and Dini Steyn, 35–52. Philadelphia: John Benjamins.
———. 1998. *Interpreting as Interaction*. London: Longman.
Waldinger, Roger, and Mehdi Bozorgmehr. 1996. *Ethnic Los Angeles*. New York: Russell Sage Foundation.
Waldinger, Roger, and David Fitzgerald. 2004. "Transnationalism in Question." *American Journal of Sociology* 109 (5): 1177–1195.
Walkerdine, Valerie. 1998. *Daddy's Girl: Young Girls and Popular Culture*. Cambridge, Mass.: Harvard University Press.
———. 2006. "Workers in the New Economy: Transformation as Border Crossing." *Ethos* 34 (1): 10–41.
Wallace, Diana. 2002. "Bilingual Teens May Do Translating." *Chicago Daily Herald*, February 15.
Walsh, Sophie, Shmuel Shulman, Zvulun Bar-On, and Antal Tsur. 2006. "The Role of Parentification and Family Climate in Adaptation Among Immigrant Adolescents in Israel." *Journal of Research on Adolescence* 16 (2): 321–350.
Waterman, Robin, and Beth Harry. 2008. *Building Collaboration Between Schools and Parents of English Language Learners: Transcending Barriers, Creating Opportunities*. Tempe, Ariz.: National Center for Culturally Responsive Educational Systems.
Waters, Mary C. 1999. *Black Identities: West Indian Immigrant Dreams and American Realities*. Cambridge, Mass.: Harvard University Press.
Weinstein-Shr, Gail. 1994. "From Mountain Tops to City Streets: Literacy in Philadelphia's Hmong Community." In *Literacy Across Communities*, ed. Beverly J. Moss, 49–83. Cresskill, N.J.: Hampton Press.
Weisskirch, Robert S. 2006. "Emotional Aspects of Language Brokering Among Mexican American Adults." *Journal of Multilingual and Multicultural Development* 27 (4): 332–343.
Weisskirch, Robert S., and Sylvia Alatorre Alva. 2002. "Language Brokering and the Acculturation of Latino Children." *Hispanic Journal of Behavioral Sciences* 24: 369–378.
Wenger, Etienne. 1999. *Communities of Practice: Learning, Meaning, and Identity*. New York: Cambridge University Press.
Whiting, Beatrice B. and John W. M. Whiting. 1975. *Children of Six Cultures: A Psycho-Cultural Analysis*. Cambridge, Mass.: Harvard University Press.
Wong Fillmore, Lily. 1991. "When Learning a Second Language Means Losing the First." *Early Childhood Research Quarterly* 6: 323–346.
Wortham, Stanton Emerson Fisher, Edmund T. Hamann, and Enrique G. Murillo, Jr., eds. 2001. *Education in the New Latino Diaspora: Policy and the Politics of Identity*. Westport, Conn.: Prager/Greenwood.
Yezierska, Anzia. 1923. *Children of Loneliness: Stories of Immigrant Life in America*. New York: Funk & Wagnalls Company.
———. 1925. *Bread Givers*. New York: Persea Books.
Zelizer, Viviana A. 1985. *Pricing the Priceless Child: The Changing Social Value of Children*. Princeton, N.J.: Princeton University Press.
———. 2005. "The Priceless Child Revisited." In *Studies in Modern Childhood: Society, Agency and Culture*, ed. Jens Qvortrup, –200. London: Palgrave.
Zhou, Min, and Carl L. Bankston. 1998. *Growing Up American: How Vietnamese Children Adapt to Life in the United States*. New York: Russell Sage Foundation.
Zúñiga, Victor, and Rubén Hernández-León, eds. 2005. *New Destinations: Mexican Immigration in the United States*. New York: Russell Sage Foundation.

Index

AB292, 152n34. *See also* legislation on child language brokering
academic engagement, 150n9
academic literacy, 162n10
acculturation (assimilation), 16, 150n11
acculturative stress, 60, 116–117, 160n30
activism, 132–133
adolescence, social construction of, 151n22
adult ideological viewpoint, 161n1
adultification, 10–11, 57, 63, 99, 116–123, 149n3
"adults in the making," 5
aesthetics of place, 139
African Americans, 44, 47, 97
age-based categories, 23
agency, 22
American Dream, 97
amusement parks, 13, 24
anthropologists as translators, 6, 149n11
apprenticeship models of cultural transmission, 102
Aries, Phillipe, 17
Ashley, 55, 69, 111
"asina," 30
assimilation (acculturation), 16, 150n11
audiotaping, 2, 29–30, 31, 38, 139–140
authentic caring, 132

Baby Boom generation, 131–132
Beatríz, 63–64, 70–72
bilingual education, 29, 30–31, 40, 42, 45, 46–48, 54, 67–68, 140, 155n13

bilingualism, 26, 160n27
bilingual resources, 48
biological (physical) limitations of children, 22
borderlands, 122, 157n2, 159n16
Briana, 20, 55, 60, 61, 63, 75–77, 110
brochure about language brokering, 162
Buccholtz, Mary, 25
bussing, 29, 45, 47

caddying, 115
California Childhoods project, ix, 37, 137, 145, 147n1, 154n4
CallerID, 57, 145
care work, 160n31
census data, 39, 42, 44, 155n17
Central America, 3, 20, 36, 39, 41, 132
changing parenting practices, 151n22
Chee, Anna, 133, 147n1
Chicago: immigration to, 1–3, 10, 29, 30, 32, 65, 155n18; as a research context, x, 37, 41–44, 96, 131, 133, 136, 138; Chicago public schools, 67
childhoods: author's, 15, 35, 133, 149n4, 155n17; beliefs about, 22; changes in, 18, 151; comparative views of, 48–49, 65; in contact zones, 20–21; in diverse cultures, 151n24; homework's shaping effects on, 51; immigrant, 3, 18–20, 103, 125, 148nn4–6, 150n9, 150n14, 158n4; as an interpretive frame, 16; landscape portraits, 35–49; meanings of, 18, 140; shaping effects of translation work, 2, 7–10, 14, 33,

childhoods: (*continued*)
96, 98, 118–119; as social construction,
14, 16–18, 152n33; as a stage, 16;
as a unit of social analysis, 16; views
of (interpretive frames), 36
child poverty, 18
children: as actors and agents, 21–22, 28;
as agents of social transformation,
21–22; capacities under the law, 77;
in educational decision-making, 67;
helping neighbors, 58; methods of
studying, 127, 133–142, 161n1,
161n13; as objects of adult evaluation,
80, 85, 93; paradoxical positionalities
of, 5, 63, 77–78, 92–93, 156n10; rights
of, 21–22
children's work, 2, 4–5, 21–22, 123–124,
148n4
child soldiers, 24
Chinese immigrants, 3
Chu, Sara, 25
Cindy, 9, 22, 27, 63, 66, 149n2
citizenship (legal status), 20–21
civic engagement, 5, 69–70
class size reduction, 154n5
collaborations in language brokering, 2,
55, 104, 109, 156n7
collective (team) ethnography, 133–135,
162n12
college, 8, 9–10, 95
Collins, Patricia Hill, 118
commercial (consumer) transactions,
70–73, 78, 145
community, meanings of, 4, 37–38,
155n20
community walks, 138
compensation, 64, 157n13
conduit metaphor, 157n5
constraints on children's actions, 22
consumer (commercial) transactions,
70–73, 78, 145
contact zones, 20, 44, 46, 49
courtroom interpreting, 158n8
critical social science of childhoods, 16,
27, 33, 104, 121, 151n15, 152n33,
154n4, 161n1

critical studies of childhoods. *See* critical
social science of childhoods
Csikszentmihalyi, Mihaly, 120
cultural modeling, 162
cultural nature of learning, 159
cultural practices, 15, 19, 100, 101, 153
cultural values, 81, 82, 86–87, 97, 108
culture, 15, 100, 153n54, 159n12
culture brokering, 25
curriculum design, 132

Darwinian evolutionary theory, 100
Davidson, Brad, 93
deficit views of immigrant families, 66,
88, 89–90, 92, 158n7
demographics, 39, 42, 44, 147–148n3,
155n17
development: bilingual, 109, 124;
changes in families, 54; changes in
language brokering, 7, 54, 98; cross-
cultural variations, 5, 11, 14, 28, 151;
interdependent (relational), 113–114;
normative, 104; ontogenetic 101–102,
112–113; phylogenetic, 100–102;
readiness, 99; social and cognitive,
110–111; sociocultural, 101–102;
sociological, 159n5; stages, 99; stage
theories of, 159n6; through
translation, 114–116, 119–121
developmental frameworks, 83–85
diversity, politics of, 44, 46–49
dual-language education (two-way
immersion), 46–48, 54, 155n21
Duncan, Greg, 160n26
Dorner, Lisa, x, 52, 114, 134, 142,
155n20, 156n4, 159n7, 160n26
Durango, 43

ecological psychology, 151n24
Ecuador, 43
Ek, Lucila, 133
El Salvador, 43
emigrant (term), 147n1
emotions: absence of, 13; ambivalence,
14; embarrassment, 70–71; of
language, 159n16; management of, 71,

73, 113, 121; negative, 13, 14, 116;
parents, 12, 90–92; positive, 13, 68;
in the research process, 130–133,
155n14; translating as a way of
cheering oneself up, 9; as unsettling,
23; varied (mixed), 62–64, 70–74,
120, 160n30, 161n4
enactments of translation encounters, 137
Engleville, 29–34, 37, 44–49, 50, 54, 68,
70, 92–93, 97, 128, 131, 139, 155n17
English Learners, 51, 150n10, 154n8,
156n6
ER, 27
essentializing culture, 153n54
Estela: changing family dynamics, 54,
103; conflicts at home, 13, 116; false
cognates, 159n21; family's home
purchase, 44; hometown, 45; home
translating 50, 51, 52, 56, 62, 108; as
"la mano derecha de la familia," 7, 8,
10, 16; mother's views of, 11;
parent-teacher conferences, 88–91,
92–94, 106–107; portraits of, 7–8, 28,
33–34, 96–97; public translations, 71,
72–73; reading to sister, 110–111, 119,
123, 141–142; sibling caretaking, 7,
158n2; siblings' schooling, 47; writing,
33, 158n10
ethnic enclaves, 4
ethnicizing discourses, 27, 73, 153n49
ethnic labels (categories), 33, 39, 42, 44,
71–72, 129, 130, 153
ethnographic present, 154–155n54
ethnographies of immigrant life,
150nn8–14
ethnography as translation, 6, 128,
159n16
expert/novice relationship, 22, 102–110

face-saving, 157n8
false cognates, 159n21
family interpreting (terminology), 1, 3, 25
Farr, Marcia, 45, 155n19
Fass, Paula, 17, 151n23
Fear and Learning at Hoover
Elementary, 154n9

feminist notions of care, 160n31
FEP ("Functional English Proficient"),
154n8
fieldnotes, 28, 162n14
fields of difference, 4, 37, 40, 43, 46, 48,
49
food (nutrition), 155n15
freedom, 19
funding for public schools, 155n14
funds of knowledge, 66

García Sánchez, Inmaculada, x, 157n4,
157n8
gender, 16, 18, 24, 53–54, 123, 128–129,
149n9, 154n1, 155n1, 160n30
generational relations, 3–5, 10, 11, 14,
23, 148n4
generationing, 16, 152n32
gerontology, 150n7
giftedness of language brokers, 25,
160n28
global economic restructuring, 17–18,
20, 124
globalization, 17
Goffman, Erving, 79
Great Depression, 15, 101
Guanajuato, 8, 29–33, 36, 43, 45, 138,
153n51, 153n53
Guatemala, 19
Guerra, Juan, 131
Guerrero, 43
Gutiérrez, Kris, x, 99

"hanging out" with kids, 134, 136
Haviland, John, 92
health promotion, 74–77
Hernández, Arcelia, ix, xii,133
Hochschild, Arlie, 71
home obligations of children: changes
over time, 54–55; children's views of,
52–53; developmental changes in, 7;
examples of, 1, 2, 4, 7, 11; gendering
of, 53–54; invisibility of, 5; literature
on, 152n31, 156nn1–3, 160n31;
Minuchin's views of, 10–11; mothers'
views of, 11–13

home-school communication, 29, 51, 67, 68, 156n6
homework, 4, 8, 32, 50–51, 54, 56, 57, 88–90, 97–98
Hong Kong, 3, 20
household contributions. *See* home obligations of children
housework. *See* home obligations of children

identity formation, 150n9, 150n11
identity markers, 127, 128
imaginaries of space, 151n29
immigrant (terminology), 147n1
immigrant child mediators (terminology), 25
immigrant fiction, 148n6
immigrant memoirs, 148n5
immigrant rights, 97
immigrant studies, 17–18, 150nn7–14, 158n4
immigration, statistics on, 147–148n3
immigration history, children's translation work in, 148nn4–5
Independence Day (movie), 50
independent cultural scripts, 113–114, 160n25
individuation, 113–114
informal interpreting (term), 25
insider/outsider relations in fieldwork, 127–130
interdependent cultural scripts, 113–114, 123, 160n25
intergenerational relations: beliefs about normalcy and deviance, 3, 10, 13, 14, 19, 24, 65, 80, 116, 132; boundaries in, 26–27, 63; changes, 14, 63; conflicts in, 148n4; differences between U.S. and Mexico, 13; power relations, 1, 2, 3, 124
internalization, 160n30
Internet, 61, 64, 96
interviews, 9, 37, 136–137
invisibility: of children, 3, 23, 40, 131, 150; of children in migration, 15–16, 148n7; of children's work, 21, 23, 51–52; of homework, 51;

of immigrants, 27; of language brokering, 3

Jacquemet, Marco, 93
Jalisco, 43
James, Allison, 130
Jasmine, 13, 14, 60, 61, 63, 67, 69
Jefferson School, 45–48, 80
Jessica, 1–2, 13, 113, 140
jokes, 59–60
Josh, 63, 71, 72, 114
journals: entries, 13, 32, 50, 51, 56, 57–58, 60, 62, 68, 69, 73, 115, 124; as research method, 2, 140
Junior: changing spheres of movement, 112; hometown, 30, 32, 36, 153n53; home translating, 50, 52, 56, 58, 60, 62, 104–105, 107–109; mother's views of, 12, 58; parent-teacher conference, 107; portraits of, 18–30, 52, 95–96, 123, 158n1; pseudonym change, 147n2; public translating, 69; reactions to book, 141–142; reading to siblings, 21, 30, 119; siblings' schooling, 47
Junior ethnographer meetings, 31, 136, 141
jury summons, 61–62, 102, 105–106

Korean immigrants, 3, 39–41

labeling (naming and framing), 23–27
labor cost equation, 21, 124
Lam, Wan Shun Eva, ix, 149n2
language: home language environment, 19, 20; as a key word, 150n14; language learning, 16, 31, 51, 54, 55, 104, 159n16; native language abilities, 109; as text, 153n44; as a tool, 99
language brokering: defined, 1, 25; domains of, 144–146; effects on school achievement, 160n26, 160n30; gendered differences, 53–54; historical accounts of, 148nn4–5; invisibility of, 3, 4; popular representations of, 27
language socialization, 151n16, 151n24, 161n2, 162n8

Latino diaspora, 154n3
Lave, Jean, 99
legal status (citizenship), 20–21
legislation on child language brokering, 22, 152n34
LEP ("Limited English Proficient"), 39, 42, 154n8
Levitt, Peggy, 147n1
Li-Grining, Christine, x, 52, 114
lines of difference, 127
linguistic equivalents, 157n5
listening to children, 127, 133–137, 140–141
literacy, 2, 50, 61, 66, 114, 119, 156n11
literacy brokering (text-based translations): comparison with school literacy, 156n11; examples of, 1–2, 4, 30; in Mexico and Central America, 11; "*para*-phrasing," 26, 32, 50, 51, 56, 57, 60–62, 96, 97, 104–106, 110–111, 119, 156n3
Los Angeles: bilingual resources in, 67, 70; as "home," 131; immigration to, xi; as a new global metropolis, 154n1; as a research context, x, 36–41, 133, 136, 137, 138–139
Luz, 9–10, 21, 22, 27, 63, 66

Madison School, 38–41, 43, 128
Malinche, 161n6
María: as a child/adolescent, 24; expanding spheres of movement, 112; hometown, 32, 44, 45, 47, 153n53; home translating, 51, 53, 54, 56, 57, 59, 63, 109, 123; mother's views of, 11, 22, 59; parent-teacher conferences, 20, 81–88, 92–94, 106–107, 110; portraits of, 28, 31–33, 52, 97–98; public translations, 69; responses to book, 141–142
Marxism, 101
Mayall, Barry, 16
Mayans, 39
media attention to language brokering, 149n7
medical encounters, 2, 3, 4, 20, 21, 66, 74–77, 137, 149n7, 150n14

medical records, 8, 9
memories, role in research, 161
metalinguistic awareness, 114–115, 136, 160n28
methodology, 2, 5–6, 37–38, 133–141
Mexican migration history, 45, 155n18
Mexico, 1, 3, 10
Michoacán, 138
micro-agressions of race, 72, 157n6
migrant (terminology), 147
Miguel, pseudonym, 147n2
Minuchin, Salvador, 10, 149n4, 149n6
mistranslations, 27, 91
Mistry, Rashmita, x, 158n7
mixed methods, 2, 127, 135–141
Moll, Luis, 66
multiple vantage points, 133–135, 137–140
MySpace, 97

NASA, 95
native translators (terminology), 26
Natural Translation, 1, 26, 152n43
New England, 35, 36, 131
new immigrant communities, 4, 44–45, 154n3, 155n17
new sociology/anthropology of childhoods. *See* critical social science of childhoods
"The Night Before Christmas," 110–111
"normal American family," 14, 149n5
Northwestern University, x, 141
Nova: awareness of xenophobia, 113; expanding spheres of movement, 112; hometown, 32, 36, 44, 153n53; home translations, 53, 55, 57, 59, 63, 123; hospital translations, 21; household changes, 103; mother's views of, 11–12, 109, 110; portraits of, 8–9, 28, 30–31, 52, 95; public translations, 69; response to book, 141–142
nutrition, 155n15

observational methods, 137–139
The O.C., 96
1.5 generation, 131

orality, 26
Oxford English Dictionary, 152n38

paradoxical positionality, 5, 63, 77–78, 92–93, 123–124, 156n10
para-phrasing (defined), 1, 26, 153n45
parentification. *See* adultification
parentified child, 10
parenting, as source of learning, 132
parents' co-participation in translations, 55, 77, 84, 102, 104, 110, 156n7
parent-teacher conferences, 4, 79–94, 106–7, 110, 157n1, 157n4
Pease-Alvarez, Lucinda, 25
perspective-taking, 141
photographs by children, 138, 162n13
points of comparison, 18
Polish immigrants, 37, 42, 43
popular representations of language brokering, 27
power relations, 10, 27, 77–78, 132, 135–136, 149n11
Pratt, Mary, 20, 44
Proposition 187, 41
Proposition 227, 41, 49, 67
pseudonyms, 32, 141–142, 147n2
psychodynamics of ethnography, 130
psychosocial stress, 44, 60, 116–117, 154n12, 160n30
Puerto Ricans, 43, 155n18
Pyke, Karen, 14, 149

race relations, 150n9
racial formation, 153n49
racialization, 153n49
racializing discourses, 27, 73, 153n49
racial micro-aggressions, 72, 157n6
racism, 70–73, 113, 117, 122, 128, 158n3
reciprocity of care, 65–66
re-enactments of translation situations, 136–7
Regan School, x, 41–44, 92, 133, 139, 140
remuneration. *See* compensation
repertoires of practice, 100
report cards, 107–108
resistance, 11, 22
Reynolds, Jennifer, x, 156n10, 157n4

Richards, I. A., 121
Ricoeur, Paul, 115
Rogoff, Barbara, 99
role reversal. *See* adultification
ROTC, 115
Rumbaut, Rubén, 131

Saler, Benson, 6
Sammy: feelings about translating, 63, 78; metalinguistic commentary, 6, 115–116, 141; public para-phrasing, 68, 73, 77, 112, 139; social skills, 110, 128
scaffolding, 55, 56, 66–67, 102, 103–110
school dress code, 109
schoolwork as work, 151n26
September 11, 2001, 31, 43, 69
service learning, 160n31
settlement processes, 98
Shannon, Sheila, 25
Sherwood, Brian, 26
sibling caretaking, 7, 10, 29, 32, 54, 156n8
social addresses (social categories), 129, 130
social class, 18, 32–33, 44, 47, 127, 157
social contexts, mediating effects of, 129
socialization, 162n8
social skills, 110
sociocultural learning theory, 5, 17, 28, 98–110, 159nn17–18
Solorzano, Daniel, 72
Spanish as a second language, 39
specialized translation encounters, 4, 14, 21
stage theories, 99, 101, 159n6
"standards," 86, 106–107
state/legal transactions, 74
structural inequalities in urban communities, 155n14, 158n7
subjectivity, 132
surveillance, 74, 121
survey, 2, 37, 52, 53, 54, 114, 140

team (collective) ethnography, 133–5, 162n12
technology, 1–2, 8, 31, 32, 96, 97, 112

teen mothers, 24
teleological perspectives, 5, 16, 100–101
telephone translations, 1–2, 8, 56, 57–59, 156n9
television shows, translations of, 59–60
Thorne, Barrie, x, 17, 130, 147n1, 154n4, 154n10
Tony, 32, 68, 69, 112, 113, 114
Toury, Gideon, 26
Toys R' Us, 73, 110, 112
traduction naturelle, 152n43
transcription conventions, 143, 149n1
transcultural repositioning, 13
transcultural skills, defined, 119, 153n48
transcultural work, 26–27, 79–94, 131–132, 158n6, 162n11
transculturation, 131–132, 158n6. *See also* transcultural work
translation, dictionary definition, 26, 152n38
transliteration, 30
transmigrant, 147n1
transnational. *See* transmigrant
transnational families, 20 •
transnationalism, 147n1, 153n53
tugs of memory, 160n5
tutoring, 56–57
"tweens," 24, 99
Two-Way Immersion programs (dual-language education), 46–48, 54, 155n21

urban school inequities, 153

Valdés, Guadalupe, 25, 114
Valenzuela, Angela, 132
Vásquez, Olga, 25
verbatim translation, 87, 89, 92, 157n5
visual methods, 162n13
Vygotskian psychology, 100
Vygotsky, Lev, 99–101

Wadensjö, Cecilia, 74, 79, 121, 127
Walkerdine, Valerie, 122, 130
Waltham, Massachusetts, 155n17
Wenger, Etienne, 99
whiteness, meanings of, 129
white public space, 27, 72, 77, 158n9
WIC, 105, 146

xenophobia: post 9/11, 43; Proposition 187 and, 41; in public transactions, 70–73, 88, 89–90, 92, 113, 117, 122, 128, 158

year-round schools, 35, 40–41, 154n10
Yosso, Tara, 72

Zelizer, Viviana, 17, 157n13
zones of proximal development, 103, 104, 159n17
zoom lens (camera metaphor), 137

About the Author

Marjorie Faulstich Orellana is an associate professor in the Graduate School of Education and Information Sciences at UCLA. She is the director of faculty for the Teacher Education Program and codirector of the Migration Studies seminar series. She was a bilingual classroom teacher in Los Angeles for ten years.

CPSIA information can be obtained
at www.ICGtesting.com
Printed in the USA
FFOW02n1530250815
16342FF